Y0-AAW-118

Hugh MacDiarmid:
The Poetry of Self

Christopher Grieve, writing under the name of Hugh MacDiarmid, was a major modern poet and founder of the Scottish Literary Renaissance. In this study of his poetry, John Baglow eliminates what has been a stumbling block for most MacDiarmid scholars by showing the very real thematic and psychological consistency which underlies MacDiarmid's work. He demonstrates the extent to which MacDiarmid's work was dominated by a desire to find a faith that could justify his desire to write poetry, a desire which was continually thwarted by a critical intellect which inevitably destroyed whatever faith he was able to construct. This constant search without a successful conclusion is at the heart of the work of major modernist writers; MacDiarmid's poetry can be seen as embracing this tradition and making it explicit.

Baglow shows that this search for justification was a focus for MacDiarmid almost from the start, but that only with the development of "synthetic Scots" did he begin to grapple with it directly. While at first the idea of a Scottish essence seemed to promise the spiritual foundation MacDiarmid was seeking, as his poetry developed this idea became less important and he came to see poetry, and ultimately the language of poetry itself, as unrealizable ideals.

This reading of MacDiarmid's poetry and its relation to the modernist movement will be of value to readers of MacDiarmid as well as to readers more generally interested in twentieth-century literature.

John Baglow is currently employed by the Social Sciences and Humanities Research Council in Ottawa.

Hugh MacDiarmid

The Poetry of Self

JOHN BAGLOW

McGill-Queen's University Press
Kingston and Montreal

© McGill-Queen's University Press 1987
ISBN 0-7735-0571-7

Legal deposit 3rd quarter 1987
Bibliothèque nationale du Québec

Printed in Canada

Printed on acid-free paper

This book has been published with the help of a
grant from the Canadian Federation for the
Humanities, using funds provided by the Social
Sciences and Humanities Research Council of
Canada.

Canadian Cataloguing in Publication Data

Baglow, John
    Hugh MacDiarmid, the poetry of self
    Bibliography: p.
    Includes index.
    ISBN 0-7735-0571-7
    1. MacDiarmid, Hugh, 1892–1978 – Criticism and
    interpretation. I. Title.
    PR6013.R735Z56 1987   821'.912   c87-093457-0

Cover photograph Hugh MacDiarmid.
Courtesy Michael Grieve

For Robert Lloyd Baglow

AUGUSTANA UNIVERSITY COLLEGE
LIBRARY

Contents

Preface

It is regrettable that the late Christoper Murray Grieve ("Hugh MacDiarmid"), who fought all his life for the principle that Scotland must take its place among the international community of cultures, died so little known outside his native land. As he himself knew, Scottish literature, in the popular mind, is Rabbie Burns and drunken sentimentalism, quaint language and earthy primitivism: a vestigial phenomenon at best. Even those familiar with the achievements of the Great Makars such as Dunbar and Henrysoun may well still refer to them as "Scottish Chaucerians." And some of those who have glanced at Grieve's work have perhaps been tempted to see in it simply a valiant but foredoomed attempt on his part to overcome his own suffocatingly parochial tradition – they "kent his faither," so to speak. To come to his poetry appreciatively means to surmount a legacy of condescension which has stifled the aesthetic life of many another culture – English Canada's, for one.

It must be said that Grieve never makes it easy. Early work, written in an enriched, synthetic Scots language which one must take the trouble to learn, gives way to vast verbal artifacts in English, ponderous, obscure in intent, vocabulary, and reference, a seemingly deliberate turning away from "what poetry is all about." Few besides his admirers in the Scottish Literary Renaissance (which he founded) and in the social realist school of literary criticism have bothered to take the plunge. And those who have tend to share one failing in particular: they, to differing degrees, take Grieve's ideas and philosophizing altogether too seriously in themselves, and by so doing have missed the real significance of his writing.

This book is an attempt to present Grieve's work in a context which transcends both his explicit, fierce nationalism, and his maverick association with communism. In so doing, I hope to demonstrate his importance, not as a Scottish poet, not as a "Marxist" poet, not as a philosopher in verse, but as a modern poet, who developed his own solutions to problems all modern poets have faced – and continue to face.

For Grieve, it will be seen, is a uniquely faithful exponent of the twentieth-century *Zeitgeist*. The modern environment, in the most general sense of that term, is perceived as disordered and fragmented: in it, individuals lacking a place in a preordained scheme of things are left to find meaning and self-justification where they may. This existential dilemma, in its aesthetic dimension, is reflected directly and indirectly in much modern poetry, and, as in the work of a number of mainstream writers such as Pound and Eliot, is a fundamental preoccupation in Grieve's poetry.

As some (mostly slight) early verse in English indicates, this problem is a concern for Grieve almost from the start of his poetic career, which spans roughly a fifty-year period from the end of the First World War. But it is only with his development of a so-called synthetic or plastic Scots language, put in the mouth of a "friend" of his, Hugh MacDiarmid, in 1922, that the dilemma emerges as a predominant theme. During this period of linguistic and aesthetic experimentation, in which he explores his situation in a series of primarily lyrical observations, Grieve appears to find hope in a quasi-mystical Scottish essence which promises the spiritual foundation he seeks.

This culminates in his long Scots poem, *A Drunk Man Looks at the Thistle* (1926), perhaps the single greatest achievement of his career. In it, Grieve actively struggles to overcome his plight through an intuition-based appeal to a transcendental Scottish realm, but his problem, exteriorized in a thistle, remains unsolved. Accordingly, in *To Circumjack Cencrastus* (1930), he decides to look to the outside world and involve himself with facts and ideas. From this arises a poetry of particulars, his notorious "poetry of facts," in which he arranges around him various gleaned fragments of a world in chaos, comparing them to stones in a mosaic. As the ideal of the Scottish essence recedes in importance, his medium modulates into English. At the same time, poetry, and ultimately the language of which poetry is composed, become ideals in themselves, and his development ends finally in what could be described as a prolonged stutter.

While Grieve's aesthetic quest, then, ended in a magnificent failure, even in this his work perhaps uniquely illustrates the modern predicament as experienced by a poet. His obsessive self-consciousness made him, in effect, explicitly his own theme throughout his career; this, and the inexorable developmental logic which his poetry reveals, allow us unusually clear access to a poet's perception of the modern environment and the aesthetic difficulties which he shared with his contemporaries.

Throughout the book I use his *nom de guerre* Hugh MacDiarmid rather than his actual name. Although this is essentially for convenience – most of his books and much of the secondary literature follow this pattern – the preference is very much his own in any case. As truth, then poetry, then language itself became ideals for him, so too did his persona take on the superhuman powers required to grapple with a problem truly universal in its scope.

Acknowledgments

Thanks are due to Michael and Valda Grieve for permission to quote extensively from the poetry and prose of "Hugh MacDiarmid" (C.M. Grieve), and to Alexander Scott for permission to reprint a stanza of his poem "Great Eneuch." The lines from "(one fine day)" from *ViVa* by e e cummings are reprinted by permission of Grafton Books, Collins Publishing Group, United Kingdom, and Liveright Publishing Corporation, copyright 1931, 1959, by e e cummings; copyright (c) 1979, 1973, by The Trustees for the e e cummings estate; copyright (c) 1979, 1973, by George James Firmage. "A, a, a, Domine Deus," by David Jones, is reprinted by permission of Faber and Faber Ltd. The lines from A.J.M. Smith's poem "Universe Into Stone," from *Poems New and Collected*, copyright Oxford University Press 1967, are reprinted by permission of the publisher. The lines from "The Statues," by W.B. Yeats, are reprinted with permission of A.P. Watt Ltd, on behalf of Michael Butler Yeats and Macmillan London Ltd, and the Macmillan Publishing Company, from *The Poems of W.B. Yeats* edited by Richard J. Finneran; copyright 1940 by Georgie Yeats, renewed 1968 by Bertha Georgie Yeats, Michael Butler Yeats, and Anne Yeats.

Grateful acknowledgments are due to the University of Glasgow and the Canada Council for generous assistance which enabled me to carry out the doctoral research upon which this study is based. My personal thanks are long overdue – in published form – to Alexander Scott, who guided me through the doctoral stage; to Rosemary Billings, for support and encouragement; and to Martin Ballard, whose rhetoric was an added spur.

Hugh MacDiarmid

CHAPTER ONE

Introduction:
Hugh MacDiarmid
and His Age

Perhaps the most pleasing and concise survey of the poetry of Hugh MacDiarmid is to be found in the *Oxford Book of Modern Verse* edited by W.B. Yeats in 1936. It consists of a chronological sequence of three poems, "Cattle Show," "O Wha's the Bride" (an excerpt from the book-length *A Drunk Man Looks at the Thistle*), and "The Skeleton of the Future": three poems from three periods in the poet's development, evincing startling differences in theme, tone, and language. The unity which nevertheless underlies them is one of the primary concerns of this study.

The poems are not all perfectly representative of the periods in which they were written. Yeats's bias towards the lyric is clearly evident, despite the two distinct, equally significant streams in MacDiarmid's poetry, lyrical and (for want of a better word) sapient. But the selection does serve as a useful introduction to MacDiarmid's poetic canon.

"Cattle Show" is easily the best of the handful of early poems in English mostly written prior to MacDiarmid's official adoption of his *nom de guerre* in late 1922, and appearing over the name of C.M. Grieve. Unlike many of the others, it does not directly address the existential questions which even then were finding thematic prominence in his work. But it does manifest a gift for hard-edged, vivid description which was soon after realized more fully, first in Scots, and then in English once again. More importantly, the tone of poetic authority inextricably linked to the formal pose which the poem actually is, is quintessential MacDiarmid, a virtual hallmark.

"O Wha's the Bride" is an exceptionally well-crafted, concentrated lyric composed during his period of experimentation with the Scots language. Finally, "The Skeleton of the Future," while atypically lyrical at a time when MacDiarmid was more interested in a swingeing polemical poetry, philosophical excursions in verse, and ultimately a rugged and open-ended poetry of facts, nonetheless contains a number of key elements – political, symbolic, and linguistic – which characterize his later work as a whole.

MacDiarmid's formal development was actually far more startling than this brief selection suggests, not only in the radical transformations which his language and structure underwent, but also in the extent to which his underlying themes and preoccupations remained virtually constant throughout. There is in fact a remorseless logic to the changes which have comprised, so far as numerous readers and critics have been concerned, a gradual process of disintegration. But this logic, generated by the obsessive, single-minded working out of the poet's concerns, cannot be comprehended solely by reference to the explicitly Scottish context set by the author and accepted at face value by so much of his audience. Although MacDiarmid's themes appear to be Scotland-centred, for the most part, it is the modern age which constituted his aesthetic environment, and it is that entire age with which he struggled to come to grips. It is essential to situate MacDiarmid in this wider context if his remarkable work is to be fully understood.

The dimensions of that work, as already indicated, are extraordinarily wide. MacDiarmid began his career with fairly conventional poetry in English – mostly stilted Georgian exercises of generally poor quality. Some of it, however, clearly adumbrates his later poetry of facts; and an overall survey reveals that the existential concerns which continued to run like threads through his entire canon were already finding expression at this time. Interestingly, this poetry, signed "C.M. Grieve," continued to be published after the birth of Hugh MacDiarmid in 1922, but it did not improve noticeably in quality, even though the poetry of his alter ego was of a high order from the start.

In September 1922 "more or less in the spirit of parody" of those Scottish contemporaries who chose to write in Scots dialect, MacDiarmid began to write poetry which employed a Scots language pastiche enriched by the resurrection of Scots words which had long before fallen out of use.[1] It was clearly an experiment, and one that produced considerable poetic results, but there was much more to it than that. It was, in fact, a major step in a lifelong struggle for self-definition. For when he began to write in Scots, the persona of Hugh MacDiarmid came into being, and with it a dynamic contradiction (or as MacDiarmid would have termed it, "antisyzygy"): C.M. Grieve-Hugh MacDiarmid. The tension is that between actual and ideal, Hugh MacDiarmid being not only the poet, but what the poet wants to be. The figure of MacDiarmid sometimes assumes god-like proportions: and sometimes there is a very real confusion between the poet and the persona, as the later work particularly illustrates.

G.S. Fraser has made the valuable observation that "one can make a much better case for much of MacDiarmid's later poetry, if one thinks of the argument in the poems as being directed not against a reader who is being bullied, but against MacDiarmid himself." It displays "an inwardness, an unending inner struggle, in a strenuously lonely man, whose loneliness can, for the reader, be an emblem of his own."[2] These are comments crucial to an understanding of the poet's work as a whole, for they apply equally well to the early poetry. MacDiarmid is a man of many conflicting voices from the beginning. One thinks of the several selves named in his early prose sketch "Cerebral" in *Annals of the Five Senses* (1923), published under the name of C.M. Grieve, and of the contending voices in *Drunk Man* (1926) and *To Circumjack Cencrastus* (1930), as well as in later poetry such as "Lament for the Great Music." Indeed, MacDiarmid's entire poetic corpus can be seen as a continual drama, with the author as protagonist/antagonist. The differing qualities and characteristics of the actual poet and of his persona serve to enhance this drama.

This aspect of his canon deserves closer examination, because it is fundamental to his poetry and also to an understanding of the modernism of his work. Looking at the poetry, one cannot attribute the creation of a persona solely to a Scottish authorial tradition, to plain cautiousness, or to a strategy for recognition. All of these may be factors, but they are not the whole story. The uncertainty and self-questioning which characterize the modern age are, in MacDiarmid's case, partly expressed in this remarkable flexibility of identity which goes well beyond a matter of pen-names.[3]

This is not without parallels. Søren Kierkegaard, for example, published conflicting philosophical tracts under various names. Of more relevance to this examination, however, is the Portuguese poet Fernando Pessoa. "Not one but several poets," Pessoa wrote volumes of verse under a number of "heteronyms" as he termed them. He went so far as to invent fictitious biographies for his personae. As Michael Wood puts it, "A person, in Pessoa's world, is a personality, a constructed self, someone more real than you can manage to be in your diffuse daily life ... but a person is also a mask, an impersonation, someone you know you are not, a further instance of diffusion."

In an anonymous article, Pessoa made an important distinction between "heteronymic" and the merely pseudonymic: "A pseudonymic work is, except for the name with which it is signed, the work of an author writing as himself; a heteronymic work is by an author writing outside his own personality: it is the work of a complete individuality made up by him, just as the utterances of some character in a drama of his would be."[4]

Of course, this phenomenon is not nearly so well defined or extreme in MacDiarmid's work, at least explicitly. C.M. Grieve soon stopped publishing poetry under that name after MacDiarmid came into being, and in many ways the two became one. The critical voices of Leslie and others are very much in the background, and could, in and of themselves, be dismissed collectively as a strategy to advance MacDiarmid's poetic and ideological enthusiasms. Yet throughout the writing of MacDiarmid runs a fundamental uncertainty, a consistent preoccupation with his self which is to some extent augmented by the easily ignored distinction between the man and his *alter ego.*

Poses and gestures in some of the poetry suggest that Grieve is playing at being MacDiarmid, like the self-conscious waiter in Sartre's *Being and Nothingness*: the two are not completely synthesized. Sometimes MacDiarmid (the persona) appears as an ideal at some remove from the actual poet who must struggle to catch up as it were, and sometimes the two are confused. MacDiarmid is a fighting Scotsman – Grieve explores and attempts to realize this Scottishness in himself. MacDiarmid makes extravagant claims for which Grieve is criticized, although the latter is clearly not always sure who is who. The *Lucky Poet* autobiography illustrates this confusion, even at the beginning where the book is credited to "Hugh MacDiarmid (Christopher Murray Grieve)," and is called a "self-study"; it has not seemed odd to any critic up to now that the authorship was not expressed "Christopher Murray Grieve ('Hugh MacDiarmid')," which is surely the more logical of the two, especially as it is to be this self-study. We might well ask, Which self? The radical confusion of the book is to a large extent attributable to this initial confusion.

The heteronymous Hugh MacDiarmid is thus related to but distinct from the actual C.M. Grieve, who does not cease to exist merely because he gives up his baptismal name. Yet this interesting phenomenon is only a part of the picture, and is actually of secondary importance in an examination of the poetry. It is only a facet of a far more profound and general aspect of the work, namely, the polarity between actual and potential or ideal, that is, the concept of the self as a *becoming*; for the ideal, no matter how abstract it becomes in MacDiarmid's verse, is almost without exception presented as an ideal state of selfhood (rather than as heaven, for example). In the Grieve-MacDiarmid polarity, MacDiarmid is sometimes ahead of Grieve in terms of this ideal and exerts teleological pressure upon the latter, but he is not the ideal itself (truth, meaning, understanding, revelation, oneness, or whatever word is used to name it) which the poet ultimately seeks. MacDiarmid is a step along the way, a man who possesses more power, wisdom, and knowledge than Grieve to achieve the ideal. Metaphorically he is a carrot on a stick, a continual urging forward even when the destination, if there is one, is unknown: "Wrang-heidit? Mm. But *heidit! That's the thing!*" as the poet himself puts it.

MacDiarmid carried his self-struggle through a series of short lyrics in Scots into his finest sustained poetic achievement in Scots, *A Drunk Man Looks at the Thistle*; and from there into *To Circumjack Cencrastus*, which is still in Scots, if a Scots of a diluted kind. Shortly afterwards (with some bravura exceptions) the "Lallans" experiment was over, to be replaced by poetry in English, much of it of that unique type termed by the poet "poetry of facts." But the self-drama continued unabated, the tension between actual and ideal still forming the crux of the work, and the problem of the modern self – of MacDiarmid's modern self – remaining the central theme.

Looking at MacDiarmid's entire poetic output, one notices a gradual but radical change in the structure of the poetry itself, exclusive of the language used. From lyrics (*Sangschaw, Penny Wheep*) he moved on to the long poem, always pieced together from shorter ones, relatively successfully in *Drunk Man*, less so in *Cencrastus*; and from there, with exceptions (primarily political verse), to long, open-ended collections of material, scrap added to scrap, any synthesis having become part of the understanding or revelation the poet seeks. It has proved an overwhelming temptation on the part of many readers and critics to regard MacDiarmid's development as a process of disintegration, and, on a purely aesthetic level, this perception has much to be said for it. At the same time, the force that drove MacDiarmid from "gowden lyrics" to what amounts to an assault on traditional notions of poetry itself is one which can be traced throughout his work, and which reflects an iron will, a doggedness, a single-mindedness that indicates that such "disintegration" has a deliberate quality about it.

So far as the poetry in Scots is concerned, once the subject of raging debate, scant controversy exists today with respect to its merits as poetry: at its best it is consummately successful and it is recognized as such. It needs little introduction. The later work, however, remains forbidding and problematic in any number of ways. It has its apologists, such as the poet Alan Bold, and a horde of nonplussed detractors; it has also attracted critics who have made some effort to come to grips with it in a more-or-less generous spirit, but who have for the most part failed to recognize it as a completely logical outgrowth of the early lyrical verse. A brief overview is essential at this point, if only to help clarify the line of approach to be taken in this study to MacDiarmid's work as a whole.

On the immediate level the later poetry, or much of it, seems to be largely a catalogue of facts, ideas, and opinions often of a capricious inconsistency, interspersed with passages of natural description of a marvellous evocative quality. Where the former appears dry, abstract, and overgeneral, clumsy, prosaic, and dull, the latter indicates a love and fascination for the particular, the concrete, and is as finely crafted and rich as much of his finest Scots work in this respect. Plainly there is no gradual withering of poetic power, but a change with deeper causes. (From the poet we get an ironic question, "Why do I write this horrible rubbish instead" of the lyrics which gained him his reputation? He follows with an intimation that he will continue to do so.) A decline in poetic power always involves a decline in energy and imagination, but both are evident in abundance in the later work of MacDiarmid.

In reading this material one soon gets the feeling that it is more the having of opinions and ideas than the opinions and ideas themselves which is important to MacDiarmid. The specific content of his polemics can be viewed as almost incidental to much of the poetry in which they appear. The inconsistency in the content is a major indication of its irrelevance, an inconsistency so glaring that one is forced to look behind the opinions and ideas in order to find what the poet is actually saying. It soon becomes evident that he is in fact saying a great deal, and that very often the opinions and ideas are counters which he arranges in interesting ways rather than a collection of lessons for the audience to master. Paradoxically, MacDiarmid is not at all opinionated in the usual sense of the word.

This is not to say that all of his positions are inconsistently held. He has been consistently anti-English since before the birth of MacDiarmid, consistently pro-Scottish, consistently concerned with human potential as contrasted with its sorry present state. But there is more than at first meets the eye here as well. His pro-Scottishness is not merely posited as a premise and allowed to become implicit but is continually reinforced and reaffirmed, indicting an underlying uncertainty, a need to repeat over and over again who and what the author is and what he is about. In the self-defining process, his Anglophobia serves to define the not-self to some degree. His concept of human potential resolves itself into a profound concern with his own potential, and this explicit theme takes on a symbolic function. It should be reiterated: his opinions, his stances, his ideas are seldom if ever what his poetry is about.

The later poetry, despite its emphasis on the literal (to the point of virtual obsession), is rich in symbolism as well. Besides the image of water (pointed out by George Bruce and John Manson, and dealt with in some detail by Roderick Watson) and the image of stone which is specifically related to it, themes, ideas and whole passages are used as aesthetic "vocabulary" and function as symbols throughout this work. A further aspect of this verse is a special kind of heroic simile, a structure deeply characteristic of his later work, in which the two terms are on equal footing and reflect each other, rather than the more usual case in which one term serves the other and functions descriptively. In the case of "To a Friend and Fellow-Poet," for example, as Edwin Morgan notes, the poem is no more about the poet than it is about the worm. Here a dialectic is set up rather than a mere description being made; it is a sort of double-barrelled metaphysical conceit. Each term is at once literal and allegorical, suggesting the same type of equivocation as found throughout MacDiarmid's poetry, where no particular voice is given unquestioned authority over the conflicting ones. Clearly there is more to this poetry than "chopped-up prose."

And yet, equally clearly, as is evident to any reader, the language, if tough and "masculine," is also frequently flat, clumsy, and obscurely phrased. Not all of this can be explained away, but some of the characteristics of this verse are due to an emphasis on the pure subject matter, the naked facts. As Watson puts it, "To popularize them or to subject them too much to solely artistic necessities is, for MacDiarmid, to do a profound disservice to the nature of their truth, and to the peculiar integrity of science ... It is the 'facts' that must attract us and not their expression, and so MacDiarmid uses a spare prose-like diction – an approximation to the language of the text-book."[5] Imagine a physics text written in poetic rhetoric, for example, and it is easier to understand (if not to forgive!) the style of the poetry of facts.

The delicate and tricky issue of MacDiarmid's notorious penchant for plagiarism is of great importance regarding this question of style, the question itself becoming almost irrelevant when one considers passages which, but for minor emendations, are not MacDiarmid's work at all. This is not a characteristic solely of his later work, but is found to some extent almost from the start, although plagiarism may be rather too harsh a word in these cases. It should be clearly pointed out that the poet is rarely if ever trying to get away with something, for his sources are usually acknowledged, and most of them are easily traced. It might be suggested that he is trying to view the world in two ways, through experience and through what he called his "strong solution of books," but this is only part of the explanation. More importantly, these passages, like the data which is also borrowed of course, form part of the arrangement which his poetry is: they too are aesthetic counters. And in all the *Times Literary Supplement* furore over this question, no one stopped to point out that MacDiarmid plagiarizes himself as well, even though this places the whole question in quite a different light. In truth, a passage of written language is often no different to him from an object like a tree. The latter, as an image, has innumerable possible contexts, and to MacDiarmid the former does as well, with the added advantage of being able to be absorbed in its entirety in a way that a tree is not.

It cannot be denied, of course, that there are negative aspects to this indiscriminate borrowing. Philip Pacey is overgenerous when he writes, in an essay on MacDiarmid's late book-length poem *In Memoriam James Joyce*, that "There can be no more questioning of a poet's re-use of other men's writings than of a painter's re-presentation of images selected from the visible world or a composer's incorporation of folk melodies in a symphony." One in fact can go too far. In his autobiography MacDiarmid lays claim to translations he did not make, and he frequently gives the impression of far wider learning than he actually possesses. In *James Joyce* he draws the reader's attention to two references, in German, to the life of Adalbert Stifter, when the relevant passage of poetry and these footnotes to it were lifted from the *Times Literary Supplement* of 15 August 1952. No acknowledgments are given, nor are they provided for many other passages in this poem and elsewhere. The untransliterated Sanskrit quotation in *James Joyce* might also be mentioned, or his "To a Young Poet" (in prose), half of which consists of a word-for-word, unacknowledged quotation from Werner Brock's introduction to Heidegger's *Existence and Being* (1949), although the unmistakeable impression is left that the voice is MacDiarmid's own.

The implications seem a little unattractive, perhaps, but bearing in mind the Grieve-MacDiarmid polarity noted above, and realizing that it is often the concept of learning rather than the learning itself which MacDiarmid emphasizes, one can at least understand what has been done, and why; especially since the borrowed passages and "translations" are often quite effective in their contexts and frequently owe their success as poetry to a judicious arrangement in lines (see "Perfect,"[6] and "The Little White Rose," an adaptation of part of a speech by Compton MacKenzie, for example) and to effective, if marginal, revisions (see the Lallans lyrics "from the German," "from the French," and so on, in *Drunk Man* which are, as Kenneth Buthlay has pointed out, "light Scots" renditions of English translations).[7]

Such plagiarism is, for MacDiarmid, a formal technique. More than any other poet, MacDiarmid works in what might be called verbal collage. Suggested as early as *Annals of the Five Senses* and already evident in *Cencrastus*, this reaches its extreme in the later poetry. Roderick Watson, using the poet's term *mosaic*, declares the method to be original.[8] Jean-Paul Sartre's distinction between poetry and prose – that the former uses words as things while the latter uses them as signs – here becomes difficult to apply: MacDiarmid is in fact attempting to use words-used-as-signs as things.

The collages (or collage, for in a sense MacDiarmid's work is one long poem) are built around the consistent centre of the self. In this he is much like Whitman, as he is in the extensive use of catalogues, another element of his collages. "At the still centre of all his varied poetry," writes David Daiches, "stands the entranced solitary man."[9]

The collage device becomes a means of making statements about the world "as it is" so as more precisely to define his relationship to it. The nature of this relationship (MacDiarmid-in-the-world) is the hard core of all his poetry, as it is of course in any artist's work; but in MacDiarmid's case it is of primary thematic importance, and there-fore explicit. He is the theme of his work, which is a continuing self-epic with no resolution. He is the only hero in it. The others – Lenin, Doughty, Korzybski, and so on – are, as Douglas Young has put it, "apotheoses of the poet himself": crypto-personae. His poetry, in fact, is in some respects like that of another modern poet, Mayakovsky, of whom Leon Trotsky said in *Literature and Revolution*: "At every step Mayakovsky speaks about himself, now in the first person, and now in the third, now individually, and now dissolving himself in mankind. When he wants to elevate man, he makes him be Mayakovsky." MacDiarmid is at the centre of his universe too, and is constantly aware of himself. He has little time for anyone or anything but the profound problem his self seems to pose. It is as a poet that he struggles with this problem, which is, in scope and importance, the essence of modernism.

As a modern writer, then, not simply as a Scottish nationalist or idiosyncratic communist, MacDiarmid wrestles with his whole age. And although one can easily lapse into dangerous superficiality in attempting to characterize an entire historical period, it is nonetheless possible to outline certain preoccupations, emphases, and percep-tions which are indubitably modern and which give form and focus to MacDiarmid's struggle.

The term *modernism*, as Irving Howe points out in his excellent preface to *The Idea of the Modern in Literature and the Arts*, is, like any general category, a vague and amorphous one.[10] There are, however, certain attitudes and ideas not new in themselves which are given new emphasis in the modern period, and which, so emphasized, can be recognized as components of modernism. (As for the modern period itself, as might be expected there is little agreement on when it began, but general agreement that it is here – or was until very recently!) One can justifiably argue, for example, that the central concerns of Thomas Hardy strike a more immediate note than those of, say, William Thackeray, and that, moreover, there is a qualitative difference between their worlds. The same thing might be said of the *Cantos* of Ezra Pound in comparison to the poetry of Robert Bridges. Existentialism is called a modern philosophy; cubism is called a modern form of painting. The pitfalls in such comparison and characterization are diverse, as Howe points out, but the emphasis on such things as the plight of the self, the absence of natural order, and artistic concomitants such as avant-gardism and formal experimentation (content becoming in some cases almost incidental) are part of a general atmosphere within which these particular creative endeavours become recognizable to us in a way that earlier ones do not. We feel an intuitive kinship with their creators, and possess the creations. We recognize them as part of our age.

MacDiarmid has much company: in fact, the predominant characteristic of the modern mind is an overwhelming self-consciousness coupled with a very real sense of being in a predicament or plight. Perhaps in no other age have we felt so betrayed by our environment; perhaps in no other age have we worried so much about ourselves. "The average educated man," said I.A. Richards in 1926, "is growing more conscious, an extraordinarily significant change. It is probably due to the fact that his life is becoming more and more complex, more intricate, his desires and needs more varied and more apt to conflict. And as he becomes more conscious he can no longer be content to drift in unreflecting obedience to custom. He is forced to reflect. And if reflection often takes the form of inconclusive worrying, that is no more than might be expected in view of the unparalleled difficulty of the task."[11] Karl Lowith proposes that "modernity begins with the dissolution of a natural and social *order* in which man was supposed to have a definite *nature* and *place*, while modern man 'exists,' displaced and out of place, in extreme situations on the edge of chaos."[12] This is the very essence of MacDiarmid, who prefers to live "whaur extremes meet" and whose writing so often consists of the "inconclusive worrying" to which Richards refers.

But if the modern world lacks natural order, this does not stop most people from believing it exists, however doubtful they are. Doubt, not certainty, characterizes modern thinking. There is a modern concept of truth (in the sense of meaning, or what in another age was given in revelation) which is captured accurately in an evocative image from a song by Neil Young of a blind person "running thru the light of the night / With an answer in his hand."[13] Truth is all around us, but it is hidden or inaccessible. And revelation, however remote the possibility, cannot be altogether discounted. Very few modern artists, for example, take a consistent existentialist or absurdist position. For most of them the notion of truth still has validity. This is hardly surprising: the alternatives to this attitude are for most of us, artists or not, fairly depressing.

If, as Nietzsche proclaimed, God is dead, it is only natural for people to look for replacements. If God does not exist, Dostoevski said, anything is possible. We are free. But what does this freedom offer us? Erich Fromm writes, "In the name of 'freedom' life loses all structure; it is composed of many little pieces, each separate from the other and lacking any sense as a whole. The individual is left alone with these pieces like a child with a puzzle; the difference, however, is that the child knows what a house is and therefore can recognize the parts of the house in the little pieces he is playing with, whereas the adult does not see the meaning of the 'whole,' the pieces of which come into his hands. He is bewildered and afraid and just goes on gazing at his little meaningless pieces."[14] Far from being exciting and challenging, such freedom carries with it such awesome responsibility (for if we are utterly free we are utterly responsible for any decisions we make) that it seems a natural impulse to shy away from it.

Fromm is specifically concerned with totalitarianism; his thesis is that freed from or robbed of a definite place in a scheme of things, many of us try to avoid this new responsibility by turning to ideology. But we can turn to other possible avenues as well. Artists can look for salvation and order in their art. If language is their medium, however, all the crushing confusion of modernism confronts them directly.

The communication of information, taking place at great speed in modern times and destroying any sense of priority or value by sheer volume, is a factor in the totalitarian urge, as Fromm claims. The puzzle cannot be put together if new pieces keep arriving. But this difficulty confronts us regardless of totalitarianism. Most of our experience of the world is second-hand; we experience it through language. Fromm writes specifically of radio, newspapers, and film, but the vast amount of printed matter available from innumerable sources, in the form of fiction, non-fiction, advertising, propaganda, and so on, completes the picture. The world – our modern world – is overwhelmed with a sea of messages as never before in history. Assuming there were infallible methods which could establish the truth or falsity and value of a datum, it would still take countless lifetimes to examine or reflect upon a minute fraction of the information we receive.

The degradation of language which results has been described by Orwell in *1984*, and is the main preoccupation of George Steiner in *Language and Silence*, in which silence is seen as the only resort in a world in which language has lost power and effectiveness.[15] The latter theme is indicated in Susan Sontag's essay on the same subject.[16] It is perhaps not so much the misuse of language as its overuse which is a cause for concern. Like any precision tool, available to people unskilled in its use or for the wrong uses, it is bound to be abused (propaganda, advertising), but this is only one factor in its loss of effectiveness. It is the continual barrage of language on all fronts which is chiefly responsible for cheapening it. Responses to it are dulled; there is too much to digest. The modern age is the age of linguistic overkill.

Reactions to this satiation are many and varied. Marshall McLuhan's reaction against Gutenberg for having engendered a "print-made split between head and heart," and against literacy in general for having "set up a gap between appearance and reality," extends by implication to language itself, against which he poses what he believes to be its coming electronically based replacement. "Electricity," he says, "points the way to an extension of the process of consciousness itself, on a world scale, and without any verbalization whatever." In the advanced electric age he envisions a "condition of speechlessness that could confer a perpetuity of collective harmony and peace."[17] Steiner introduces the concept of "meaningful silence" as a necessary concomitant of the increasing powerlessness of language. He seems of two minds whether language is losing power as a result of a changing view of the world or whether the "retreat from the word" is a result of the overuse and misuse of language – that is, that the changing view of the world is a result of the increasing degradation of language. But that degradation is not questioned.[18]

The reaction of modern writers to the erosion of the power of language has often been to reinvent it, to develop new forms of expression which recapture some of its original force. *Finnegans Wake* is a clear example, as are the verbal experimentation of e e cummings, the dense rhetoric of Dylan Thomas, the notorious Chinese ideograms of Ezra Pound, and the reclamation of unusual words by a host of poets from Eliot and Auden to the present day. Hugh MacDiarmid's experiments with Scots and later with English are readily recognizible in this context. Language is not simply taken for granted by MacDiarmid and his contemporaries, but becomes itself a theme, a central preoccupation in a world where common language no longer seems adequate for aesthetic purposes.

Moreover, the sheer quantity of experience (through language), coupled with the absence of an accessible natural order, can itself be expected to give rise to marked artistic consequences. Writing specifically of William Carlos Williams, but in a passage with far wider application, R.H. Pearce says: "Granting the fact of [the poet's] essential alienation, he can find no certain means in his culture of giving form and wholeness to his knowledge. He can only 'invent' it. There are no *topoi* to help him along; for, overwhelmed by his sense of the general divorcement which is the type of his own, he can trust for guidance in no one. Who can tell him where to go and what to do? Perforce, he is thrown back upon himself, imperfect as he is, only the rhythm of his own sensibility and its perceptions can get him moving."[19] The phrase "thrown back upon himself" is a striking one, conveying as it does a sense of violent abandonment, almost the sense of having fallen. Stephen Spender writes of an "urban consciousness" which "has thrust the poets ... back upon their own resources, so that they must create out of themselves the luminous values which may still envelope the earth."[20] Once again, with the word *thrust*, a sense of rejection or of being cast out is implied, the feeling Heidegger refers to as *Geworfenheit*, or "thrown-ness."

"In a world of fragmented values the imagination cannot illustrate accepted doctrines, cannot refer to symbolic meanings already recognized by the reader, symbols of the faith he believes in, and imbibed with his education," writes Stephen Spender.[21] F.R. Leavis speaks of the "breakup of forms and the loss of axioms." Referring to *The Waste Land*, he says, "no one [cultural] tradition can digest so great a variety of materials, and the result is a break-down of forms and the irrevocable loss of that sense of absoluteness which seems necessary to a robust culture."[22] If, as Richards states, the poet orders experience, the modern poet can expect no help from the outside.[23] As Spender notes, "works like the last novels of Henry James ... *Finnegans Wake*, Yeats's Byzantium poems, the *Duineser Elegien*, put these writers in the God-like position of being isolated within their own creations, of having to reinvent the world and all its values within their art."[24] The sense of having been thrown into their situation, left utterly on their own, quite naturally gives rise to this stance on the part of modern artists. If no order is "given," they quite literally must make sense. Jean-Paul Sartre, writing of Baudelaire, puts it this way: "The conscious self derives its laws from itself ... It must accept complete responsibility and create its own values, must give meaning to the world and to its own life ... with the conscious self something comes into being which did not exist before – meaning."[25] Artists become lawgivers; they create a world out of what appears to be chaos.

If the common impulse is to shy away when confronted by a world consisting of Fromm's "little meaningless pieces," to take refuge in ideology or to succumb to despair, then modern artists might well be seen, and frequently see themselves, as heroic in their attempts to impose or discover order where none is "given." It is no small task, after all, to recreate a smashed universe. MacDiarmid, with his god-like poetic persona, his insistence upon facing the brute, discordant facts, his angry challenging of all moribund orthodoxies, his arrogant and uncompromising stance against anything less than the quest for perfect understanding and against anyone who fails to assume the entire burden of this struggle, takes his place among the other hero-poets of the modern era fighting their lonely battles with chaos.

And lonely it is – the audience scarcely seems to matter. MacDiarmid's disdain for his audience is manifest throughout his writing, a continual contemptuous hectoring of admirers and detractors alike. His own self-doubts are exacerbated by what he senses as an uncomprehending, listless readership, one which lacks what Sartre calls "generosity." Readers might give themselves to a work, but only until something else captures their attention, at which point it is as though the work never existed, except as entertainment or yesterday's book. Far from mitigating the inward-turning of the writer, the audience contributes to it. Makers of literature in modern times write more than ever about and for themselves.

"The Romantic poets break loose from the classical-Christian tradition, but they do not surrender the wish to discover in the universe a network of spiritual meaning which, however precariously, can enclose their selves," writes Irving Howe. "They still seek to relate [a preoccupation with psychic inwardness] to transcendent values, if not sources, in the external world. For them the universe is still alert, still the active transmitter of spiritual signs." Contrasted to this attitude is the modern one: "[To] the modernist writer the universe is a speechless presence, neither hospitable nor hostile; and after a time he does not agonize, as did nineteenth-century writers like Hardy, over the dispossession of man in the cosmic scheme. He takes that dispossession for granted and turns his anxieties inward, toward the dispossession of meaning from inner life."[26] But this last statement is not entirely true, for surely the "inner life" and the "cosmic scheme" are not divisible. The two dispossessions are one and the same. The modern takes nothing for granted. We continue to agonize and continue to hope. But for the Romantics, truth was at least theoretically accessible in a way which to the modern writer it is not. The former had moments of creative ecstasy when they knew; the latter has these moments too, but isn't sure. The modern writer stands at a distance from his or her beliefs, poking them at short intervals to see if there is still life in them. A whirling chaos of conflicting opinions on the one hand, and scientific, sceptical rationalism on the other have conspired to kill certainty.

Modern poetry which makes use of beliefs of the "pseudo-statement" variety (to use Richards's term) often displays a thematic concern with the whole problem of belief. For example, it is the struggle into religion, not the religion itself, which is indicated in the later poetry of Auden and Eliot, just as it was the process of writing a poem, not the poem itself, which concerned the Symbolists. One finds that in modern writing, belief engenders its justification rather than self-assurance, and that the problem of believing is much more a thematic concern than any belief *per se*. Even Yeats, whose tone is relatively self-assured, felt it necessary to publish *A Vision* as a justification for his belief system. Beliefs too are a form of data; the choice of any one is now a hazardous undertaking. A belief no longer serves as an underpinning or as a set of aesthetic axioms which can be implied and left alone, but is now a vexing question in itself to the modern writer. "He offers his *struggle* with dilemmas as the substance of his testimony; and whatever unity his work possesses, often not very much, comes from the emotional rhythm, the thrust toward completion, of that struggle. After Kafka it becomes hard to believe not only in answers but even in endings."[27] The problem of belief for many modern writers is such a dilemma.

But underlying all such dilemmas, as has been indicated, is the primary problem of the "thrown," "displaced," "dispossessed," or "lost" self. Sartre, in his often brilliant book *Literature and Existentialism*, summarizes the whole question of the modern writer-in-the-world: "But if we ourselves produce the rules of production, the measures, the criteria, and if our creative drive comes from the very depths of our heart, then we never find anything but ourselves in our work. It is we who have invented the laws by which we judge it."[28] The most fundamental problem facing the modern writer is the self, or, as Kafka puts it, "You are the problem. No scholar to be found far and wide." Whereas in neoclassicist writing, as Sartre argues, the present was confused with the eternal (the myth of perenniality), and reading was a ceremony of recognition, modern writing demonstrates in contrast an awareness of ceaseless and random change into which the self is unceremoniously thrown.[29] And the self, stripped down to essentials, is the fundamental theme of modern literature. To dismiss modern writing on the grounds of fragmentation, obscurity, or self-preoccupation is to dismiss modern humanity.

The writers themselves offer manifestos on occasion. "There is no more beauty except in struggle," says "A Manifesto of Italian Futurism."[30] And Evgeni Zamyatin considers continual revolution a cosmic law. "Some day," he asserts, "an exact formula will be established for the law of revolution. And in this formula nations, classes, stars – and books will be expressed as numerical values." He writes of "molten rock ... encrusted with dogma." "Weak-nerved minds unfailingly require a finite universe, a final integer; ... [they] do not have the strength to include themselves in the dialectic syllogism."[31] What we have here, of course, is no solution at all to Zamyatin's proposed goal. The contradiction in these statements is of crucial importance, for it occurs in much modern thought. "There is a goal but no way; what we call the way is only wavering," says Kafka, echoing his main influence Søren Kierkegaard.[32] For "wavering," "struggle" can be substituted, since both are reactions to the predicament in which the modern self feels enmeshed. Zamyatin wants an "exact formula," but his wish to plunge into dialectical struggle and his rejection of those who demand a "final integer" indicate that his primary concern is struggle, revolution for its own sake. In one way or another the goal is always a unified understanding, but the modern writer, made sceptical of beliefs and finding in the prevalent atmosphere of scientific rationalism an objective knowledge which is "not of a kind upon which an equally fine organization of the mind can be based" (that is, it fulfils no spiritual needs), is divorced from a "way" and is left to waver or struggle as the case may be.[33] The self is incapable of providing its own foundation. As MacDiarmid expresses it, "The mind creates only to destroy."[34] So that, whereas in previous ages writing presupposed a unified context within which it took place and which it reflected, the process is reversed in the modern period. That context has become the goal. Yeats's system-building, for example, as Richards points out in *Science and Poetry*, involved "an effort to discover a new world-picture to replace that given by science."[35] Leavis agrees, substituting the word "create" for "discover."[36] As for Hugh MacDiarmid's explicit faith in raw data, one does not detect any end to his restlessness or struggle in the later poetry of facts. In the very act of writing, modern writers such as Eliot, Joyce, MacDiarmid, or the Williams of *Paterson* are attempting to construct a reality, to indicate a direction along which the self can move, to codify experience, to establish some sort of continuity of the self through the chaos of sensations and thoughts the world presents to them.

It may be useful at this point to note the work of a poet who is transitional, not fully modern, but in many ways a harbinger of literary modernism: Walt Whitman. He was the first to produce poems of the type Donald Davie terms "open-ended" and which

Duncan Glen describes as *"individual* and free-growing forms which seem to most fully express our modern consciousness" – the "poetic main-stream of our age in American/English literature."[37] Whitman's world was young America, seemingly ripe with promise, a new Zion. His occupation was journalism. His "Song of Myself," which in many respects is cosmic journalism, marks a turning-point in poetry, in terms of both theme and structure, for it is concerned with the self, has no conventional resolution, and quite clearly uses the material of young America as a means of expressing the self-in-the-world. Alexander Pope would never have claimed, "I am large, I contain multitudes," for that is a radically modern doctrine. William Blake's self, while seeming perhaps to be more similar, is in fact much more like Pope's than like Whitman's, positing as it does a plane upon which the self does not function. Pope said, "Presume not the heavens to scan," and Blake inverted this, attacking "natural religion." But Walt Whitman appropriated heaven and earth for his self, even if it is true that heaven is in the background in his work. The self for Whitman is never in doubt, and nothing is off limits to it. It is neither ultimately absorbed into a depersonalizing transcendental unity (Albion) nor is it reduced to civilized Augustan proportions.

Being-in-the-world, Whitman's central theme, is at the core of modern thought. The concept, it should be noted, is neither an idealist one (in which everything is the self) nor a materialist one in which the self is objectively part of the world.[38] Being-in-the-world is a constructive process. The focus of creation becomes the experiencing self. Whitman experiences the world and the world is available to him: it grows as he grows. His America too is large and contains multitudes. And his poem has no conventional ending because no experience is final except death. A poem about the self ("about" in both senses) cannot end or be resolved in a conventional manner. The ending of MacDiarmid's *To Circumjack Cencrastus* is markedly unsatisfactory for this very reason. The lack of an ending in Pound's *Cantos* does not trouble the reader – there is always room for yet another Canto, as there is for more material in *The Waste Land, Paterson,* or Olson's *Maximus Poems,* or, returning to Whitman, in "Song of Myself." Poetry is a partial synthesis of self and not-self in the writing of it; the creative act is "having" at its fullest. There is always more to write. For poets not content with lyric moments there is the long poem, and where the poet's own being is the theme, explicit or otherwise, that long poem has no ending while the poet lives and continues to be a poet. Unity in this poem is what Leavis, struggling to show *The Waste Land* as unified, called the "unity of the inclusive consciousness."[39]

But Whitman is not the first purely modern poet, for he does not abandon the concept of a soul. This is of primary importance. He does not write out of chaos but out of a calm assurence that things have their place in some scheme. The tone of his work is boisterously affirmative; his soul is, after all, indestructible, and glides easily in and out of the body. His catalogues, a sort of existential shorthand, are not clusters of fragments shored up against his ruin but exciting series of images generating a consistently joyous atmosphere, a garden, not a wasteland, a network of spiritual meaning, if only by implication. Here is the influence of Romanticism by way of New England Transcendentalism. We do not find this body/soul dichotomy in MacDiarmid, Williams, or Pound. And yet, interestingly enough, the moment of ecstasy for Whitman is not the soul's escape from the body but the very opposite, in which body and soul become one. The soul, set free to attain identity with the life of America (seen in successive images, in a girl's body, a horse, etc.) returns to the body, and the two-become-one are enriched. The "I" of Whitman is never in doubt at any time.

For modern poets, however, that tenuous grasp on the absolute which was sufficient to permit Whitman his joyous, unquestioning affirmation of being has faltered. What was for Whitman an Eden has become a Waste Land, in which they wander alone, and wonder, and agonize, handling bits and pieces they chance to find, perhaps even collecting them, although they offer at best only the ghosts of clues as to their place in a structure, or their meaning. These poets might try to assimilate what they find, but the pieces fit into no universal scheme, instead littering a dead land where a mighty battle seems to have taken place. Here are bits of things barely recognizable for what they are, other things which cannot be identified at all, the whole presenting to the optimistic (or less pessimistic) a gigantic jigsaw puzzle, or, to the more pessimistic, a mere heap of garbage with no hidden meaning upon which crawl the lonely shapes of human beings vainly trying to make sense of it all (see Samuel Beckett's novel *How It Is*, or his playlet *Breath*, for example).

As an alternative, these scattered things can appear as equipment which we use to create ourselves, utterly on our own responsibility; their meaning grows out of this use. It is difficult to think of many modern writers who have consciously adopted this attitude, however. The prevalent attitudes consist of various reactions to the Waste Land, either an acceptance of it, nostalgia for what came before, an attempt to rebuild from the ruins, or a rejection of it from the vantage point of some belief.

Long poems, for fairly obvious reasons, offer a greater idea of the poet's confrontation with the age than the short poem or lyric can do, especially in regard to form, even if the long poem, or at least the loosely structured open-ended poem which has been discussed, presents the critic with severe problems of evaluation. What are the structural elements which predominate in these poems? Plainly there is more to Pound's *Cantos*, for example – or to MacDiarmid's later long poems – than pure associationism, even if critics show a truly modern wavering: Yvor Winters, writing of the *Cantos*, says "there are a few loosely related themes running through the work, or at least there sometimes appear to be,"[40] and Kenneth Buthlay, considering MacDiarmid's poem "Cornish Heroic Song," can say only that its theme is "fairly certain."[41] There is a question of perception here: Jacques Maritain writes of the creative process: "Art begins with the mind and the will to select. The spontaneous welling up of images, without which there can be no poetry, *precedes and nourishes* the activity of the poet: and doubtless it is never the result of premeditation and calculation: this must be emphasized. As a general rule, however, the mind not only regulates but invites such an activity and gives it a direction. It then waits for the results, stops them as they issue, makes a selection and forms a judgement."[42] The mind referred to in this passage is the conscious mind. The way the conscious mind perceives reality is clearly of importance in determining what kind of poetry is produced: this is truistic. The beliefs (that is, systems of belief, world theories, standpoints) of a poet influence his or her perceptions. A poet who floats in a sea of such beliefs perceives reality on a much more elemental level, upon which the comforting inevitability of cause and effect no longer operates, resolutions do not take place as a matter of course, patterns prove illusory or meaningless, "things fall apart," and there is no metaphysical backdrop of moral or natural order placing the poet in a scheme of things. The beliefs themselves, in vast numbers and confusion, seem to battle among themselves for acceptability, with scientific rationalism as the umpire, addicted to technicalities, disqualifying all participants with impartiality; the latter try desperately to adhere as best they can to rules which make the game impossible: a Kafkaesque situation.

Two contrasting examples of reactions to this situation can be found in the poetry of W.B. Yeats and David Jones. As R.G. Billings has shown in her unpublished thesis, "The Mood and Plan of Yeats' *Words for Music Perhaps*," Yeats employs a dramatic structure in this cycle of poems so that in reality there is only one poem which moves towards a resolution – Plotinus sailing to Byzantium, the symbol of Yeats's transcendental realm. The immediate homely situation of Crazy Jane, for example, is seen to progress against this backdrop which transcends immediate situations but infuses them with meaning. Armed with his personal "religion," then, Yeats uses what is in fact a religious sensibility to produce a long poem where an ending of the traditional sort can take place. The movement of the poem is able to have a direction, and be concluded, and one is given a complex of cause and effect in which one observes immediate situations such as Crazy Jane confronting the bishop deriving from or evidencing a web of spiritual meaning. Structurally, what seems to be several poems proves to be one in the same way that what seems to be the many proves, in Yeats's system, to be the one. His vision provided him with a sense of certainty and meaning which perhaps no other modern poet, with the exception of later Auden, has achieved. But in his whole emphasis upon recognition, upon demonstrating the truth of his belief, letting it be the theme rather than the underpinning of much of his poetry, Yeats is indicating a reaction to the Waste Land: his poetry is the exception which proves the rule.

David Jones, also a man of deep religious sensibility, has no system by which this sensibility can be codified, shaped, and transmitted within a comforting transcendental framework. He becomes, therefore, a sort of religious historian, rescuing fragments of value from a historical grab-bag. His poem *The Anathemata* is subtitled "fragments of an attempted writing," and he himself describes it as "a series of fragments, fragmented bits, chance scraps really, of records of things, vestiges of sorts and kinds of *disciplinae* that have come my way by this channel or that influence ... a coat of many colours." And he writes that "no 'external discipline' can be real, invigorating, and integrating unless it comes to us with the imperatives of a living tradition."[43] Harold Rosenberg, writing of Jones in his essay "Aesthetics of Crisis," sums up the problems: "if art is a language of signs, these signs, Jones knows, are constantly being invalidated by the speedy rhythms of cultural change and interchange ... And though art must display the sacred otherness of fact, our minds and spirits have been shaped by science to treat fact as fact and nothing more." Jones assembles his fragments like an archaeologist, knowing each piece has value and meaning, and "displays the overlapping layers of time by a technique of jamming together data plucked from different cultural 'moments.'"[44] There is no "living tradition," but rather a collection of heirlooms which Jones values and wishes to preserve. Conclusions or resolutions are not called for. In the absence of a viable present "external discipline," Jones has resurrected the past and grouped a series of historical pieces around himself like a montage. He is in the centre of it all, choosing his fragments. His world, assembled out of history, is shaped by his process of choice and thus is self-centred *de facto*; and the same is true of Pound, who turns to history as well. When one has no system to make the world coherent and meaningful, one turns to the available data: history is studied exhaustively, we see it struggle towards the status of myth but never quite reach it. The poet is alone with his objects, in the absence of an all-encompassing order, and Pound, Williams, and others find history the richest category of objects, a series of relics to be revivified in the Waste Land. Poets become the planners of their world, for the objects are not given but chosen, and any form which arises does so only in terms of these choices; very little is presupposed or "understood."

MacDiarmid's objects are not, as a rule, derived from history – he prefers, as has been indicated, the comforting feel of facts and words which seem irreducible, the quarks from which the universe can be reassembled. But the aesthetic techniques involved, if far less polished than those of David Jones, are nonetheless essentially similar, consisting of the arrangement of material around the "I" of the poet, without a conventional beginning, middle, or end.

In order to give any sense of coherence to these aesthetic objects at all, there must be more than the mere process of choice. The objects themselves (data, ideas, images, and so on) are given, willy-nilly, a life of their own when used by a poet. He or she must in fact set up a dynamism rather than a collection of parts unrelated except by the process; otherwise we have merely noise without even Irving Howe's "unity of purpose." A poem is a construction – even *The Waste Land* is built out of mutually reinforcing images of sterility and desolation – and this presupposes some relation between the parts. Even if the unity of purpose is the only unity that exists, the parts of the poem as a whole should reflect or point to that purpose. In the absence of what William Soutar called an "architectonic of belief," the components of many modern long poems (and novels) are related to each other by means of an elemental linking process in which the separate parts reflect and struggle with each other in dialectical fashion. In some way they are related to a whole, even if this whole is only implied and turns out to be neither theme nor underpinning, but some unguessable poetic intention. At the same time they are important in themselves, and their distinctiveness and differences, coupled with their relationship to each other in terms of a whole, provide the dynamism of the poem.

The "centripetal" force which relates the components often appears as a mirroring. Yeats writes in his poem "The Statues," "Empty eyeballs knew / That knowledge increases unreality, that / Mirror on mirror mirrored is all the show."[45] The statues "see" with Yeats the illusory nature of what he proceeds to call "this filthy modern tide," its "formless spawning fury." Eliot writes despairingly in "Gerontion" of "a wilderness of mirrors" which is, in fact, the Waste Land itself. Franz Kafka in his novels and in many of his short stories uses a technique of piling parallel situations upon each other without causal relation between them. Hugh MacDiarmid uses a similar technique in many of his long poems. Here the mirror concept is implicit as an actual structure in the work. What Eliot and Yeats evince is a despair in the loss of a system of values and its replacement by an associationist perception, a despair shared by Yvor Winters as a critic. The components of many modern long poems mirror each other, in that each reflects, in one way or another, some factor common to all of them. What is modern in all this is the vagueness of the factor and the fact that the components are not placed in some overall scheme, and thus de-emphasized, but rather are all on a level, the common factor being no "architectonic of belief" but in a very real sense the poet's existence.

The "centrifugal" force which renders the components distinct and individual completes the dialectic. If "mirror on mirror mirrored," parodying the mimetic principle (a mirror held up to life becomes a mirror held up to other mirrors), merely makes us look beyond the poem, as it were, the attention is focused once again upon the poem by the dynamics occasioned by the opposing forces. A continual synthesizing process takes place upon a metaphorical landscape. Greek myth and contemporary reality are juxtaposed in *The Waste Land*, for example, and the result transcends them both. Tiresias, the central figure in the poem, is at one time a woman-turned-man by the gods and a symbol of the ambivalence, sexual and otherwise, of the outsider, a modern man on a journey through the Waste Land unsure of who he is or what he is about, detached from it all like Camus's Meursault. The synthesis of the two is striking. Tiresias in Eliot's poem is more than the ancient Greek character, but his modern role is emphasized by his former one in Greek mythology. We have on a symbolic level two parallel situations of ambivalence which are synthesized in one role transcending either: Eliot's Tiresias is Tiresias and at the same time a contemporary. The two components of this figure are different and yet mirror each other, and from this, exactly as in metaphor, a synthesis arises. In Kafka's novel *Amerika*, to give another example, the parallel situations of Karl aboard ship and Karl in New York form part of a continual process in which Karl's immediate situations, the same only different, reinforce each other and emphasize his plight, which transcends ship and city. The rhythm of the novel arises from this dialectical tension.

In this connection it is interesting to note a study of one poem of

Fernando Pessoa by Roman Jakobsen which "reveals a dazzling play of symmetries, mirror images, contraries, contradictions, and balanced cancellations."[46] It would be absurd to imply that traditional poetry, or literature in general, lacks these elements. What is modern is the considerable emphasis placed upon them, or, rather, the way in which they emerge as central structures in work lacking the traditional beginning, middle, and end. They are not ancillary to some scheme, in other words, but appear to take the place of a scheme.

In his development MacDiarmid more and more comes to rely on the barest of centripetal/centrifugal techniques to hold his material together and give it life. Extended metaphors are linked to others; his lists and verbal collages proliferate as his writing becomes a lengthy statement of intentions, a description of what is required to achieve the ideal poetry he wants, a vast collection of building materials. The particularity of the fragments highlights the enormity of the ideal task of assembly. In the midst of them MacDiarmid gropes for the light: the swirls and eddies of his progress are the dramatic tensions which do, to that extent at least, make the fragments cohere as poetry.

Hence in MacDiarmid's work, in particular his later work, we can see a unique approach to the Waste Land. Without the religious sensibility of Jones, the hermetic vision of Yeats, or the relatively disciplined literary/historical consciousness of Pound, MacDiarmid's own presence is magnified in his creation as he stumbles, changes direction, encounters more obstacles, and stumbles again, complaining loudly the while. There is a deepening sense of confusion as his poetry develops – and of tragedy. In his pursuit of the missing ideal through art, MacDiarmid's art itself becomes idealized and rises out of his reach. He is mired in his reading, his facts, his words, his ideas, unable at last to do more than thrash about. But as other poets have paradoxically created poetry from mourning the failure of inspiration (Coleridge and Yeats come immediately to mind), so MacDiarmid produces an idiosyncratic later work which is often unlovely, often tedious, but is nevertheless full of the drama of one trapped but never losing hope.

In this, he poignantly expresses the frustration of the modern condition. MacDiarmid's entire work, in fact, early and late, consists of reiterations of the fundamental existential dilemmas of our time as they are expressed in the practice of poetry. His self-consciousness and single-mindedness allow us deeper insight into the poetry of his fellow-travellers in the Waste Land, all of whom have developed their own ways and means of coping with an environment hostile to earlier notions of art as revelation. That environment, and its influence on the modern writer, are nowhere so completely and pitilessly delineated as in the long, tortuous canon of Hugh MacDiarmid.

CHAPTER TWO

The Early Lyrics:
The World and the Self

I am the tongue of that vast bell
    Inverted over me –
The voice, the victim, and the god
    Lost in infinity.
(A.J.M. Smith, "Universe Into Stone,"
from *Poems New and Collected.*)

In his early work Hugh MacDiarmid began to develop themes which form the basis of his later verse; it is a far from seamless web of social concern, Scottish nationalism, preoccupations with the immensity and ultimate meaning/meaninglessness of the universe, an anything but sublime egotism, and an accumulation of theories, judgments, cultural "bits," and vocabulary. In effect he had gathered together most of the building blocks of his life's work prior to the publication of *A Drunk Man Looks at the Thistle* in 1926, and thus a close examination of this early material provides a sound basis for a study of his entire poetic career.

Christopher Murray Grieve had been writing for over a decade previous to the creation of "Hugh M'Diarmid" the poet in the *Dunfermline Press* in 1922. One of the fascinating aspects of the early verse written in the period when "M'Diarmid" and Grieve were publishing side by side is how different the quality of the two streams of poetry is, and yet how similar the underlying preoccupations remain. It required the development of a new medium, "Synthetic Scots" or "Lallans," to bring out the first-rate qualities of poetic expression one finds in the work of MacDiarmid. The "Grieve stream," almost entirely very minor poetry, has been virtually ignored by the critics. Yet for two reasons it is of great importance. First, it contains themes of poetic creation and the self in-the-world similar to those found in "M'Diarmid"'s work. Second, the later work of MacDiarmid, that is, his post-1935 poetry which is largely written in English, can in many ways be regarded as an extrapolation of the poetry and to some extent the prose appearing over the name of C.M.

Grieve. In order to indicate the importance of this work, it shall be examined separately from the Scots poems of "M'Diarmid"; the connections between the two streams will be made evident in the course of this chapter.

In J.K. Annand's painstaking presentation *Early Lyrics by Hugh MacDiarmid*, the earliest poetry of MacDiarmid is revealed as slight, giving little or no indication of his later success. "She Whom I Love"[1] might be a precursor to "Trompe L'Oeil" in *Penny Wheep*,[2] for in both poems there is a disturbing image of a multiple-eyed lover. But perhaps only the poem "Two Gods" contains anything of real interest.[3]

MacDiarmid composed this poem about the present moment from a reading of Goethe. He writes, "Now is a mighty God / Then an unknown." The philosophy expressed in this poem is similar to Pirandello's conception of life being made up of an endless series of instants without relation to each other, so that the continuity of change (and of the self, whose perception is thus fragmented) is destroyed. The past, continues MacDiarmid, shall have "The dreams I dare / Not let my own heart share." This is certainly striking a poetic pose, but nevertheless the idea of an ever-changing present moment and a removed and therefore irrelevant past indicates the lack, at this point, of a clear, continuous poetic direction, since the continuity of dreams is explicitly rejected by MacDiarmid. The philosophy of this poem, in other words, lies in a thematic treatment of the poet's unrest, and is a means of expressing his situation as an uncertain one. From this one slight poem it is obviously risky to infer too much about the poet at this stage; but as examination of later work indicates, it is no passing fancy, no theme adopted and as quickly forgotten.

MacDiarmid as C.M. Grieve shows little development in his poetry, published in *Northern Numbers*, the *Scottish Chapbook*, and other periodicals, as well as in his *Annals of the Five Senses*. The *Early Lyrics*, in fact, are a fair indication of what MacDiarmid was doing at this time under his real name. There is an over-reliance upon diction to carry the weight of his poems, coupled with occasional very real poetic insights, as a closer examination of this material bears out.

Several poems of the "Grieve stream" appear in the first series of *Northern Numbers* (1920) edited by himself. It is in this anthology that we are first introduced to the explicit theme of silence, in a poem called "Allegiance."[4] Duncan Glen suggests that the poem is an early statement of Scottish nationalist interests,[5] although Kenneth Buthlay points out quite rightly that the "cause" in this poem may be just a girl after all.[6] Nevertheless, Glen's suggestion cannot be entirely discounted. There is a comparison of the rich and beautiful Mediterranean with the Scottish landscape where a "brown stream chunners in my heart always." His allegiance, says the poet, is not to the queen (whose identity is mysterious as well: as a First World War poem, Victoria cannot be whom he means) but to the "cause forlorn" in a land where "timeless silence in the far blue hills / Hangs like a ready bell!"

The theme of silence recurs again and again in MacDiarmid's poetry. Burns Singer has pointed out the importance of this concept in his work as a whole.[7] Singer is largely mistaken about his later work, however, in taking explicit statements from *In Memoriam James Joyce* and applying them as keys, and it is clear that he makes no distinction between two equally valid concepts of silence. One is that area of understanding beyond language, the silence of which George Steiner writes. The other silence reflects the absence of a universal order given intuitively to the poet. Its use as a theme in this and other poems indicates MacDiarmid's awareness that he is on his own and must proceed at his own risk without any outside guidance insofar as song is concerned. It reflects a sense of his entire responsibility for his work. That poetry is indicated thematically is evidenced by the music of the "ready bell" which is ready for him to make, and by the theme of Scotland whose voice or clapper he might well wish to be, just as in the later Scots lyric "Ex Vermibus" he wishes to provide the "worm" which will make the unfledged bird of Scotland take wing and sing. Silence, like the theme of darkness which is also common in his poetry, is Jean-Paul Sartre's *néant* or nothingness, a void in which one can only "possibilize," which at every moment characterizes the self in-the-world and cuts it off from the security of Being. In this void, the very essence of human freedom, one must construct his own self *ex nihilo* as his "fundamental project."[8] The "ready bell" of the poem can easily be understood as an indication of a coming *magnum opus*, the delineation of a universe focused in Scotland soon to be outlined in "Braid Scots: An Inventory and Appraisement." Scotland, as Daiches says, is to MacDiarmid a "mode of knowing."[9] MacDiarmid, in the guise of a prophet coming to make Scotland realize its potential, is in fact concerned with his own sense of potential, which is his actual theme: if Scotland is to be the hub of the universe, MacDiarmid is to be the hub of Scotland, for the underlying situation is invariably MacDiarmid-in-the-world.

This explanation is not making too much of these lines. In a continually recurring context, the theme of nothingness appears time and time again in his work. It is that which must be escaped – the silence must be filled with music, the darkness with light. But silence and darkness are always there to be filled, are never eliminated or resolved, and represent a continual sense of lack. In "Mountain Measure" the speechless presence of an overwhelmingly immense universe engenders a mood of despair: "And all man's thoughts are but as winds / That in the valleys still / Spin gravel!"[10] Here two concepts are united. On the one hand we have the inaccessibility of Being, the theme of nothingness being expressed in physical terms as tiny man, vast universe, with the gulf between them clearly implied. On the other is the more literal idea of perception – the poet, confronted with such vastness, must do what he can to take it all in, must use the data of experience even if it amounts to a mere shifting of gravel, an exercise fundamentally devoid of meaning. For the situation of humanity, as implied in these lines, is a perennial one. We resist the world, the world resists us, some gravel is moved. Or, in Sartre's words, "Man is a useless passion." In the poet's despair this arises as a distinct possibility: the self is cut off from the world, and its thoughts are incapable of establishing it in a scheme of things.

The themes of silence and cosmic immensity (the latter symbolizing both nothingness, in that a gulf between the self and the universe is implied, and also the availability of endless amounts of material) are amplified somewhat in *Northern Numbers* (second series, 1921). One device often used by MacDiarmid in his work as a whole, that of proceeding from the particular to the cosmic, perpetually revealing in this way his fundamental plight which underlies all immediate, particular situations, is quite noticeable here. "Edinburgh" provides one instance: the city is a "mad god's dream / Fitful and dark," he writes, after dismissing Glasgow, Dundee, and Aberdeen. The last line of the poem is "Earth eyes Eternity."[11] The world is viewed from a strange angle in "Playmates," in which a goddess, described as a childhood playmate "upon whose breasts / The pale skies dangle," is said to have kept with MacDiarmid a spare star upon which nations were confined. All these nations killed themselves except America, who "went wrong in the head" and had to be killed. "You were merciful then," says MacDiarmid.[12] On one level we have overtones of history and culture; more basically, the innocence of childhood is presented as a cosmic scheme, an Eden overseen by a goddess who, as a childhood playmate, no longer exists. (The Eden subtheme occurs elsewhere in this poetry: for example, in "First Fruits" in which he sees himself outside the garden where he had experienced perfect love, in a sort of exile.) This loss of innocence is the explanation of the above line – MacDiarmid no longer has his cosmic scheme, the goddess has absented herself. Compared to that, destroying nations is merciful. MacDiarmid has been left to himself, cast out, and his nostalgia for childhood reflects his sense of *Geworfenheit*. In Sonnet II of "Sonnets of the Highland Hills," "Heaven," the cosmic theme is once more apparent. What if paradise is just another "void of skies," asks MacDiarmid? The Scottish hills will suffice for heaven, he continues, if "thought is but a cranny in the wall" whereby we can get a brief glimpse of the world even if we are "blindly borne away."[13] Once again there is an expressed sense of human limitation in which thought provides mere glimpses as we are caught up in a meaningless flux which denies us a fixed point from which to view the world. (Compare Blake's dictum "One thought fills Immensity.") This poem can be compared to "Ex Ephemeride Mare" in *Penny Wheep* in which the limitations of human thought are even more forcefully expressed. At any rate, thought seems to be implied as a possible way out of the dilemma, for if thought merely allows us glimpses, a development of thought might allow us more. In much later work the theme of human limitation arises as an imposed limitation which can be overcome by knowledge. There is in this poem a suggested alternative as well; that of paradise, carrying with it connotations of a fixed universal order in which the self has an appointed place. But this is rejected out of doubt. MacDiarmid sees himself left with his immediate world (Scotland), facing limitations of thought which place the universe out of his mental reach, and being borne away blindly by change without apparent direction or meaning.

Sonnet IV (in which MacDiarmid displays a knowledge of Yeats by beginning "Rain-beaten stones ..." a phrase which occurs in "Magi") gives voice to the inner confusion evoked by the awareness of immensity, whether of experience or as a symbol of nothingness. Immensity reflects the boundlessness of our freedom expressed as innumerable possibilities from which to choose, none of them the right one, or is, as pointed out above, a vast universe from which the self feels itself to be detached:

> And I, in bold and boundless consciousness,
> A brooding chaos, feel within me press
> The corpse of Time, aborted, cold, negroid ...
> Involuntary thunders slip from me [!]
> And growl, inconsequently, hither, thither
> And now converse, see-saws of sighs and groans,
> Oblivion and Eternity together![13]

In this abominable sonnet one is again presented with MacDiarmid's sense of freedom and being lost, a feeling which is communicated regardless of the pompous, stilted language.

The third series of *Northern Numbers* (1922) contains very little of merit or interest. "Water of Life," for example, where one might expect to find adumbrations of his later preoccupation with water as a symbol, reveals little more than empty rhetoric and poetic gesturing.[15] "Cattle Show," however, displays a fine handling of language, and is in fact one of his best lyrics in English.[16] A talent for vivid description is already here in evidence. In "The Universal Man," MacDiarmid writes, "All ecstasies and agonies / Within me meet," shadowing forth his later declaration that he likes to be "whaur extremes meet."[17] The scope indicated in these lines shows an unwillingness to be confined to the local, to the immediate situation. "Spring, A Violin in the Void," although of slight poetic merit, contains in its title at least an interesting parallel with the lines from "Allegiance" quoted earlier. Here a void is filled with music, as though the awakening life of spring were bringing order to a silent world.[18] The theme of music recurs again and again in later poems, although it is usually that of the poet in one guise or another rather than that of an impersonal life-force.

The *Scottish Chapbook* appeared in 1922 shortly before the first appearance of the poetry of Grieve's "friend," "Hugh M'Diarmid." For the purposes of this examination, the work of Grieve qua Grieve will continue to be traced through to his *Annals of the Five Senses*. Thereafter, with the exception of one of MacDiarmid's better known Scots lyrics, "The Bonnie Broukit Bairn," printed over the name of C.M. Grieve in John Buchan's *Northern Muse*, no more poetry over this name appeared.

"A Moment in Eternity," dedicated to his schoolmaster and friend George Ogilvie, is the first of the "Grieve" poems to appear in the *Chapbook*.[19] Joseph Chiari finds it an accomplishment of "extraordinary intellectual power,"[20] and Roderick Watson sees it incorporating a Bergsonian "philosophy of Heraclitean flux and duration into a neo-Platonic system" of MacDiarmid's own.[21] David Daiches, however, is less impressed, referring to its "comparatively facile eloquence."[22] The poet, using philosophical ideas which Buthlay and Watson point out are picked up from the Russian philosopher Vladimir Solovyev, tries to convey the optimism of one who has, momentarily, glimpsed the truth and knows therefore that it exists. But the poem has a hollow ring to it, and Daiches is closer to the mark than the poem's apologists. As an attempt to fuse intellect and passion it is highly unsatisfactory, being too self-conscious to be passionate and far too muddled and vague to be intellectual. Visionary imagery of a confused kind, and verbal tricks such as "shining shadows" merely indicate a set piece which has not come off. Language is used with appalling imprecision, such lines as "Lassoing cataracts of light / With

rosy boughs" (how can boughs lasso anything?), or "Lapsing again /
To incandescence and increase" (how can something lapse to
increase?), or "I shone within my thoughts / As God within us shines"
(what does this mean?) being all too common. A poem demonstrating
such sloppy use of language cannot possibly present a coherent
argument, and it is useless to look for one here. As an optimist
MacDiarmid is less than convincing, and it is worth noting that this
entire poem is used again in *Cencrastus* when an optimistic note is
called for; the poet's heart is absent from such unqualified bubbly
affirmation even when it seems necessary to balance a very real
despair.

In "The Rhythm of Silence," written "On Seeing a Lonely Bird in
Space," the mood of despair is once more expressed, as the poet
writes of the meaninglessness and emptiness of the universe. The
transition is easily made from a lonely bird in space to a lonely man
who is, to use F.H. Heinemann's phrase, "gliding over standpoints,"
unsure of how to deal with the world in which he finds himself.[23]
Silence is the theme once again in another sonnet, "High Over
Beauty," within which, the poet suggests, creations can take shape.[24]
And eventually he poses a possible way out of his dilemma – the way
of knowledge, whether science or learning. In "Science and Poetry,"
he writes,

> All-conscious Earth serenely swinging
> In its appointed place
> Is flawed by no least trace
> Of chaos to it clinging;
> And all that men are and have
> Is one green-gleaming point of light
> In infinite night.[25]

Confusion and uncertainty are eliminated, and the idea of an
"appointed place" is no longer a concept tinged with pessimism.
Knowledge seems to shrink the vastness of the cosmos by making the
unknown known. In fact, as knowledge increases, so does the
complexity of the world, making it more and more difficult to
conceive of a coherent scheme into which it all fits. This becomes a
major problem in the later poetry of facts which is adumbrated in this
poem. At this point in his development, however, the possibility that
science might prove to be the absolute spiritual foundation he is after
is only a suggestion, and the imagery itself is more striking than the
idea behind it.

The way of learning often involves a Poundian approach, a sifting over of cultures in order to isolate bits and fragments which might, when enough are gathered, "cohere" (see "Canto CXVI"). MacDiarmid's "Continental Sonnets" shadow forth what are, in fact, important preoccupations in later work such as "The Kind of Poetry I Want."[26] They are a cycle consisting mainly of reworkings of other people's ideas, sonnets grand in conception and loftily executed, which indicate an attempt to grasp what might be called informational aspects of culture. On the one hand (in "Acme," for instance, not one of these sonnets) MacDiarmid writes of a world of men forgotten by God, and calls dramatically upon the creative force in God to aid him, a theme which occurs again in the Scots poem "Sea-Serpent."[27] But in these sonnets, on the other hand, he turns to knowledge of a pedestrian kind, and the energy of the poet appears to be held in abeyance. One must look to the voluminous prose writings of this time in order to see MacDiarmid grapple with knowledge in an energetic way: it is only in the later work that the poet has been able to synthesize the practice of poetry, his great energy, and a "strong solution of books."

His prose, unlike his poetry, shows little or no development throughout his career, so that a discussion of his prose at this time is really a discussion of his prose at any time. Here the way of knowledge is given full expression. His cultural interests, for example, are indicated in an essay such as "A Russo-Scottish Parallel," in which one feels he is attempting to understand culture and indicate common concerns or preoccupations which are transcultural and transmundane.[28] Solovyev, whose philosophy is discussed in the essay, conceived of a "Russian Idea" of these dimensions, and MacDiarmid was later to propose a "Gaelic Idea" based on this conception. Further examples are numerous – of politics, culture, and science being brought into a general struggle for comprehension in a bewildering world of experience on all levels. In his "Causerie" in the *Chapbook* of May 1923 MacDiarmid explores theories of poetry, looking at those of Frost, Aitken, Pound, and Aldington, and then quotes Dr A.M. Clarke with approval when the latter says "if the Romantic Revival was the realization of the ideal, this, the Realistic Revolt, is to be the idealization of the real."[29] And in June 1923 he quotes Denis Saurat equally approvingly when the latter attacks the lack of intellectual calibre in contemporary writing. MacDiarmid continues, "it may be that Science may be the father Poetry needs for the Super-Sense that is to be ... [The] paramount function of poetry must be to increase and *eventually to complete* our knowledge of [reality]" (emphasis added).[30]

In his prose MacDiarmid evinces an uncontrollable flow of ideas, and immensity becomes an immensity of information (which in actual fact reveals nothing) mined, for the most part, from his omnivorous reading. His prose work has become notorious for such statements as "we Scots are Oriental, the descendents of the lost tribes of Israel,"[31] and his later assertion that Stalin's homeland was ur-Gaeldom; for contradictions such as his simultaneous espousal of Social Credit and Marxism; and for sheer incomprehensibility, especially if one tries to follow his endless arguments on a purely intellectual level. Yet all is not merely a chaotic jumble, despite appearances: he is indeed "getting at something."

What then is MacDiarmid saying behind this welter of opinions, theories, and raw data? The answer to that is part of the concern of this study; the question arises naturally enough from the inconsistency one observes between his intellectual quackery on the one hand and his first-rate poetic craftsmanship on the other. This will be examined in more detail later on, but it is worthwhile noting some general aspects of this odd phenomenon where it begins to arise. The inconsistencies which abound in the prose have been noted. The actual "bits" of data and theory have by and large a curious quality of otherness, as though they are not possessed by the poet/polemicist at all. They come too quickly and are often gone as quickly. There is no real attempt to systematize his polemics, and this is as true of the later poetry as it is of the prose from the beginning, and little real argument – it is more a series of pronouncements. One feels as though MacDiarmid were "writing around something" rather than writing about it. In his book *Scottish Eccentrics*, for example (the prose of which is atypically clear; and one sketch, on William McGonagall, is a masterpiece), it is easy to suspect that the author has an ulterior motive; that he is referring to himself in an oblique fashion, that his catalogue of Scottish eccentrics is almost a catalogue of personae. Or, at the very least, we can agree with Donald Carswell who states that MacDiarmid is not after personalities here but "practices ... peculiarly Scottish."[32] Even in a book so seemingly straightforward, one has a sense that there is something behind it.

The vast amount of prose in the MacDiarmid canon falls almost entirely into two categories: on the Scottish essence, involving by implication things Scottish, Scottish culture, Scottish nationalism, and, indirectly, politics and economics; and on the potential of humanity, involving the mastering of knowledge, the concern with facts, the stupidity of his fellows, the wastefulness of orthodoxy, "mob cowardice," and, once again, politics and economics of what appear to be a progressive kind. These two categories are obviously linked together in several ways: for example, Lenin, a powerful symbol (a poet in concrete, in fact) embodies both, offering Scotland and humanity a direction in which to develop; Stalin is presented as a

Gael; communism is presented as a system which will destroy the wastefulness of the class system which enslaves Scotland and prevents human beings from realizing their potential; Scotland and the universe are linked so that the human potential for grasping the universe becomes a problem of Scottishness and vice versa – the list is all but endless. And these two categories assume major thematic importance in the poetry: MacDiarmid is a very single-minded man.

What we have almost from the start are two complementary modes of expression, prose and poetry, in which MacDiarmid develops and explores related themes. The poetry of this time is often expressive of a self-conscious sense of being in a plight, of looking for answers, and the prose can be seen as a sifting over of material which might lead to such answers. Because of its complementary nature, the prose is worth examining in the light of the poetry; in a sense it can even be regarded as notes to it. We are saved from a detailed examination of all the minutiae by its repetitive quality, which is actually one of its most important aspects.

Underlying the two themes mentioned above, and implicit therefore in the "Causeries," the articles on his own and other poets' work, the endless political chit-chat, and so on, is a continual feverish struggle to define and establish himself in the universe. The human potential theme reflects his own sense of potential. The Scottish theme reflects his abiding concern with who and what he is. MacDiarmid grapples with his plight by insisting, over and over, that it is possible to resolve it. This possibility is crucial, but it is not a certainty to MacDiarmid, and this is revealed by the repetition which characterizes his pronouncements, a continual reaffirmation of what he always insists is true anyway.

He is never content merely to "be Scottish" but clearly feels a deep need to define explicitly what that is. The concept of the "Caledonian antisyzygy," for example, which supposedly defines the Scottish character, recurs throughout his work, both prose and poetry, having been seized from the pages of Gregory Smith, who himself tried to define Scottish literature using this concept.[33] The idea of sudden and violent juxtaposition of contraries may well serve, in part, as an excuse for bad craftsmanship, and, at the same time, be expressed as a self-conscious technique; but it is impossible to do more than speculate. What is more important is that this concept is brought into play as an attempt to define a sort of ideal Scot, a Scot far removed from MacDiarmid's "fower million cretins." By continually attempting this description he is exercising Sartrean "bad faith," for in the act of defining himself within some wider, external concept of Scottishness he is trying to place himself within an immutable framework of values and characteristics for which he himself cannot be held accountable. The fact that this framework is neither self-evident nor an explicit system in his immediate Scottish environment, that it actually has to be constructed and verified, results in an underlying doubt manifested by MacDiarmid's unwillingness to say it once and have done with it, his incessant reaffirmation of it by example and more often by bold statement. John Speirs writes, "To be deliberately and self-consciously 'Scottish' in one's writing is not to have regained that lost consciousness."[34] Saying "I am a Scot" seems to substitute one uncertainty for another. That his fellow-countrymen are continually attacked for not being Scottish enough, or for not being Scottish at all, or for not even being human is a clue to the fact that MacDiarmid's struggle is existential, that the problem of "being a Scot" is felt to be uniquely his. Being a Scot, it is often implied or explicitly stated in his work, means being an outsider in contemporary Scotland.

He attempts to establish his own Scottishness by grasping at a number of drifting straws – every conceivable theory and fact which could be of help is drawn into the struggle. It is foolish to take MacDiarmid's prose outpourings as a ludicrous failure in arguing a case, because they are not based on argument at all in the usual sense. They are a consistent reaffirmation, in the guise of this example and that opinion, that MacDiarmid is a Scot with unlimited potential. The closest examination of his essays and polemics in general reveals hardly a trace of anything but assertion. By trying to establish this absolute frame (we hear of a "Scottish psychology," a "Scottish physiology," and so on), MacDiarmid tries to root himself in Being, for by penetrating the Scottish mystery he establishes or founds himself. Those things in Scotland worth having, he says in *Cencrastus*, are attached to everything else no matter how far removed, thus indicating that being one with an objective Scottish essence "places" him in the universe at large.[35] "My native land," he is to say in later life, "should be to me / As a root to a tree" – but "This Scotland is not Scotland."[36]

The other major theme, potential, is clearly linked to the first. It is a means of expressing, for MacDiarmid, the idea of founding oneself in the existentialist sense, although the concept of truth lies implicit in it. Not self-creation but self-realization is the way he conceives of his struggle, thus implying that there is something specific to be realized. It is also, of course, a simple recognition of his freedom to be, since it is often presented as a violent contrast to any idea, system, or attitude that seems to deny freedom. MacDiarmid tends to project his own sense of "unrealized-ness" onto Scotland or humanity in general, but the masses always remain an abstraction to the poet, and come to symbolize his sense of lack in himself. They are appropriated as a concept in what remains an essentially lonely quest for understanding which perpetually eludes him.

The above points will be illustrated in the course of this study, but it has been necessary to introduce them here because these themes became evident in his work very early on. From a recognition of his plight, clearly expressed in the poetry which has already been discussed, comes the suggestion of ways and means of approaching the problem. Even in the slight early English poems these themes, representing approaches, can be recognized.

In what might be regarded as the culmination of the "Grieve stream," *Annals of the Five Senses,* one finds a synthesis, creative prose displaying a poet's sensibility, in which his sense of the problem his situation poses is given forceful expression. "I [have] deemed it desirable," writes the author, "for the most part to show the psychological movements, with which I am mainly concerned, reflected through the current reading and cultural conditions of the characters involved." His material is to be "not only ... books but ... magazines and newspaper articles and even ... speeches."[37] It is interesting that the theme of Scottishness is not a concern in this volume. For the most part the writing is over-psychological and overdone, but it is also wildly energetic and imaginative. In one passage there is an explicit confession of a kind of paralysis in which, surrounded by a myriad of ready-made explanations, the writer, in the guise of one of his characters, all of whom are easily identifiable as alter egos, is unable to seize upon any one of them to solve the problem of lostness which has been outlined: "He was already wary ... keeping a corner of his head open and free for the opinions of his friends – not to put his reliance on opinions, least of all on his own opinions, and was becomingly fearful of that 'cursed conceit of being right which kills all noble feeling'"(14). This quotation, which arises again slightly modified in *Drunk Man,* indicates the poet's sense of being on his own in his confrontation with the world, no current explanations of it being relevant to his particular situation, none providing the answers he seeks. The modern age is the age of opinions: but to "internalize" any one of them requires irrefutable knowledge of its truth (and the falsity of conflicting ones), and such knowledge is clearly unavailable as shown by the very fact that so many opinions exist. At best they are assumptions and hunches based upon evidence which is never complete and very often contradictory. MacDiarmid seeks certainty.

At one point the poet sees himself as a series of fragmentary selves, a poet, a prig, a social man, a beardless boy, and so on (14). His poetry will be an attempt, ultimately, to make himself whole. But he is beset with difficulties: "Every one of his separate egos became violently anarchical, creating an unthinkable Babel"(20). He feels "the effect of his sense of personal insignificance, of physical inadequacy, of having paralyzed his creative faculties by over-reading – of being merely a 'strong solution of books' as 'full of quotations as Shakespeare' – and so forth" (20). His world is far from reassuring: "In the words of the Irishman 'there [is] no beginning nor end to it, and it [hasn't] any bottom'" (23).

Although MacDiarmid never ceases to propose that somewhere, somehow, there is an explanation of the world, the immediate world presented to him appears distressingly absurd, and there are passages in *Annals* remarkably like ones in Sartre's *La Nausée*, in which the absurdity of the world is met by the author's nauseated awareness. Here are some passages from "Café Scene": "Every cell of his body and his brain seemed, separately and conjointly, posed on the very edge of an unknown that was both ludicrous and fatal" (42). And, "Worlds might go smash but bills must be met" (51). The routine demands of the world are inanely poised against the dreams and spiritual struggles of the artist; absurdly, the trivial outweighs the cosmic. Nausea and vertigo are clearly evoked in these passages which arise from such recognition of the meaninglessness of his situation: "Finally his fingers closed on a great round of metal, and he drew it forth, and with an air of mastery which he instantaneously felt had been crassly premature, tossed it on the throbbing counter" (51). And again, "A line between two flagstones on the pavement, suddenly a yawning chasm! A cough behind him which gave him the feeling of having been buried under an avalanche! Feet splaying at angles suggestive of the most irreconcileable and meaningless divergences! A tall man instantly precipitous! A woman's waist expanding equatorially! Hands like starfish or stars! Noses like fallen towers!" (48) It is interesting to compare these with the following passages from a café scene in *La Nausée*:

I felt my shirt rubbing against my nipples and I was surrounded, seized by a slow, coloured whirlpool, a whirlpool of fog, of lights in the smoke, in the mirrors, with the benches shining at the back, and I couldn't see why it was there or why it was like that. I was on the doorstep, I was hesitating, and then there was a sudden eddy, a shadow passes across the ceiling, and I felt myself being pushed forward. I floated along, dazed by the luminous mists which were entering me from all directions at once. Madeleine came floating up to me to take off my overcoat and I noticed that she had drawn her hair back and put on earrings: I didn't recognize her. I looked at her big cheeks which stretched endlessly away towards her ears. In the hollow of the cheeks, under the cheek-bones, there were two isolated pink patches which looked as if they were feeling bored on that poor flesh. The cheeks stretched away, away towards the ears and Madeleine smiled:

"What will you have, Monsieur Antoine?"

Then the Nausea seized me, I dropped on to the bench, I no longer knew where I was; I saw the colours slowly spinning around me, I wanted to vomit.

... There's a spring inside me that's broken: I can move my eyes but not my head. The head is all soft and elastic, as if it had just been balanced on my neck; if I turn it, it will fall off. All the same, I can hear a short breath and now and then, out of the corner of my eye, I can see a reddish flash covered with white hairs. It is a hand.[38]

In both cases a sudden suspicion that things have no meaning leads to a highly excited state, where the self seems to be spinning about aimlessly without any means of imposing perspectives upon a world which now seems to lack any coherence. There is no given angle of vision. MacDiarmid is very aware in *Annals* that any such viewpoint is arbitrary in such a world: "If ... he must look at things from an unaccustomed angle, see the unfamiliar and unsuspected aspects of all the everyday familiar things that in the sinful arrogance of his individualtiy he had taken as fixed and fundamental, given and unchanging, it did not matter what sort of angle it was" (43-4). The choice is his, and no choice is right.

The remote or inaccessible understanding which will put things right is presented as a fixed order from which MacDiarmid is separated: "There was always this reviving trust in a centre of unity, a reassembling of his faculties for action in the faith that some inner purpose would be developed and confirmed. He believed recurrently that his own thought was part of the consciousness which sustained the world, and he expected to find a rational quality in its final outlines as well as in human history" (69). Thus a theme of search arises, for the order/meaning is presented as something to be found. His trust in the existence of a "centre of unity" is reaffirmed further on: "He pulled himself together again ... His memory was like the shooting of frost crystals on a window-pane: never was there a crystal which was not attached by traceable lines to the main body, yet no one could prophesy whether each fine filament might strike out on its undivided adventure. What he sought would come slowly, and in its own way. When the great music came [A reference to the author's own work, symbolized as in the later 'Lament for the Great Music' by the *Ceol Mor* of the Scottish pibroch] it would not be such and such a bit of tone-colour, nor this or that sonority, but the soaring or tender curve of the themes, their logical yet ever-new unfolding, the embodiment in the whole composition of richest variety with completest unity"(86).

But where to begin? MacDiarmid sees "his brain [as] a hall of mirrors in which he caught countless reflections of every theme in as many shapes and sizes" (105). The parallel with Eliot's "wilderness of mirrors," and the relation of this felt state to the modern situation in general as described in the introduction to this study, is fairly obvious. The story from which this is quoted, "A Four Years' Harvest," is itself a series of reflections, political ideas, human types, verses, odd bits of fact – but "there was so much to be read that there was hardly time to think" (110). The printed word, making the poet aware of so much, leaves him adrift in a sea of bits and pieces without pattern or meaning. It is impossible for him to choose a system which makes everything understandable, since there are so many conflicting alternatives and so much material to integrate. Explanations lack the confirmation of some inner authority. In his doubt he hesitates to reject anything:

His aim [was] to complete every thesis, to see all round every problem, to study a question from all possible sides and angles ... And thus his dreams were edged with the redeeming inconsistency, the saving dubiety, and he held with Browning the great central liberal feeling, a belief in a certain destiny for the human spirit beyond and perhaps even independent of, our sincerest convictions (195).

His tendency was always to the whole, to the totality, to the general balance of things. Indeed it was his chiefest difficulty (and an ever-increasing one that made him fear at times cancellation to nonentity) to exclude, to condemn, to say No. Here, probably, was the secret of the way in which he used to plunge into the full current of the most inconsistent movements, seeking – always in vain, until he was utterly exhausted, not having failed, however, to enrich every one of them – *to find ground upon which he might stand foursquare* (194) (emphasis added).

MacDiarmid outlines the way of knowledge in terms of a vague hope: "He fell back upon the old, old feeling that something of everything is wanted to make a world ... and that if every opinion is equally insignificant in itself humanity's bewilderment of thought is a mighty net which somehow holds the whole truth" (194). For within this chaos, he says, all activities, efforts, and enterprises presuppose the hope of an end: "Once kill this hope and his movements become senseless, spasmodic and convulsive, like those of someone falling from a height" (190). But as we have already seen, MacDiarmid oscillates between despair and straw-grasping; his optimism, if such it can be called, is expressed only in terms of the possibility that there is truth to seek, and in fact, as the last quotation illustrates, the negative possibility is ever present. The passages from "Café Scene" which have been noted do in fact seem to present a "senseless, spasmodic and convulsive" existence. MacDiarmid refuses to admit that the world is radically contingent, although this possibility haunts him throughout his work as a perennial seed of doubt which renders it essentially tragic.

A projection of his own aims is made, as he states his ideal, merging himself with humanity which merely becomes a larger MacDiarmid: "new kingdoms of the spirit set far above the aspiration of the politicians, beyond all the projects of social betterment, a republic of souls in which, above mere right and sordid utility, above beauty, devotion, holiness, heroism, and enthusiasm, the Infinite would have a worship and an abiding city. But ... it would be essential to eliminate all such suffering and iniquity as is preventable and germane in defective social arrangements, before it would be possible to return to spiritual goods" (191-2). As a "physical-intellectual" being, a mirror in which the world is viewed, as he puts it, but "also part of the world," MacDiarmid senses that he is at a far remove from the ideal of universal order: and in this passage the process of history indicated is an analogue of the process he himself wishes to undergo (154). The actual-ideal polarity, a conscious obsession throughout the poet's work, is here "exteriorized," as it frequently is, but MacDiarmid himself, as always, remains the focus of it.

An article in his *Northern Review* called "The Theory of Poetry" illustrates once more what he is confronting, and his gnawing uncertainty as well, for the article is really a question: What is the correct theory of poetry? He quotes Middleton Murry: "to register the mere facts of consciousness, undigested by the being without assessment or reinforcement by the mind, is, for all the connection it has with poetry, no better than to copy down the numbers of one's bus tickets." Here is the trap MacDiarmid sees before him, undifferentiated experience with no inherent priorities or values, a shapeless world in which knowledge increases its bulk and complexity without revealing anything. MacDiarmid continues, "The tendency among our poets to 'register the mere facts of existence' is still on the increase," and adds that the attitude of the new school is Whitman's, that is, the feeling that past cultural history must be gone over and carefully sifted, demonstrated, for example, in the approach of Ezra Pound.[39] He has not, as the tone of the article indicates, really made up his mind about this school. He sees the trap, but he himself has shown interest in cultural history, and his ever-elusive answer, as the quotations from *Annals* have shown, is felt to be present somewhere in the confusion, the goal of a diligent search. At about the same time, however, "M'Diarmid" is writing that "wee bit sangs are a' I need," and in this article Giovanni Papini is quoted: "We have no law, no discipline: the myths and divinities of all the ages are dead and turned to clay ... We feel the lyric ... Shakespeare, a portent of dead ages, is not great enough or pure enough in his lyricism to entitle him to immortality even in anthologies: he moves within the sphere of dramatic action and suffering in those ambiguous, impure and external forms which are steadily sinking in esteem."[40] Forms which in past ages reflected not only external but internal authority (the poets made these forms their own) seem to the modern mind (Papini) solely external, an imposition upon the poet's energy. If the absence of these forms indicates a formless world, harmony and form are restored to experience by the lyric. But the single lyric is only a temporary refuge for MacDiarmid, who nearly always has his eye on the long poem.

The actual poetic merit of most of the verse discussed so far is slight. The poet's feelings are cloaked in diction, and a pretentious quality is often evident. But, as has been pointed out, it is a curious fact that this continued even after the creation of Hugh MacDiarmid, whose poetry contrasts so strongly with Grieve's. In September 1922 two lyrics written in a rich pastiche of Scots vocabulary appeared in the *Dunfermline Press*, introduced by MacDiarmid (as C.M. Grieve) as being by a "friend" of his. One was "The Blaward and the Skelly," which is only an exercise in the medium, and the other was "The Watergaw," which is one of MacDiarmid's finest lyrics. From then on the persona of "M'Diarmid" revealed creative powers which in Grieve had never even been suggested. Lyrics, tough prose in a style indistinguishable from Grieve's, and some short plays and prose in the new medium came pouring out in an enormous spate of energy. And for all the changes in quality, form, and medium, the underlying concerns reflected in the themes which have been discussed remain the same.

The new medium of "synthetic Scots" exercised a powerful discipline upon MacDiarmid, including the attention which had to be paid to each word in order to possess it and use it, and his work in Scots is for the most part highly polished, precise, and controlled. Poems such as the aforementioned "The Blaward and the Skelly" and "Modern Poetry," which merely seem vehicles for "auld-farran" words and in a sense serve a propagandistic function, are the exception: the lyrics brought together in his books are usually self-assured and technically unselfconscious, in marked contrast to the experiments of predecessors such as Lewis Spence and those of many of his own followers since.

MacDiarmid continually connects themes, so that most of his poems form part of a grand design, if somewhat diffuse at this stage. They are not momentary disconnected fancies. One work of great importance in this respect is not a lyric at all but a long rambling philosophical poem called "Braid Scots: An Inventory and Appraisement," which appears in a shortened version, "Gairmscoile," in *Penny Wheep*. It provides what amounts to a theoretical framework for his lyric poems in Scots, at least insofar as it maps out an exploration of his new medium and relates it to the theme of Scottishness itself. The line, "It's soon', no' sense, that faddoms the herts o' men," the poetic rendition of an observation made elsewhere a little earlier, illustrates a conception of poetry and the poetic process which seems at variance with the previously outlined views on knowledge.[41] Poetry, as is implied also in the above-mentioned quotation from Papini and the line "wee bit sangs are a' I need," becomes a refuge from the complexity and disharmony of the world. Feelings become truths in themselves, and a unity of mood is established and enhanced by sound and imagery. But MacDiarmid, whose eyes are always on the whole world, is not to remain satisfied with this means of escape for very long.

The poem as it appears in the *Scottish Chapbook* is several stanzas longer than it is in the collected version, and it clearly indicates one element of concern left vague in "Gairmscoile," namely, MacDiarmid's plans for a poetic career. In a fine couplet he expresses what he feels to be his vocation in life: "As the mune moves the seas but leaves the wells / Unstirred, only a poet's hert to poesy swells."[42] Scotland, he continues, needs freedom to gain its voice, so he will draw himself through Scotland's misery "an' towards the sun!"[43] It can be observed that there, as elsewhere (notably in "Ex Vermibus" where he is, or his poetic talent is, a worm to be fed to the unfledged bird of Scotland), the poet places himself at the disposal of Scotland, as it were, becoming a means by which Scotland is to realize herself. On the logical level his existence is subordinated to that of the Scottish essence, but one misses the note of humility which usually accompanies such a gesture. Much as the poet might like to fulfil the role outlined here, thus solving his existential problems, he is unable to convince us that he puts Scotland before himself. Scotland, as continually revealed by his grappling with it, remains so much of a question mark that any such subordination remains theoretical. Scottishness too becomes an object of search.

At the end of the poem comes a note in which MacDiarmid announces new parts of the poem to come, and provides a list which amounts to a partial skeleton of his subsequent thematic development: IV The Voice of Scotland, V Invocation to the Old Makars, VI Scotland as Mystical Bride, VII Braid Scots and the Sense of Smell, VIII Braid Scots, Colour, and Sound, IX Address to the World-Poets of To-day, X Edinburgh, XI Glasgow, XII Sunrise Over Scotland, and Epilogue.[44] These themes recur in prose and poetry throughout his career to come. Scotland as a mystical bride, for example, is a thematic element in *Drunk Man* and elsewhere. "Braid Scots and the Sense of Smell" is explored in "Scots Unbound" which appears years later. "Braid Scots, Colour, and Sound" is likewise explored in later poems such as "Water Music" and "Balefire Loch." "Address to the World-Poets of To-day" can be found in fragments quoted in *Lucky Poet*, and might almost be another subtitle for the very late *In Memoriam James Joyce*.

Clearly the Scots language was of vital importance to MacDiarmid because it is a medium carrying with it a rich and profound series of connections with the Scottish essence he desired. To develop and use an actual language distinct from all others would more than anything else define the poet as a Scot. The vocabulary, over and above its texture of sound, carries with it overtones of culture, history, and psychology which seem to place the user within a transcending context of Scottishness. The impersonal nature of the language when considered as material, as MacDiarmid clearly considers it to be – he often tries to relate it to the Scottish landscape, for example, as in "Scots Unbound," so that Scotland and the Scots are united in language, which reflects an essence transcending both – seems to affirm the existence of a Scottish essence made available by the use of this language. Using it becomes almost a ritual by which the speaker (or writer) puts himself into contact with this essence as by prayer or incantation. Scottishness is a noumenon. MacDiarmid's references to "Scottish psychology," "Scottish physiology," and so on, and his references to Spengler (for whom culture had a pattern transcending the individual and even the people, becoming a sort of *Kulturgeist*) reinforce this explanation.[45] Jamieson's *Dictionary* is a collection of sacred objects.

MacDiarmid's attitude towards his new medium was one of excitement. "Words," he says in an article in the *Scottish Nation*, "have an emotional significance as well as a literal."[46] The Scots language offers a splendid chance to bring into one frame emotion, thought, and the Scottish essence. He goes on to quote several Scots words for different smells, many of which he is to use later in "Scots Unbound."

Scots vocabulary is highly particularized for smell, and for sound, as a glance through Jamieson's *Dictionary* makes evident. MacDiarmid as a poet is highly concerned with particulars, so that this characteristic of Scots made it even more attractive. He was in fact quite fortunate in having so much raw material at hand. In his later poem "Water Music," for example, a vast fund of echoic and imitative words for water-sounds and water-movements are brought together in a poem which exults in sound, a poem like a display case but forcing no awareness of this upon the reader. The powerful feelings evoked by these unfamiliar and highly expressive words result in a view which, in the context of his work as a whole, is at variance with his concern for knowing and for understanding through knowing. He begins to feel that the meanings of words are of less consequence than their sounds; as he says in "Braid Scots: An Inventory and Appraisement," "It's soon', no' sense, that faddoms the herts o' men." The imaginative potential of old Scots words was plainly delighting him, and in a striking synthesis with the theme of universal order he writes that these words have "evolutionary momentum [which] in our constant search for totality" must be made use of. Specifically, he is writing of a language to be made whole, but in the context of his entire work this can be taken to refer to a language which can express the whole.

MacDiarmid was finding his feet in these experiments, practising the use of his new Scots in plays such as "The Purple Patch" and of course in his verse.[47] At this time as well, his interest in politics, which had begun years earlier with his attachment to a Fabian group, began to take a radical turning. At this stage he preferred Bakunin to Marx and fascist Italy to bolshevik Russia: "Fascism, then, may be regarded as a form of reaction against Marxism: but it can only succeed for a while – Italian Socialism on the new basis, not of Marx but of Bakunin, will eventually overcome it."[48] Elsewhere he argued that fascism was tending towards the left, and that it was "the only thing that will preserve our distinctive national culture."[49] It is interesting, incidentally, that in the light of his cultural preoccupations he was able to resist becoming further embroiled in fascist theories, although his almost consistent damnation of the masses throughout his career and his exaltation of elitism might be considered by some an indication of leanings in this direction, as might be his support in the 1930s for the Hitlerian concept of *Blutsgefuhl*.[50] At the same time as the latter, however, he had declared himself a communist, with the publication of "First Hymn to Lenin"; just one more piece of evidence that he was – and remained – no political thinker, and no consistent adherent to any doctrine.[51] His interest in politics, however inconsistent, is always related to the "Scottish" and "potential" themes.

The themes of estrangement and potential are illustrated in two uncollected poems from MacDiarmid's *Northern Review* which are here quoted in full:

Eyes
The frost lies glumpin' i' the pool ...
But my ain hert that mirrors a'
The haill braid warl's delight an' dule
Deeper than its reflections fa',
Hauds sic anither pair o' een
Lyin' toom 'yont a' that plies atween ...

Creation
Cells o' my brain are trauchelt yet
Wi' daiths o'airmies an' the birth
O' wild floo'ers owre their burial pit
For ilka heid has a' the earth,
Its past an' future, for its load.
What fin's himsel' fin's Man an' God.[52]

The first poem conveys the sense of the poet somehow being two people separated by a vast, empty gulf. One of these, by metonymy, is an ideal who mirrors the delight and sorrow of the whole world; the other is the poet now, to whom the eyes of the ideal seem empty, that is, offering nothing in the way of guidance, advice, or encouragement. The feeling of despair is heightened by the emphatic "my *ain* hert"; the ideal and the actual are linked, and yet they still remain utterly apart. Implied here also is the idea that feelings (the heart) are incapable of being synthesized with thoughts (the poet consciously reflecting). Even if the heart holds the answer, the mind cannot receive it. One senses here a doubt that feelings in themselves are valuable in solving the problem of existence. "Creation" seems almost a sequel to "Eyes": the actual possibility of knowing the universe in the sense of making it accessible and possessing it, past, present, and future, is the theme here. In this poem the head contains everything rather than the heart reflecting everything. And yet the same problem – separation from Being, from certainty – is expressed. The affirmation of potential here, the potential of becoming God, is only a restatement of the problem, not a solution. Like the ever-elusive serpent Cencrastus (for example), this complete self-knowledge is at a remove from the poet. As Kafka says, "There is a goal, but no way."

The themes which have been outlined above are given new force in MacDiarmid's first two books of Scots poetry, *Sangschaw* and *Penny*

Wheep, in which the poet's excellence of craft, expressed in poetic skill and thought, first become readily apparent. Many of these poems deal thematically with nothingness, the gulf between MacDiarmid and Being which the poet senses and attempts to traverse. But there is more in these collections than a dull reiteration of this central concept which provides the focus, in fact, for a dazzling series of variations. From these poems emerges a giant lonely figure who not only explores the problem of being, but revels in the sheer joy of being a poet.

MacDiarmid in many of these poems becomes a Nietzschean superman grappling with the entire universe on his own. His perspectives are usually grand, befitting his self-appointed role which in his career as a whole assumes heroic proportions. In this he is similar to John Davidson, a poet whom MacDiarmid admired greatly and who may have influenced him. Davidson's poetry is riddled with such phrases as "I will sing though men be deaf!" and "master of the universe";[53] evolutionary ideas found in MacDiarmid's work have parallels such as "every atom in the earth / Aches to be man unconsciously,"[54] and "Out of the beast came man; from man comes God."[55] "In me," writes Davidson, "the infinite Universe / Achieves at last entire self-consciousness,"[56] and, he says elsewhere, "I devour, digest, and assimilate the Universe; make for myself in my Testaments and Tragedies a new form and substance of Imagination; and by poetic power certify the semi-certitudes of science."[57] Here again the concern parallels MacDiarmid's in the poetry of facts. To Davidson, the scientist was the "inspired interpreter of holy writ" and science "the true theology": "Free from the forbidding past, / Knowledge only now begun / Makes an actual world at last."[58] The poet as a hero and as prophet is a conception clearly shared by the two men, some of whose preoccupations were remarkably alike, but the likeness to a great extent would seem to be less a matter of direct influence than a common confrontation with the modern age. In *Sangshaw* and *Penny Wheep*, and foreshadowed in the earlier verse and prose, the heroic type is not imposed as an idea which the poet struggles to vivify, but is an organic conception taking shape from within.

Sangschaw is by far the better collection of the two. The preface, by John Buchan, introduces the task of writing in "synthetic Scots" as the central concern here – "a task ... at once reactionary and revolutionary." MacDiarmid liked this phrase so much that he used it in his *Albyn, or Scotland and the Future* to describe the developing Scottish Renaissance.[59] There is much more than an exercise in linguistics in this work, of course; the lyrics do not appear merely as attempts to justify a revival of the Scots language. This in fact is precisely why MacDiarmid attacked the Scottish Vernacularists.

The first thing that one notices as a characteristic of these lyrics is the use, and sometimes the overemphasized use, of contrasts or comparisons out of which many of the poems seem to arise. The comparative "like" or "as" is often of structural importance. Much of the dynamism of these particular poems arises from the linking together in this fashion of dissimilar images. The contrast (or comparison) between an indistinct rainbow (MacDiarmid's gloss) and the "last wild look" of someone dying, in "The Watergaw," is what this poem is based upon, for example.[60] Once more, the contrast between the farmer's death and the life which continues on the farm, in "Farmer's Death," is central to that poem.[61]

Some more examples demonstrate the various uses to which the poet puts the contrast/comparison device. "Trompe l'Oeil," the first poem in *Penny Wheep*, is a comparison between five blue bird's eggs and the blue eyes of a girl, "blue" being the connection which brings eyes and eggs into jarring contrast made even more jarring when MacDiarmid says the eggs are like a five-eyed glance.[62] The net result is a peculiar type of repulsion in which the emotional impact is out of harmony with the quiet lyric tone of the poem. The comparison fails to convince because it is not in fact a very good one. The quality of blueness is not enough, one feels, to suggest immediately a five-eyed glance in consequence. The "jostling of contraries," in Gregory Smith's concept, the "Caledonian antisyzygy," was very early taken to heart by MacDiarmid (see his "Theory of Scots Letters") and one might at least speculate whether he is attempting, in his continual and marked use of contrasts, to conform to this abstract principle of supposed "Scottish psychology."

Certainly they can be startling, if not always effective. "Scunner," for example, provides the violent contrary of love and disgust which are seen as an unattractive unity. The body hides in its graces, he says, as the "tedious" ground hides in the grain, and both the body (nerves, blood, and so on) and the ground (dirt and rocks) are inherently "scunnersome."[63] A body is thus compared to a cornfield by means of their similar inherent contrasts. "Parley of Beasts" contrasts Noah and his animals with the narrator and his self, almost a "Circus Animals' Desertion" without the benefit of original possession, but the poem seems a little too self-conscious.[64] In "Servant Girl's Bed" a girl is compared to a candle, but a possible surrealistic effect is cancelled out by an almost homiletic ending, and in "The Fairmer's Lass" the golden glory of a cesspool in the sun [!] is contrasted with the darkness of the daughter's heart, a contrast which, for all its inventiveness, remains ludicrous.[65]

It is in lyrics such as "The Eemis Stane" and "The Bonnie Broukit Bairn" that the contrast/comparison technique comes into its own. In the former poem the image of Earth is linked to a complex series of images involving a carved, teetering stone, images which are returned to the original "Earth" by the phrases "fug o'fame" and "history's hazelraw."[66] (The whole effect, despite the word "like," is that of an extended metaphor rather than a simile.) The latter contrasts Earth with other heavenly bodies, weeping with gossip, appearance with reality. This poem gives a perfect illustration, in fact, of the technique at its best, as well as of the theme of potential indicated earlier. Mars looking handsome in a red suit, Venus beautiful in a gown of green silk, and the "auld mune" in golden feathers are carrying on a silent conversation, "starry talk." The first three lines are description, in which the two planets and the moon are given a grandeur abruptly cancelled by the fourth line, in which their conversation is revealed as "a wheen o' blethers," mere stairhead gossip. (MacDiarmid often juxtaposes the vulgar and the cosmic for effect.) They have ignored Earth, a beautiful baby with a dirty face; but should this child cry, says the poet, the whole chattering group will be drowned in the tears.[67] This poem allows many interpretations, but perhaps the most satisfactory one is this: the apparent grandeur of the cosmos is as nothing to what Earth can be – that is, to what the human race, or MacDiarmid himself, can achieve. Even the cry of a child, signifying its awareness of being neglected, is enough to drown this grandeur. A child, of course, is a potential adult; in terms of the human race, the poet says that, as a race, we are in our infancy, but that even the cry of awareness that our collective face is dirty – an incoherent wail – is a giant leap forward. Humanity must recognize that it is in a plight before this can be resolved. We have been left on our own and can expect no guidance from whatever gods there be.

MacDiarmid's own sense of potential, then, is projected onto Earth as a whole, a common practice in his work, poetic and otherwise. It is reassuring to involve everyone in the struggle he himself is undergoing because by doing so he overcomes some of the loneliness necessarily associated with a struggle which is purely personal. There is no doubt that he feels himself to be an outsider, and any love for the human race is shown to a human race, as the *New York World* said of Trotsky, "none of the members of which are yet born."[68] In practice, MacDiarmid is no respecter of persons. The unrealized potential of humanity symbolizes his own, and we know this because the category of humanity nearly always remains abstract for him, and its possibilities for achievement as MacDiarmid expresses them nearly always mirror what he feels to be his own possibilities, such as super-genius, vast learning, and great aesthetic development. A later poem, "Glasgow, 1960" (first published in 1935), is a fine illustration.

Thus the neglect of Earth by the planets can be seen as a way of expressing MacDiarmid's own sense of estrangement from Being. On this level the gossip symbolizes the apparent absurdity and confusion of the universe, an awareness of which is heightened by the contrast between the appearance of the two planets and the moon and the actual substance of their conversation. The "starry talk" gives us no answers and is not even directed at us, implies MacDiarmid, which is to say that the grandeur of the cosmos, as the poet sees it, gives a false sense of security, almost of decorum, to existence, when in fact it is irrelevant to it. We are still awed by beauty and superstition, so much so that we do not realize that our collective face needs cleaning. The poet is aware of the plight of living, so that he is arguing against this fascination; if the heavens are indeed populated with the colourful gods and goddesses, they are not paying any attention to Earth and certainly do not reveal any profound wisdom. Just by realizing the predicament we are in (not nurtured but neglected by the heavens – the cry of the child signals the awareness of this neglect), we can drown these fantasies and get down to the serious business of realizing our potential.

"The Watergaw" is a far simpler poem.[69] There is one main contrast/comparison here, that between a dying man's last look and an indistinct rainbow. Both are "ayont the on-ding." At the threshold of death the man gives a "last wild look" which means whatever the watergaw means. Both meanings are uncertain; no one know what follows death, and the rainbow is indistinct. The chaos of the storm has its counterpart in the storm of life, an interpretation which is not too far-fetched when it is observed that the poet is preoccupied with wind in *Drunk Man*, for example, which serves as an image of the aimlessness of life, energy without apparent direction or meaning; and when one keeps in mind his more general theme of finding the hidden order in the chaos surrounding him. The existence of such an order is perhaps revealed, albeit indistinctly, by the rainbow and the wild look, the first being an obvious contrast with the storm (as calm, beautiful ordered colours) and the second a transfiguration, a sudden understanding of "what it is all about," perhaps even a glimpse of heaven (the order the poet seeks, in a sense). But the poem remains ambiguous: what one really observes here is a linking of two uncertainties, and a host of other interpretations are equally valid.

The watergaw is, after all, ephemeral, so that the wild look might with some reason be taken as one of despair, for example. The concept of order versus chaos, however, is certainly of importance in the poem, which thus illustrates a perennial concern of the poet's.

The feeling of lostness as a theme recurs in such poems as "In the Hedge-Back," in which the night is an engulfing threat, a void which surrounds us and separates us from the world.[70] "Ex Ephemeride Mare" opens with a description of gleaming fish which vanish in an emerald sea, and this situation is then compared to MacDiarmid, who sees himself as equally ephemeral; then, we are told, dreams are glimpsed "through Time's shawls" and are lost in "dowf [unimpressible] immensity," so that the image of fish in the sea is compared first of all to MacDiarmid and then to dreams and a cosmic perspective.[71] These glimpses, of a possible answer perhaps, may well be those expressed metaphorically as loops of a sea-serpent in *Drunk Man*, but in all the feeling is one of lack or of failure. The glimpses tantalize, nothing more. In this poem, dreams (visions) are glimpsed but quickly lost, as the poet senses himself to be lost, a mere silver flash seen against the whole of Being which remains inaccessible and obscure. There is a difficulty here, in that dreams are not glimpsed, but had. Quite possibly what is meant here is that dreams are glimpses, of that explanation or universal order which the poet seeks. What is certain is the emphasis on the poet's being on his own, denied access to what he can merely glimpse through vision, and himself only a brief appearance with no more significance than a momentary silver flash from a fish in the sea. Here, order is expressed as a transcendental realm, since vision in the conventional sense derives from such a plane and reveals the one in the many – the "a'efauld form o' the maze" to use MacDiarmid's own phrase.

This concept is even more forcefully expressed in one of MacDiarmid's finest lyrics, "The Eemis Stane."[72] The world is compared to a precariously balanced rock in the sky, covered with writing, which has become obscured by the moss of fame, the lichen of history, and the snowstorm of the poet's "eerie memories." Several critics agree that the stone is a tombstone, Kenneth Buthlay indicating a possible precursor to the poem in the *Scottish Chapbook*, and Iain Crichton Smith and others making this interpretation.[73] If it is correct, the writing on the stone might be the memorial to a dead God, the name of God in fact, and thus the truth the poet is looking for. The idea of God being dead is suggested in "Farmer's Death," for example. But the critics make no attempt to justify this interpretation on internal evidence. There is no reason why the stone must be a tombstone, either: it could be a Rosetta stone or the cornerstone of a ruined building. But this is little more than speculation: what we have in the poem is an image of stone with words carved into it, words which are obscured. The understanding the poet seeks is hidden. The images of darkness and the snowstorm evoke a sense of desolation. The poet himself is at the centre of all this, confronted by fame and history on the one hand and his own "eerie memories" on the other, all of which combine to throw confusion in his way. The complex, endless mass of data called history allows no revelations to burst through suddenly with the immediacy and clarity of writing carved in stone. The poet's own personal history, too, his past life rising like a ghost before him, is a confusion of memories likewise offering no vital insights and no pattern, a past as elusive and inaccessible as the truth he seeks. The difficulty in this poem is the word "fame." Whose fame? Or does "fame" in this case have its other meaning, rumour? The most probable explanation is that fame, the abstract category, is a temptation which turns the poet away from his search for the "words cut oot i' the stane." In practical terms the business of being a poet and writing to fulfil a public role arises as a temptation. If "rumour" is meant, however, the "fug o' fame" becomes another means of expressing uncertainty. Even what the poet learns of the world might be ill-founded, so that he cannot take knowledge as a jumping-off point with absolute assuredness. There is always the danger that what is presented as fact is only rumour. In any event, the poet once again sees his essential situation as estrangement from Being. It should be noted also that there is an implied connection here between physical reality and language, his chosen artistic medium. The belief that the rest of reality can be expressed in, or subsumed in language, at least implicit in this poem, becomes firmer and firmer in the course of MacDiarmid's development, as will be indicated in later chapters.

A cycle of four lyrics, "Au Clair de la Lune," would seem in its symbolism to prefigure the use of the moon in Drunk Man.[74] "The moonbeams kelter i' the lift, / An' earth, the bare auld stane, / Glitters beneath the seas o' Space, / White as a mammoth's bane." Here Earth has no words carved into it at all. It is lifeless and ancient, and reflects the light of the moon with which it is contrasted. In another of the lyrics the moon has such an effect upon MacDiarmid (he is "moon-struck") that the cosmos is suddenly dwarfed by the poet's gigantic perspective: "An' the roarin' o' oceans noo / Is peerieweerie to me: / Thunner's a tinklin' bell: an' Time / Whuds like a flee." The title of this cycle, and the emphasis in these lyrics upon the moon, suggest that the light of the moon symbolizes understanding. In the light the true Earth is revealed as a meaningless object, or dwarfed to insignificance. Yet there is no note of despair here. The emphasis is entirely upon the poet, who in the light of the ideal becomes a superman. He is alone in the universe and rises to overcome it. Even if the universe is absurd (and the moon seems to be above the universe in the poet's cosmography), with time buzzing randomly about like a fly, the moon seems to offer promise that he can create the order it lacks. As a thought, MacDiarmid is "lifted owre the gowden wave" to have "keethin' sicht o' a' there is, / An' bodily sicht o' nocht." In the last lyric, MacDiarmid is no longer alone, as he promises that "Earth's howlin' mobs" will be hushed by "the sang / That frae the chaos o' Thocht / In triumph braks or lang." Those last two lines reflect a hope which remains with the poet throughout his career. The cycle as a whole presents the poet in a meaningless world seeking a truth that seems to be promised him, and assuming god-like proportions in the process; in this it is almost a précis of his poetic canon.

This affirmative tone is not repeated in his poem "Somersault," in which the Earth is presented as hurtling through the cosmos, no longer a spinning top as in "Moonstruck" but a massive, noisy juggernaut.[75] MacDiarmid professes to love this "rumpus," but the tone of the poem becomes progressively more foreboding. The impersonal nature of the universe becomes frankly threatening. The sea glowers, the West hurtles down like the Gadarene swine only to find the East waiting; East meets West like a sow devouring her young. There might perhaps be a mythic element of eternal return in this endless somersault of the Earth, in this futile, meaningless continuation. (Could the poem on one level be an expression of historicism? Spengler's *Decline of the West* had been noted earlier by MacDiarmid. If so, the poet could be making a connection between the apparent absurdity of the world and that of history, reinforcing the use of "history" in "The Eemis Stane.")

This more usual view of the world as it appears is expressed in poems such as "Thunderstorm," in which the narrator becomes all but insignificant in an empty cosmos, and "Hungry Waters," in which the destructive forces in the universe seem predominant, as in Thomas Hardy's world view – we are told that the sea will devour the land.[76] The very ground under the poet's feet becomes uncertain, and the formless sea triumphs. (In *Drunk Man* the sea is a symbol of disorder as well.) "The Long Black Night" eliminates the poet as a participant in a situation, and presents instead only a black void decorated with star jewellery, beautiful but uncaring and unknowing whence it is going, a beauty devoid of meaning and without relation to humanity.[77] The tone here is one of despair or resignation. Universal order in the last four lyrics discussed does not appear as a possibility at all. This mood, which often recurs in MacDiarmid's work, is summed up in his "Bombinations of a Chimera": "I rise and fa' in my restless way / And earth seems big syne or sma' / But it'll be the same at the end as tho' / I'd never flown ava!"[78] This echoes the feeling of futility conveyed by "Ex Ephemeride Mare," the sense of merely existing, and nothing more. The universe (Being) remains inaccessible, and the poet's eventual death renders all attempts to seize the universe futile and meaningless. In this stanza the poet sees himself as unjustified, part of no pattern, a voice in the wilderness eventually ceasing. Death defines life as meaningless; the poet consciously becomes Heidegger's being-for-death. He has no place in the universe guaranteed him, for things remain the same whether he lives or dies.

In several other lyrics, however, MacDiarmid employs a Yeatsian device; in order to affirm the existence of some meaning behind everday events he provides sharp contrasts between the immediate and homely and the cosmic. Yeats uses the choric line for this purpose, in some of his "Crazy Jane" poems and in others such as "Beggar to Beggar Cried" in which ordinary beggars with ordinary earthly preoccupations are given a metaphysical significance by means of the repeated italicized line "Beggar to beggar cried, being frenzy-struck" (frenzy in the Yeatsian vocabulary being the madness of inspiration deriving from a transcendental realm). MacDiarmid does not reveal such a realm, but merely affirms the existence of trancendent meaning by means of vague symbols such as God and heaven. In "Crowdieknowe" he imagines the provincial mentalities of the people from that town being expressed on Judgment Day when confronted with the majesty of God.[79] This superb satire does not merely mock the townsfolk but demonstrates a gulf between all human beings and cosmic order. The people are actually unaware of what is happening to them; understanding (symbolized by God) escapes them. They can only interpret events in this narrow fashion. Human limitation prevents them from seeing their situation. Even God, MacDiarmid suggests, might well quail before such assertive ignorance! "Feery-o'-the-Feet" is a poem along similar lines, in which a jealous husband, it is said, will rise from the dead on Judgment Day, his only thought being to kill his former wife and her new husband in a jealous rage.[80] With all the cosmic implications of this day, such a person can think only of what must be seen as ludicrously petty in relation to it. In neither of these two poems is there a synthesis of the miraculous and the common. The common remains common; the miraculous, though "here," remains inaccessible. MacDiarmid is not merely satirizing lowbrowism but is making a profound comment upon the inability of human beings to seize what should be in their grasp. There is an underlying principle in the world, he is implying, a pattern somehow available, but for one reason or another we are unable to perceive what is right in front of us.

The humour of these two poems is muted by the element of death, which is treated directly in several of the *Chapbook* lyrics. It indicates perhaps a preoccupation with horror, which Edwin Muir has pointed out particularly in the poem "Country Life."[81] This is a collection of homely farm objects and creatures, a tableau of country life, but there are aspects of it which indicate, by nuance, another dimension, such as the peculiarly expressive "golochs on the wa'." "The Last Trump," yet another poem about Judgment Day, makes the idea of death far more important than the humour: a corpse, ashamed of its decomposed state, is afraid to rise and face God.[82] In "Farmer's Death" there is no humour at all.[83] The farm animals are full of life, the farmer is dead. Roderick Watson points out as characteristics of the animals their "avidity of ... *consumption*, and the visionary intensity of their being (feathers like fire, hide like silver) [which] constitutes a terrible triumph over the master who once kept them as a source of food."[84] From the evidence of "God Takes a Rest" and other poems in which God is said to have separated himself from or forgotten about His creation, such as "Sea-Serpent," the farmer, as Peter Thirlby suggests, might well be God.[85] An alternative might be that the world continues as usual after a person dies (the message of the lines from "Bombinations of a Chimera" quoted earlier), indicating the tragic fact of his or her irrelevance to the world as a whole. Perhaps this is the crux of MacDiarmid's preoccupation with death. Faced with the vast universe, he worries about being overwhelmed by it or lost in it, as we have seen in other poems, and thus fears that his death will have no importance at all in the absence of a clear cosmic scheme. In order to overcome this fate he attempts to increase his stature (see *Lucky Poet*, for example, his references to himself as Christ, and so on), to see the world in larger perspective (as in "Au Clair de la Lune" and elsewhere), even to swallow it entirely (the possibility of doing so is indicated in the poem "Jimsy: An Idiot," even if Jimsy is not necessarily the poet himself). In these poems we note the continual presentation of a gulf between humanity, or the poet himself, and a plane upon which universal order is manifested, or sometimes the presentation of humanity or the poet without any such order being suggested. This theme and its companion theme, the search for order, are continued in several other lyrics. "Blind Man's Luck," for example, a poem reminiscent of Yeats in its presentation of a contrast resembling that in some of the "Crazy Jane" poems, shows a poor old blind man squatting in front of a fire. Suddenly the scope widens – he has pillaged the nest of heaven, he says, and has placed the empty eggshells of the sun and moon where his eyes were, "for luck."[86] Here is a man on familiar terms with the cosmos, or else a pathetic old man with delusions. The poem is based entirely upon this ambiguity. Blind prophet or half-crazed blind beggar with eyes like two addled eggs who mumbles to himself by the fire? Certainly he believes himself to be a prophet, but we see only a poor huddled figure. How does anyone know that he himself or anyone else has stumbled upon the answer?

"I Heard Christ Sing" is built around the contrast between Christ and His disciples, who seem very much men of this world: to accentuate this difference, they are described in Braid Scots, whereas Christ's song is in almost pure English (and thus, MacDiarmid suggests, is remote from the world of experience!); their dance (around Christ, the still centre; the whole group forms a Boethian wheel) seems homely indeed compared to Christ's song.[87] The poem is worth comparing to Yeats's "Long-Legged Fly" in which the dance of the girl has similar connotations, the steps reflecting a transcendental order or meaning. But the dichotomy remains in MacDiarmid's poem, as indicated by the difference in language.

"Jimsy: An Idiot" goes much further.[88] A laughing idiot assumes incredible powers – the light of heaven is his mouthwash, his jaws mix North and South together; he travels over the Earth like a snake (an unmistakeable connection here with "Sea-Serpent" and ultimately with *Cencrastus*) swallowing an egg. As the process of swallowing continues, only a glimpse of the sky is left, like a rabbit's tail peeping outside its burrow. And before God knows where He is, Jimsy is swallowing Him. The poem begins with the idiot's laughter, all that is apparent says MacDiarmid, as though Jimsy had turned himself inside out. By doing this, of course, he would of necessity hold the universe inside him! Perhaps the poem illustrates Blake's motto, that if the fool persists in his folly he becomes wise. Madness, even idiocy, can be a sign of miraculous possession, so that the idiot, like the old blind man, may be a poet or a prophet. But here again the alternative may hold as well. The poet, attempting to encompass the universe, is an idiot; and the only result of taking the universe to himself is meaningless laughter, the only possible mimesis of an absurd world. The ambiguity is created by the description of swallowing the world, not in itself an act guaranteeing wisdom, and it reflects perhaps MacDiarmid's uncertainty about the existence of objective meaning. Perhaps there is no underlying pattern at all, and the laugh of the idiot is desperate: if, as the poem "Creation" suggests, "ilka heid" contains all there is, one is no further forward in one's search for a pattern underlying it; and if it turns out that there is none, only wild laughter will come from that head, not song or prophecy.

"The Currant Bush" makes a connection between a woman who died in childbirth and her reincarnation as a currant bush growing in the place where her house, now vanished, once stood.[89] She is "still at odds with nature" because she died in the natural creative process of giving birth, and now in her new form is struggling to grow against the natural destructive process of nature which destroyed the house. Her situation remains struggle, a struggle to survive, and the world is presented therefore as impersonal and threatening. Here there is no life/death, birth and rebirth theme; instead of an ordered progression from death to rebirth, we have a parody of this process. A woman dies in childbirth, and then is reborn as a currant bush which must struggle to survive the same blind forces (of life or of death, equally threatening to her) which originally killed her. The recurrent situation is meaningless, and the forces of life and death present no pattern, merely a random interplay of struggles and counter struggles.

But MacDiarmid, as we have shown, does not despair all the time. In several of these poems he affirms the possibility of overcoming his difficulties, although inevitably managing to imply the negative possibility as well. "In the Pantry," for example, gives the image of a pantry full of mouldering food, a landscape of rotting victuals which corresponds to the landscape of the world itself.[90] The necessity of replacing all this ruin with something new is emphasized, and the role of the Creator is once again taken. "Ex Vermibus" presents a converse, linking the problem of Scottishness to these more general concerns.[91] Here, as noted earlier, the poet's energy is likened to a worm in the craw of an unfledged bird (Scotland), a worm which will give that bird a wonderful song (the voice of Scotland). One cannot help comparing this pronouncement, in which the poet's craft, while compared to a worm, is proudly affirmed as an instrument of some greater good, to the conventional Christian attitude of humility ("miserable sinners" and so on) whereby one becomes part of a greater purpose and plan by rejecting one's individual independence (the sin of Satan and the rebel angels being to affirm the latter). To become part of Scotland, as was pointed out earlier, roots the poet in Being and thus "establishes" him: "If there is ocht in Scotland that's worth ha'en / There is nae distance to which it is unattached" he is to say in *Cencrastus*, so that being one with Scotland is to be one with the universe.

But "Whip-the-World" once again demonstrates his sense of prophethood.[92] He promises to put the world in a permanent whirl someday, saying that the force of song, a cosmic force, makes the world spin. The world, once more like a top, requires some time to stagger out of this whirl, so that poets in fact make the world go round! But he indicates that he will render this continual respinning unnecessary, by means of a song which the world will never be able to overcome. In one obvious sense he is speaking of an answer which history and discovery will never supersede, song being equated therefore with prophecy. Here his work is no worm for Scotland's belly; he is the man who keeps the world turning.

The poem "Song" treats of the poetic gift itself.[93] A strange windborne tune is heard, the same inescapable one sung by an unborn, formless man. It is his essence, the potentiality of life. MacDiarmid says to note the tune and put words to it if one would have peace. The poet therefore must express a meaning, implied in this poem to be universal, a tune there to be found. The concept of the poet shaping himself by his writing is opposed to the concept of an anterior order (the tune) in the one poem. It is precisely this contradiction which is indicative of MacDiarmid's work as a whole. He writes of a formless man, and implies that the man's shape arises from putting words to a pre-existing tune, so that the separation from this order, symbolized by formlessness, is resolved as the tune is realized – that is, made song. This is surely the elemental situation of the poet as MacDiarmid sees it; lost in chaos he must discover order – and realize himself – by writing. His poetry, or song (the two are identified by MacDiarmid throughout his work), will, as a process, take the form of an anterior scheme of things. In other words, MacDiarmid is writing here of inspiration, in a sense akin to the dictionary definition of divine influence. The mystical tune is the answer. Putting words to it in a sense gives it substance. The tune, a potential song, is sung by a potential man; as words are put to it, the man takes shape (self-realization). The contradiction noted above is resolved by the analogy of discovery: one is free and responsible for one's explorations, but what is discovered has been there all the time.

At this point, when MacDiarmid is realizing himself as a poet, he might seem to be interested primarily in short polished lyrics which set off the potential impact of Braid Scots words. Thus, in "To One Who Urges More Ambitious Flights" he insists, as has been noted above, that "wee bit sangs" are all he needs.[94] But his eye is always on the great music, and the giant-like stance he assumes in so many of these poems seems quite at odds with the vehicle by which it is expressed. "Krang," for example, presents the poet as prophet once again.[95] The world is like a whale flensed by the sun. The prophet, with an invocation, asks for a whirlwind (an allusion to Moses and the whirlwind; MacDiarmid is asking for what Moses received) to give him a tune for a song, by blowing through the ribs of the world-whale as though playing a harp. Here perhaps is an indication of a planned *magnum opus* – he says the resulting song will reverberate around the world – but more importantly it reinforces the idea, expressed in "Song" and "The Eemis Stane," of an objective order to be reached or grasped. "Krang" presents a world laid bare by light, within which resides the pattern or meaning sought. The invocation is a poetic gesture and no more, for it is directed at no God nor other being. MacDiarmid is again writing of inspiration, but once again also it is the world which will inspire him, in some mysterious way, not a god or a muse. The mysterious wind-borne tune of "Song" is in this poem not even available for words to be put to it. Yet the possibility of such a song is felt to exist. The tune can be evoked perhaps. But is there not a note of uncertainty reflecting the alternative possibility that no whirlwind will appear? The invocation seems to take place in a vacuum as though the poet doubts that he is addressing anyone and crosses his fingers just in case. On one level it is inspiration he asks for; on another it is the order he wishes to affirm which he wants, a song arising from the skeleton of the world, the latter symbolizing order, the former revelation.

It is perhaps worth digressing here for the purpose of indicating, by means of another reference, why a skeleton represents the order which has been stressed as a major concern of the poet. This is a short story called "The Dead Harlot" which appears in *New Tales of Horror* [1934]. The following quotations show that the prostitute's skeleton symbolizes universal order, or rather, has the symbolism thrust upon it:

1) What artistry has wrought such sculpture from such chaos, with this finality of form, this economy of means, this undeluded surety of touch? Think of the antiseptic vision, the unnerving eye for essentials, the ruthless mastery – the consummate finish! No mawkish sentiment here, no pandering! He has probed his subject and come to unanswerable conclusions, profound, exclusive, universal! No straining here after originality, no needless elaboration of the theme, no moralizing! His work has the impersonality of all great art. It lies before us, stark, simple, pitiless, unpalliated ... a study in the elimination of unessentials.

2) Who would rather have diffuse heats, blind hot livingness, than this keen hard separateness?

3) Who does not envy such a faculty of sharp incontrovertible response to all the lapping, suffusing, swamping, endless conspiracies of life? ... Complexity has laboured and brought forth the most signal of all the simplicities.

AUGUSTANA UNIVERSITY COLLEGE
LIBRARY

4) [T]he clean cold light of death streams straitly through her liberated, bare, and unvibrating bones, ranking in silence here, radiate in finality, cradling the invisible, unpulsating heart of eternity.[96]

The language is that of the *Annals,* an over-inflated rhetoric which nevertheless clearly expresses the idea of order hidden in chaos, and of ultimate revelation. The skeleton of the harlot is forced to become symbolic here: MacDiarmid seems very anxious to make a point. Because it represents the final truth, the bones do not vibrate as the poet wishes the whale's skeleton to do since the song arising in the latter case links or is to link the poet to the order gradually revealed by that song, order which is completely revealed here as an ideal. Putting words to the tune is a way of expressing the communing of the poet, exercising his craft, with Being; but in the other case the mystery of Being is resolved, the end is revealed without it being necessary to refer to the means by which it is attained. Quite clearly "Krang" and "The Dead Harlot" share the same symbolism.

Three long poems, "Ballad of the Five Senses," "Gairmscoile," and "Sea-Serpent" take some of the themes discussed in this chapter onto the level of philosophical musing. In the first of these poems, MacDiarmid begins by describing how he revelled in the full use of his five senses in the attempt to know God and the world as it really is.[97] But this was not enough; he was not after subjective impressions and glimpses but wanted the whole "objective" truth. Putting sense-impressions and thoughts aside, he came to quite a different plane from what he expected, a limbo of ghostly living thoughts which were indescribable and each one as different from the others as day and night or life and death. There were an infinite number of these thoughts. All the sense impressions of the world, which MacDiarmid has treasured (comparing his full sensual appreciation to the mere "shaddaw-show" vouchsafed to other people), and his thoughts of God, became trivial, he tells us, reflecting his despair in *Cencrastus* that "There's naething that a man can be / That's mair than imbecile to me / In the licht o' totality." These living thoughts seem themselves inaccessible to the poet, so that the "flourishing tree" that is the world, and the sun that is God, are even further away. His situation in this limbo represents the realization, in another gigantic perspective, of the magnitude of his problem. The poem ends with the hope, much tinged by despair, of seeing the truth which lies far beyond the Gods of others.

"Gairmscoile" shows the poet more hopeful, and the poem is itself of more importance to MacDiarmid's work as a whole.[98] He begins with a description of the monstrous elemental forces in people's hearts, forces connected with sexuality and also with the destiny of Scotland. This in essence is a theory of a Scottish collective unconscious, although he uses the theory only as a kind of metaphor; he is writing of unity once again. The past and future, he continues, are one, and time will be cast aside some day. As he struggles towards a conception of oneness in the poem, MacDiarmid focuses upon the problem of language. As a poet and an exponent of "synthetic Scots" he is under some pressure to evolve a concept of the potential and the use of language in general. Language, he feels, is a part of a national culture, an essential part of it, organic and not artificial: "Wull Gabriel in Esperanto cry / Or a' the warld's undeemis jargons try?" As a Scot, MacDiarmid writes,

> It's soon', no' sense, that faddoms the herts o' men,
> And by my sangs the rouch auld Scots I ken
> E'en herts that ha'e nae Scots 'll dirl richt thro'
> As nocht else could – for here's a language rings
> Wi' datchie sesames, and names for nameless things.

In Scots, then, lies perhaps the complete means of expressing the Scottish destiny and the universe in a "Scottish context," and ultimately defining the poet himself: "For we ha'e faith in Scotland's hidden poo'ers, / The present's theirs, but a' the past and future's oors." It is in language that these "hidden poo'ers" will find expression, and the song of the poet will be in recreated Braid Scots at this stage. Language is in fact the central preoccupation of this poem, and the potential of the Scots vocabulary, pointed out earlier when the first version of this poem was examined, promises to be a major factor in establishing the poet in the universe. The theme of language here prefigures his later preoccupations with "world language."

"Sea Serpent," because of its obvious connection with *Cencrastus*, is perhaps the most important of these three poems as a key to later work.[99] In this poem MacDiarmid treats of the corruption of the soul, the deadening of the human spirit through the ages, a sort of fall in fact. The poet is clearly trying to relate his sense of *Geworfenheit* to some all-embracing scheme or cause – that is, to give it a necessary rather than a contingent character. The sea-serpent fills the universe, and is the soul of the universe, a concept of immanence similar to Stoic and Hindu ideas. God is not the sea-serpent. He planned the shape of life, but the force of life itself remained unshaped until God gave it the sea-serpent's form. God, says the poet, is in the serpent's belly, just as he was in Jimsy's; the poet, as MacDiarmid says in *Cencrastus*, belongs in the serpent's mouth! God has become so preoccupied with the particulars of His creation that He has forgotten the "a'efauld form o' the maze," which is the sea-serpent itself. MacDiarmid appears like a star or a note in a symphony, sensing the sea-serpent forgotten by God. He sees himself in this poem, then, as part of a universal process.

Nature and humanity are struggling, he continues, and he asks if God will return to His old position. (In this poem, MacDiarmid uses a device later used to good effect in *Drunk Man*. He sets up a system of moving parts, in this case humanity, the serpent, God, and nature, each in a fairly well-defined relationship to the others, a relationship primarily logical rather than intuitive.) The sea-serpent is central in the situation: perhaps, suggests MacDiarmid, it has a wound in its side, and the sudden surges of feeling which come over us are only its death-throes. Perhaps it has no more power to fill countless lives with what the poet calls the single movement of life; in other words, just as we find ourselves incapable of bridging the gulf to order, so that order, personified, cannot bridge the gulf to us. So MacDiarmid invokes the serpent, asking it to reveal itself, to be "to oor lives as life is to Daith." He exhorts him to spring from the spirit of God and give new life to God, making Him relevant to our lives so that the world and the "meaning' o' ilka man" will be part of a perceived whole. God's present concern with particulars reflects the poet's own growing awareness of the innumerable particulars of the world he confronts. The poet is saying in effect that more and more particulars are created, but no pattern embodying them has been made evident. Our own (or the poet's own) inability to see more than these fragments merely indicates that God, our inspiration of old, is in the same fix. The wound in the serpent's side, and the possibility of his dying as a result, might be an allusion to Christ, but is probably of more general significance: the order the serpent represents may well have become unattainable because our degradation has torn the very fabric of that order.

It cannot be stressed too strongly that these three poems are of interest only because the poet's approach to the problem of existence shifts to a semi-philosophical attempt to clarify the issues. The poems themselves are not very good, and the philosophy they contain is not profound. The struggle with the problem of the self through this type of musing does adumbrate much of the later poetry, however. The concept of poetry is here widened from "wee bit sangs" to admit speculation, philosophy, and opinion as he seeks to make his problem intelligible. The poet places no narrow limits on his craft. What might seem in these cases to be a lamentable absence of self-criticism represents in fact the beginning of an attempt to carve out and develop an alternative approach to that of his lyricism. These poems too are experiments.

The work which has been discussed in this chapter was succeeded by two long poems, *A Drunk Man Looks at the Thistle*, which was already in the planning stages during much of this earlier publication and is quite possibly his greatest single poetic achievement, and *To Circumjack Cencrastus*. The poetry which has been examined, and much of the prose, establishes many of the thematic, and some of the structural, ingredients of these long poems and, indeed, of his poetry in general. MacDiarmid never ceases to experiment, but in many ways these poems represent his most intense period of experimentation where he is developing an aesthetic vocabulary and grammar, having already established through an obsessive self-consciousness his major poetic theme: the poet in the modern world.

CHAPTER THREE

Uncouth Dilemmas

MacDiarmid's being-in-the-world defines a problem. Confronting the fact of his existence (and it is seldom less than a confrontation), he faces his loneliness, his uncertainty, his lack of place in a scheme of things as a quandary to be resolved. Life is to him a trap from which he must struggle to escape, not into death but into some ideal state. This solution remains abstract; it is presented as an eventual understanding, revelation, or truth, an explanation for his existence, a goal for which to aim. And it is within the sphere of poetry that this goal is to be realized. All this is the central concern of two book-length poems which follow the outpouring of lyric verse examined in chapter 2, *A Drunk Man Looks at the Thistle* (1926) and *To Circumjack Cencrastus, or the Curly Snake* (1930).

With the publication of *Drunk Man*, MacDiarmid revealed that he had developed from an accomplished and sometimes brilliant miniaturist into a major poet. The poem represents the high-water mark of his work in Scots and probably of his writing as a whole. Maturity of utterance and sophistication of expression combine in a swingeing, energetic exploration of his situation which he never surpassed. But MacDiarmid is not the sort of person who is satisfied merely to describe his plight of existence. The writing of verse is rarely if ever an end in itself for him, but a means by which truth might be attained. Thus, more than an exploration, *Drunk Man* is the written record of an actual attempt to win personal revelation through the practice of poetry.

By means of a persona (the drunk man) and a carefully staged situation which epitomizes the poet's own, MacDiarmid engages in his struggle for understanding. The drunk man, on his way home from a pub, has lain down upon a bracken-covered hillside, facing the moon, against which is silhouetted a thistle. It is a dark night, illuminated only by the moonlight. The man is too drunk to do anything but lie there and dream; the poem is that dreaming. He is not a character in his own right, but a "translation" of MacDiarmid himself, so that his fantasizing and the poet's writing are the same occurrence. The drunk man's highly contrived elemental environment (so contrived that in the hands of a lesser poet it would have had little aesthetic credibility) defines the space within which the poet confronts his problem. This "literal" situation forms the underpinning of all the poetic flights which ensue, and for all the rambling and diffuseness of the poem as a whole it is remarkable that this focus never wavers. Every waking dream of the poet on his mental hillside can be referred back to it. It anchors his fantasies, and at the same time provides the symbols of which the fantasies are constructed.[1]

Many of these symbols are introduced in the first few lines: the thistle, the moon, whisky, and the dark night. The thistle growing on the hillside is the dominant image throughout the poem, and it symbolizes MacDiarmid's being-in-the-world. Committed as he is to the idea of the Scottish essence which he, being a Scot, embodies ("For a' that's Scottish is in me"), the emblem of Scotland seems a fit shape to give to his reified existence (72, CP 145). Thus, exteriorized as a thistle, the poet's being-in-the-world stands before him as a challenge, a problem to be solved. The moon clearly symbolizes the goal of understanding which the poet seeks. It is an archetypal image, except that its unattainability is open to question; it seems to represent the realization of a potential the poet feels he possesses. The dark night surrounding the poet continues to symbolize, as in the earlier lyrics, the nothingness which encompasses him and cuts him off from certainty. It has the additional useful effects of forcing the gaze to the moon and thistle by obscuring the rest of the world, and conveying a pervading sense of mystery which heightens poetic intensity. The whisky is a device by which the "literal" environment of the drunk man is allowed to achieve symbolic proportions while retaining its integrity as a "real" unchanging basis of operations. Other symbols appear later on. The sea and the wind are images of energy and chaos – formless change, for example. The element of woman adds another dimension to the movement of the poem, that of sexuality and of a neoplatonic pull such as that imposed upon Dante by Beatrice. All these symbols recur and combine in a sort of poetic calculus.

The poem opens with a dissertation on whisky, "no' the real Mackay" these days, like everything else merely called "Scottish," says MacDiarmid (1, CP 83). Whisky on the level of poetry is of course poetic energy, the power of imagination or inspiration, a good Scottish substitute for the wine which is the more conventional blood of poets. It is the essence of Scotland, but it has, he says, become adulterated over the years. On one level MacDiarmid is describing the state of Scottish culture, which has lost its vitality and identity as a result of Anglicization. Whisky has become tea, or merely "A laxative for a' loquacity" in a Scotland which is, as Roderick Watson puts it, his own personal Waste Land. On a deeper level the poet is describing the modern plight in which inspiration or vision is subject to a corrosive scepticism, having seemed to have lost an authority it once possessed. His drunkenness is not only poetic frenzy, but symbolizes the instability of the modern condition.[2]

In the midst of this peroration, the first of three intrusions by MacDiarmid as poet takes place, as he expresses his desire to take his fellow Scots on the trip he has embarked upon, raising them to the heights and casting them into the "nether deeps." This might seem to strain the fabric of the poem, but in fact it serves to put the drunk man in his place, as the poet's persona. The reader is made aware that the man on the hillside is MacDiarmid writing his poem, an identity the author obviously feels is important enough to be made explicit regardless of aesthetic risks (2, *CP* 83).

After setting the scene, MacDiarmid makes a beginning by announcing his intention to plunge into the swill – the confusion of the world – and keep an open mind. He has no ready explanation for things as yet, unlike most men, he says. He will not "filter truth / In fishy gills through which its tides may poor / For ony *animaculae* forsooth." He wants it all, and becomes increasingly aware of the difficulties involved as the poem progresses. At this point he sees the immensity of his self-appointed task contrasted to his "crazy little brain." A well-known passage follows:

> I'll ha'e nae hauf-way hoose, but aye be whaur
> Extremes meet – it's the only way I ken
> To dodge the curst conceit o' bein' richt
> That damns the vast majority o' men. (5-6, *CP* 83)

To be where extremes meet is to be in the thick of struggle at its most intense. Extremes are limits; MacDiarmid is interested in understanding, and the exploration of extremes means the determination of the very boundaries of his existence. Life lived to its fullest means life amid a clash of extremes. It is here that any dialectical synthesis takes place (the revelation the poet seeks). For MacDiarmid, being is believing. To adopt safe positions, to accept a system of beliefs rather than engage oneself fully in the pursuit of truth, is to forgo that truth. Faith is no substitute for whole-hearted investigation. No system provides the ironclad certainty MacDiarmid strives for. To him such structures seem the comfortable illusions of those too timid to face life.

Using more than the senses, the poet says he will "stert whaur the philosophers leave aff, / Content to glimpse its loops I dinna ettle / To land the sea serpent's sel' wi' ony gaff" (6, *CP* 87). The "gaff" is any system which tries to explain everything. The sea-serpent is the same one as in "Sea-Serpent" discussed in the last chapter. It is understanding, the one in the many, the universal order which MacDiarmid seeks but which, snake-like, eludes his grasp. There is a suggestion here that by trying to land the serpent, one does it an injury; MacDiarmid's approach is more cautious and, as *To Circumjack Cenrastus* indicates, more humane.

A chance thought of his wife gives rise to an apparition, a mysterious woman. She is the mystical bride, the personification of the Scottish essence (as indicated in his list of sections to be added to "Braid Scots") on one level, perhaps Robert Graves's White Goddess, the perennial muse, on another. The noise of the revellers in the pub from which MacDiarmid has come can be heard in the distance; in a sense it is humanity at a distance from the poet, the tavern with its uproar being a microcosm. His situation is a lonely one. The moon looks over the world. It becomes for a moment a liquor glass in which he sees, first, his own reflection, and then a "silken leddy." She is not an imperious muse but a lonely one, moving "darkly" as though to a "trystin'-place undreamt." The essence of this vision is promise. The woman seems inaccessible but leads him on. She would seem to be the personification of the moon, and thus of the ideal which MacDiarmid wants to possess. She seems authentic enough, and endless faith gathers around her. The poet defines his actual state as captivity from which he seeks escape by penetrating the dark veils which eclipse her. His dark secrets, the unrealized and thus unknown part of his self, full of turns and twists (like a sea-serpent?), might be revealed through her. A sun (enlightenment) is given to him to use, and the whisky in his blood searches the inner recesses of his self. She appears once again, gazing at him through the sea, which itself symbolizes the ever-changing, confused, and chaotic nature of the world he confronts. It is implied that he will reach her by plunging in. All this promise is hoarded by his soul, but he is as yet unable to "spend" this "wealth." The final affirmation of *in vino veritas* is marking time, as the poet awaits further revelation (7-9, *CP* 89).

But this vision fades, rather than intensifying, and MacDiarmid begins to question its validity. "The munelicht's like a lookin'-glass / The thistle's like mysel'," he says, returning to imagery similar to that just previous to the woman's appearance (9, *CP* 89). He asks himself whether, after all, it was only his own reflection he was seeing. Next time he will make sure, he says, but a few lines later, when the vision does return, he fails to do so in any obvious fashion.

The thistle now becomes the focus of his attention. Is this ugly shape his own reflection? MacDiarmid feels as though he has been turned inside out (see the *Penny Wheep* poem, "Jimsy: An Idiot"), as though he were a contrary in one being, Jekyll looking at Hyde. Descending to the "literal" plane for a moment, he complains that he needs a shave, suggested, of course, by the prickly appearance of the thistle, after claiming rather uncertainly that the thistle cannot frighten him. A mysterious wind, symbolizing energy, as in the *Penny Wheep* lyric "Krang," whistles in his ears, and the mystical bride reappears. He makes an unmistakeable connection between her and the understanding he seeks ("I bide in silence your slow-comin' pace"), and questions his situation anew, this time bringing the thistle into it. Does she make a thistle of him, he asks? For otherwise he would be "happy as the munelicht, withoot care." But thinking of her, and of her contempt and anger, presumably aroused by his having failed to reach her, has transformed half the world into the itchy thistle on the hillside. Its curious existence inside and outside the drunk man is emphasized by this choice of adjective. It feeds upon the moonlight, turning it into part of itself. It will not let him be (9-10, *CP* 90). Plainly, romantic dreaming will not do. The reality of his situation will not permit it.

The thistle, abruptly within the drunk man, appears at first to be conscience, placed in him by the woman. It seems to plague him like conscience, and it could certainly be an image of morality. But he quickly realizes that it is much more than this. "The need to wark, the need to think, the need to be, / And a'thing that twists Life into a certain shape / And interferes wi' perfect liberty" feed the thistle. It has become his very existence, taking shape as he does. For every choice a man makes, he says, every course of action he takes, destroys all the other possibilities of choice and action so that this life is like a thistle compared to the moon. The thistle, he concludes, is "Mortality itsel'," it is "Man torn in twa / And glorious in the lift and grisly on the sod" (11, *CP* 91). He generalizes here, but it is himself he is talking about. The thistle is MacDiarmid, its head in moonlight, representing the aspiration towards the ideal, but securely rooted in the ground nevertheless. MacDiarmid's existence is in-the-world. He is trapped in the actual. The moon is an abstraction; it is the thistle he must deal with.

He is not quite ready to begin grappling with it, for some doubts must be dispelled. What if he is merely an exhibit preserved in spirits? What if he is in bed dreaming all this? He deals with these questions effectively enough. "We maun juist tak' things as we find them," he says, and so the struggle is to be an authentic one as far as he is concerned, regardless of 103 objective possibilities which he realizes are quite irrelevant. The thistle is not in front of the moon by accident, he says, suggesting an underlying meaning or justification for this existence, but a new doubt occurs a little later; what if it is no more than a composite diagram of cross-sections of his forbears' organs and his own? If this is the case, the problem of existence is no concern of the mind at all. A non-conscious procreative series renders consciousness superfluous. But this doubt vanishes as the thistle reasserts itself, staring him in the face as though it were his soul, and Scotland's soul as well. The mental challenge is restored. He realizes what he must do:

> To meddle wi' the thistle and pluck the figs
> Frae't is *my* metier, I think. (13, *CP* 93)

The "figs," glimmers of truth, glimpses perhaps of the sea-serpent's loops, are rewards for the risky enterprise of meddling with the prickly thistle, for facing the difficult and painful problem of living.

The thistle almost immediately becomes an octopus, and then, by suggestion, a sea-serpent (not the other way round as Roderick Watson states) which seizes MacDiarmid, stinging him and disgusting him with its embrace.[3] Its poisoned scales are like shafts, but at the same time are not sharp but flabby. He feels his life being drained away. He becomes aware at last that this "whale-white obscenity" is his own soul (14, *CP* 94). The adjective "whale-white" gives the clue to this passage. MacDiarmid has set out on a pursuit of truth with the same single-minded determination that Captain Ahab displayed in his pursuit of Moby Dick. One of the manifestations of this truth is the sea-serpent. But a doubt, so profound that all previous ones seem trivial, and so chilling that he is drained of energy, has suddenly occurred to him. What if the sea-serpent is not truth at all, but merely a manifestation of his own being? For his "soul," as becomes evident in the course of the poem, is his actual being, not an immortal part belonging to a transcendental realm. In this passage the doubt, for so it is in the context of the poem as a whole, carries all the force of conviction.

It has been seen that the thistle takes shape from a continuing past of choices and actions. Being-in-the-world is a process. And as surely as it leaves a past, it flies towards the future. Sartre defines a consciousness as just this flight towards the future, as it vainly tries to coincide with itself. MacDiarmid experiences Sartrean nausea, arising out of his awareness (so it seems at this time) of his "facticity" – that is, that he exists for no reason or purpose, but just exists. His whole quest is an illusion – the sea-serpent, which he has been deluded into thinking is truth that, when attained, will provide the foundation for his existence which he seeks, is revealed as just that unfounded existence. He sees that its "purpose whole" is to be a snare and a delusion. The solution is only part of the problem after all. Seeming to be free to pursue the truth, he is in fact a victim of illusion, and trapped in a mode of existence which lacks not only a foundation but now the hope of one as well. It is worth noting here that after this doubt has been dispelled, the white whale appears again later in the poem – as the moon.

The moonlight has grown leprous, but MacDiarmid begins to recover, even in the depths of his despair. The wind comes up once more, and even though it may be his skeleton that it whistles through, and it makes a noise rather than a tune, it is clearly suggested here that there *are* forces which do not originate in him and which signify external verities (14, *CP* 94). A calmer, reflective tone takes hold as he considers the ebb and flow of his visionary power; he seems to have banished that soul-shaking nightmare forever, for it never recurs in this poem or in later work. The abruptness with which it is abandoned suggests that he found it a possibility too terrible to contemplate.

The moonlight seems to ebb and flow, and MacDiarmid's thought does the same. His brains, he says, are like seaweed, bladders full at high tide, left knotted like wrinkled old blood vessels at low tide. The moon, it seems, influences the tides of vision. What the poet is describing here is the rise and fall of poetic intensity which one in fact perceives in this poem, his shifting between the "literal" and symbolic planes. By attributing the ebb and flow of imagination to the action of the moon, he cleverly avoids responsibility for it (perhaps this too is "pairt o' a Plan"?), but whatever the cause, he has been unable to win through to the fullness of revelation. This passage ends only with the stark affirmation that life and death, the physical fact of existence, for no man is enough (15, *CP* 95).

In these first 384 lines of the poem, the drunk man ascends to an elusive vision and descends into utter despair, concluding only with the assertion that there is more to a person that mere living and dying. He has returned, in effect, to his starting point. So he begins his struggle anew in what starts out as a far more precise and methodical analysis and exploration of his problem. The petty cultural nationalism of his compatriots is scornfully compared to his own heroic

struggle with the Scottish soul (his own); even here a note of self-irony
creeps in as the drunk man compares himself to Ulysses wandering
on wine-dark oceans, but the contrast holds for all that (15, *CP* 95).
From this affirmation of the uniqueness and epic quality of his quest,
he proceeds immediately to make an explicit contrast between two
opposing possible poetic attitudes open to him.

The moon, says MacDiarmid, makes his soul obedient to "her" will
(the mystic woman and the moon are united here), and he perceives
"the sensuous windin's o' her thocht." But each winding, he becomes
aware, has a counter-winding in the thistle, which bursts, "green wi'
jealousy," between the moonlight and his heart (16, *CP* 96). His
fancied rapport with the moon, a romantic ecstasy, has been proved
false; he cannot win through to the ideal with idle poetic dreaming.
The thistle, like conscience once again, awakens him to his responsi-
bilities. All he has done in trying to avoid the problem of the thistle is
to produce a mirror-image of it which he has mistaken for his goal.
The easy route to truth is countered by his own being-in-the-world as
a mute and inexplicable fact. He must face the "wild kinks" of his
existence, previously given as the turns and twists of dark secrets and
expressed in later work as eddies in water, and hope to discover the
one serpent of which these are coils.

He begins anew by describing the thistle's appearance with a series
of comparisons between its characteristics and other things. These
become steadily wider-ranging and more fantastic, but somehow they
leave the thistle untouched. One is merely left with a confused series
of imaginings which, inevitably perhaps, ends in low comedy. The
poet recalls a Scottish soldier sitting on a thistle and yelling; there
seems to be at least a suggestion here that in order to meddle with the
thistle a more direct approach is needed (17, *CP* 96). This is followed
immediately by a reference to his own poetry, in which, continuing
the comic mood, MacDiarmid attributes the foreign references in his
poem to his Scottish schooling. This second attempt to grapple with
the thistle has ended in confusion, at any rate:

> Guid sakes I'm in a dreidfu' state.
> I'll ha'e nae inklin' sune
> Gin I'm the drinker or the drink
> The thistle or the mune. (17, *CP* 97)

But MacDiarmid remains the drinker and the moon remains his
goal. He presses on anew, this time allowing a memory of Langholm
Fair to assume cosmic importance. But his promise to "dance the
nicht wi' the stars o' Heaven" comes to nothing as he becomes

suddenly aware of a very literal sexual desire for his wife (18, *CP* 98). The problem with the thistle seems to be one of approach: letting his imagination flow seems to have no permanent results. The thistle is a symbol, but he realizes that it must be more than that. He must live the thistle, which, as noted before, has a curious simultaneous internal and external existence in the poem. "The thistle yet'll unite / Man and the Infinite!" he affirms, and describes the joys and power of living life to the fullest in terms of it (19, *CP* 98). The roots of the thistle stir in the hollows of man's heart, he says, like the sea-serpent, whose coils are like the thistle's leaves; this curious simile, which doubles back upon itself, indicates the power MacDiarmid senses in life, the potential in human (his) existence to be like the serpent, or, as can be seen in his next volume, the potential to "circumjack," or be circumjacent to, this universal snake (19, *CP* 98). This idea is developed in three more stanzas, the third one replacing the general "man" with the first person singular. The stanza which follows deals with the fall of humanity, but a rather different fall from the conventional one:

> The howes o' Man's hert are bare,
> The Dragon's left them for good,
> There's nocht but naethingness there,
> The hole whaur the Thistle stood,
> That rootless and radiant flies
> A Phoenix in Paradise! (20, *CP* 99)

The Christian attitude towards existence is clearly wrong, according to MacDiarmid. He is at one with William Blake in this. Christianity has separated the soul from the body, and made life after death more important than life on earth. Such a waste of human potential appals the drunk man. By inventing a supra-mundane paradise, this doctrine has left humanity with an empty heart. MacDiarmid rejects this approach out of hand, and goes on to explore a related approach to the thistle which seems at first a tempting possibility. Taking a pair of opposites, Masoch and Sade, he complains that in his being this pair is turned into one; he is in the thick of clashing extremes, and these two signify them all. They are turned into one only in that they occupy the same space, as it were, for there is no synthesis, only havoc. Perhaps, suggests MacDiarmid, if he could see "A' that they've been" in the thistle – that is, remove them from himself and impose them upon a symbol exterior to himself – he might "wun clear." But the realization comes swiftly:

Thistleless fule,
You'll ha'e nocht left
But the hole frae which
Life's struggle is reft! (20, *CP* 100)

He would merely, in a disguised form, be˙ succumbing to the life-denying Christianity described previously. He cannot turn his struggle into an abstraction to be solved from without. To solve his problem he must live it. One is reminded here of one of the reasons for the anti-scientific bias of the existentialists, that science reduces humanity to an abstract series of properties to be treated as dispassionately as other phenomena. The thistle functions as a symbol, but it cannot be allowed to be only an object. This explicit understanding defines the poet's relationship to his central symbol. It will not be used merely to represent, but in a very real sense it will be, the poet's being-in-the-world. This prefigures MacDiarmid's attitude to the outside world in general, examined in chapter 4.

Having established what approach not to take, he falls back on philosophical musing. Reason serves the end of pleasure. Truth (in the abstract, it is implied) is a means to wider knowledge and interest in life, not an end in itself. Poets and artists await flashes of vision amid states of boredom, he says. Poets are proud spirits amid the "feck o' mankind (21, *CP* 100)." This self-administered fillip propels him from stock-taking into active struggle once again.

In a short song, the image of the sea is reintroduced. Using Christian allusions he makes another beginning, one similar to that of Pound in "Canto I." "And then went down to the ship / set keel to breakers, forth on the godly sea" becomes, in MacDiarmid's case, "We're outward bound frae Scotland." All Scots, past and present, he says, go outwards in confusion. The mizzenmast is a monkey-puzzle tree, another manifestation of the thistle. The captain (God) has never been seen, and "the first mate is a Jew" (Christ). "We've shipped aboard Eternity," he concludes (21, *CP* 100). Scotland serves as the starting point for every Scot, including himself. As he is to say in *Cencrastus*, "If there is ocht in Scotland that's worth ha'en / There is nae distance to which it's unattached." But each individual (including himself) is left on his own, "in a creel." The tone of this passage is one of despair. The thistle becomes the unclimbable mast of a possibly undirected ship; the situation seems permanent, without resolution. His problem of existence, that is, carries him along in a confusion which threatens never to end.

Having thus redefined his situation, and expressed the fear that his quandary is running away with him, the poet makes his second intrusion, as poet, into the narrative. He says defiantly that his readers may see only foolish fuss in his confusion and struggle, but he cannot stop his "galliard" in order to teach them the steps. His poetry is his struggle, so that it and the thistle merge:

> You vegetable cat's melody!
> Your *Concert Miaulant* is
> A triumph o' discord shairly,
> And suits my fancy fairly
> – I'm shair that Scott'll agree
> He canna vie wi' this ... (22, *CP* 101)

The poet and the drunk man coincide for a moment in their respective modes of existence, and then the drunk man is re-established as the protagonist.

Sexual awareness returns, and Christianity becomes Christianity between the sheets. Just as the Christian attitude deflects one from the essential struggle, so sexuality becomes a trap as well. His mind tells him that his wife laughs to see him thus enslaved. "I wish I kent the physical basis / O' a' life's seemin' airs and graces" he says, indicating perhaps that freedom is the consciousness of necessity, that knowledge will allow him to transcend this powerful drive which now keeps his spirit entwined in his entrails. His whole being at this moment seems sexually determined, so that the thistle becomes his erect phallus. A lyric already published in *Sangschaw*, "A Woman's Love," sums up this possibility. A woman, says MacDiarmid, reduces a man merely to his sexual appetite (23, *CP* 101).

But this bodily desire undergoes a sublimation into some of the most intense poetry in *Drunk Man*, as his wife becomes neoplatonically transformed into the mystical bride. As a poetic gesture of self-abasement, the drunk man expresses his overwhelming relief at this apparent deliverance from brute carnality by stating that the intense light of the bride's eyes blinds her to his baser aspects. Following this is the finest lyric in the poem and perhaps in his entire canon, "O Wha's the Bride." Here the muse is revealed as the Scottish muse, carying a bouquet of thistles which in this context are purely emblematic. She has been raped, but her virginity remains, paradoxically untaken. This "evil deed" took place before she was born. She promises herself to the drunk man, saying that in her arms he will forget the desecrations perpetrated by other men (24, *CP* 102-3). On one level, of course, MacDiarmid is referring to the cultural rape of Scotland which has prevented her from being born as a nation; now, having at last emerged (in essence), she offers herself to him. On another level there is a clear allusion to the Virgin Mary, who appears explicitly in a passage only a few lines further on, but a childless Mary in this case. This places the poet in the not unfamiliar role of God Himself, a "God in Murray tartan" as he puts it in *Cencrastus*. On a third level she embodies the goal of understanding which he struggles to possess, a goal framed in a Scottish context. Outward bound from Scotland he now doubles back. The promise of success seems closer to fulfilment here than at any other point in the poem, as the bride actually seems on the point of being won.

Since so many worthless children are born, MacDiarmid claims in the next passage, he hopes that the result of his union with the bride will be worth something; already the doubts are creeping in, lessening the effect of his vision (25, *CP* 103). His tone turns wry and sardonic. The bride becomes the moon once more, and the thistle becomes her child, born not of union but of separation (25, *CP* 104). MacDiarmid's being-in-the-world, that is, is defined by this separation; it is in essence a perpetual flight towards the ideal. The drunk man realizes his perennial plight yet again. The thistle, as in the earlier passage discussed above, cannot be bypassed in the search for truth. Nourishing the hope that he might find "sudden birth," he says, identifying with the thistle, that his roots "hauf-publish" him upon the air, so that "the struggle that divides [him] still" is plainly seen. The parallel here with Sartre's conception of the *pour-soi* or consciousness as "project" is striking. Other identifications are made, and finally, he says, "My self-tormented spirit took / The shape repeated in the thistle." At length he promises an eventual resolution of the struggle: "The impossible truth'll triumph at last, / And mock [the thistle's] strife" (26-7, *CP* 105).

Having resumed the centre of the stage, after the mystical bride has proved false (the moon even acquiring associations with death), the thistle becomes, as Scotland, the barren fig tree withered by Christ. The drunk man says he will make it flower (27, *CP* 105-6). The mention of Scotland introduces a series of comments upon the decadent state of contemporary Scotland. The thistle's rose, a symbol which embodies both achievement and failure (it crowns the plant, but it is not the ideal), is contemptuously dismissed as English (29, *CP* 107)! After yet more criticisms of the state of his land, his elemental chase is redefined. The moon is a white whale pursued by the protagonist on a ship whose deck is the Earth and whose sail is the thistle. This mystical voyage is contrasted with the banality of his fellow Scots, whom he tells to go drown in their beer (30-1, *CP* 109).

The drunk man then breaks into a drinking song of his own, "To

Luna at the Craidle-and-Coffin." The moon is seen as an old hag which MacDiarmid rejects in disgust. Describing his innumerable attempts to possess her, each ending in failure as has been seen, the poet feels he is being drained of vitality to no purpose. She becomes "Cutty Sark" dancing naked, tantalizing him; he is forced to watch, and wants to see all of her, but in a despairing mood he complains that all his pleasures end like a drink taken yesterday. He continues on his theme of being drained, this time like a barrel of ale; his "freaths" (plumes of froth; semen, on another level) hang in the sky like rainbows, as he ends on a note of desperate exhilaration (32-3, *CP* 109-10).

The central images of moon and thistle appear again. Presumably by insulting the moon as he has done, he has succeeded in reducing Eden to something of no value. The thistle seems as much a part of this world, and inseparably linked to it, as the man in the moon is to the moon (33, *CP* 110). MacDiarmid's quest seems doomed to failure. Various images of despair follow. All has been illusion. "A' the ferlies o' natur' spring frae the earth, / And into't again maun drap (35, *CP* 112). He asks that the moon give him freedom from the darkness or remove all the light, for this tantalizing half-light is intolerable. He desires, in short, to be "clear o' chaos" so that, like the thistle in front of him, he might "brak' in roses owre a hedge o' grief" (35, *CP* 113). Here the thistle, always available to the poet for the symbolic use it has been put to, is left at a remove from him, so that the thistle's roses become the symbol of the ideal he wishes to achieve. So preoccupied with the moon has he become that the identification between thistle and himself is momentarily allowed to lapse.

Having reached a dead end, MacDiarmid engages upon a disquisition on love, and the visionary gives way to the discursive (35-7, *CP* 113ff). It is passages like these which suggest, erroneously, some underlying philosophy in the poem, but this adapting of commonplaces (love caught between the extremes of lust and law, for example) seems more a retreat than anything else, as the poet seeks refuge from a problem which has become too much for him. Exhorting his heart to cast out its dead wood, he considers the possibility that humanity (himself) has unsurpassable limitations and is superfluous to any scheme of things. There seems to be no guaranteed progress. Genius seems detached from any human purpose and irrelevant to God's. In MacDiarmid's experience, as has been seen, flashes of insight have proved irrelevant to the problem the thistle represents. This problem remains in all its complexity: a "mongrel growth," a "jumble o' disproportions, / Whirlin' in its incredible contortions." It is, in fact, "A' the uncouth dilemmas o' oor nature / Objectified in vegetable maitter." But this latest in a series of redefinitions of his plight leads to no solution. His ability to reach truth is doubted: "For naething's seen or kent that's near a thing itsel'!" The "routh / O' contrairies that jostle in this dumfoondrin' growth" remain unsynthesized (41-2, *CP* 116-19).

A long passage, explicitly concerned with the General Strike in 1926, follows next, in which the promise of the thistle eventually being transformed into a lovely flower represents on one level the aspirations and struggle of the working class to realize their potential. The rose which leapt out from the thistle is, on this level, the General Strike itself. As it failed, so the rose shrivelled. "The vices that defeat the dream / Are in the plant itsel'," he concludes. The workers are crucified upon the thistle. But the poem ends with MacDiarmid himself so crucified (42-6, *CP* 119ff). One can thus look upon this poem as a clever use of history as personal metaphor, a not uncommon practice with this poet, so that the rose which died could refer to any or all of the visions the poet has had in the course of the struggle which is his poem, and this passage itself might therefore be taken as a summing-up or commentary upon his exertions so far.

The reader becomes aware, as the poem progresses, that MacDiarmid grows more reflective and depressed about the thistle and the problem it embodies and sees himself more and more as the helpless prisoner of cirumstances rather than the heroic wrestler with his situation that he begins by being. Despite periodic affirmations, he suffers a marked loss of confidence after the failure of the mystical bride to become his. False romanticism or not, she did appear real, and she promised him a solution to this plight that seemed at that moment almost tangible. One senses a growing bafflement as the drunk man grows repetitive and the thistle becomes more impersonal and threatening. His frustration grows. People (MacDiarmid) are like quarts squeezed into pint pots, he says. Progress may well be an illusion. The thistle appears now as a "stranglin' rictus," a "sterile spasm" (46-8, *CP* 122-4). The problem of approach arises again: "Nae chance lunge cuts the Gordian knot," he realizes. He asks that the understanding he seeks be revealed to him and exhorts his soul to increase in him. The "ootrie gangrel frae the wilds / O' chaos" might yet be transformed, but the tone of these passages is one of ever-growing despair:

[S]till the puzzle stands unsolved.
Beauty and ugliness alike,
And life and daith and God and man,
Are aspects o't but nane can tell

The secret that I'd fain find oot
O' this bricht hive, this sorry weed,
The tree that fills the universe. (50, *CP* 126)

"The tug-o'-war is in [him] still," he complains. And the drunk man is getting dry. He despairs of his "empty dreams" (51, *CP* 127).

As inspiration wanes, the intellect defines the problem afresh. The thistle becomes "the facts in ilka airt / That breenge into infinity, / Criss-crossed wi' coontless ither facts / Nae man can follow, and o' which / He is himsel' a helpless pairt." On the level of knowledge, "The less man sees the mair he is / Content wi't, but the mair he sees / The mair he kens hoo little o' / A' that there is he'll ever see, / And hoo it mak's confusion aye" (54, *CP* 129). The world in the absence of a unifying intuition is unutterably complicated. It appears "eemis," or precariously balanced; it lacks foundation, spiritual or rational. MacDiarmid's struggle has served only to reveal in greater clarity and depth the dimensions of his problem.

From one man's confrontation with the thistle, the poem now opens out into wider and wider generalizations. His plight becomes everyone's, and he turns from engagement to discourse. A frustrated God is straining to be born of him – his potential is as yet unable to be realized – and general ideas of progress occur to him, such as evolution, which carries with it the implicit guarantee of inevitability (59ff, *CP* 134ff). This concept is not the Darwinian one, but the older philosophical idea which MacDiarmid probably picked up from Davidson's poetry, or perhaps from his reading of the philosophy of Vladimir Solovyev. A.O. Lovejoy deals with this in *The Great Chain of Being*: the absolute order of the universe came to be seen as "temporalized," so that the universe is fulfilled in time and is once more in God.[4] Charles Darwin, in fact, produced his *Origin of Species* in the midst of philosophical speculation about evolution which had begun much earlier. MacDiarmid's choice of this concept as another personal metaphor (for there is no question of his remaining on the sidelines as an observer of human evolution; it is his own potential he is concerned with) is perhaps explained in part by Sartre's analytical description of a human as "the being whose project is to be God," consciousness becoming its own foundation, stasis achieved.[5] The poet would naturally be attracted to a concept which reflected a powerful impulse within himself.

The "spirit o' strife" might well destroy illusions, but it seems to offer nothing positive in their place. MacDiarmid now allies himself with Dostoevski, but, in so doing, reduces even that "spirit" to an abstraction. Asking for Dostoevski's genius is a rhetorical gesture in a way which the invocation of the mystical bride, for example, was not. The poem as a poem becomes markedly more complex and obscure from this point, and less interesting as well. His affirmations become less effective every time they are repeated: when he states in his "Letter to Dostoevski" (as the section is labelled in *Collected Poems*) that he will open his heart to the pain of the thistle, that he·will proceed free of public opinion, that he will rise above the thistle like the moon, that the thistle's growth will be a process through which his spirit has gone, the reader has more than a distinct feeling of *déjà vu* (63ff, *CP* 137ff). MacDiarmid cannot of course be criticized for failing to win the moon, but it is an ever-deepening flaw in the poem that he becomes increasingly garrulous about his predicament and the potential he feels he possesses. The first suggestion of what is later termed "the kind of poetry I want" occurs here:

> For a' that's Scottish is in me ...
> And I ... 'ud be an action
> To pit in a concrete abstraction
> My country's contrair qualities,
> And mak' a unity o' these. (72, *CP* 145)

The "concrete abstraction" is an ideal poetry, a poetry which embodies the synthesis which the poet has been unable to make. All this writing of what he is going to do, or wants to do, is a substitution of a kind of speculation for active engagement. Too often in the later stages of the poem the force, immediacy, and free flow of his imagination give way to an overly intellectual mode of approach that renders his situation an abstract proposition at times.

This is certainly not to suggest that the poet has damped down his imagination. His ever-increasing sense of being dwarfed by a thistle which has grown monstrous, his images of crucifixion, and so on, have a living force in the later parts of the poem. He feels his plight, and this is conveyed to the reader. But his "meddling" with it becomes theorizing, as it grows larger and more grisly. His "waeful plicht" seems beyond all power to solve.

As the poem continues, his agony forms a thistle around him made of lines of torture, a thistle which is a "symbol o' the puzzle o' man's soul," but despite his suffering no revelation comes (74, *CP* 147). The thistle becomes a many-branched candelabra filling the sky, and an octopus floundering about in the sea. (A stylized thistle readily suggests these images; Watson's contention that they are manifestations of the sea-serpent in this context seems rather fanciful.)[6] MacDiarmid realizes that

I am the candelabra, and burn
My endless candles to an Unkent God.
I am the mind and meaning o' the octopus
That thraws its empty airms through a' th' Inane. (75, *CP* 148)

The octopus flails about in the sea of confusion which is the
phenomenal world; all is inane because nothing offers any clue to
salvation. The candles on the candelabra will "sune gang oot" as well.

A conventional treatment of light and dark follows which illustrates
the poet's weakness at this stage for philosophical chatter. The poem
progresses, and the problem continues to be restated. The perennial
question is now merely rhetorical:

> Hou can I graipple wi' the thistle syne,
> Be intricate as it and up to a' its moves?
> A' airts its sheenin' points are loupin' 'yont me,
> Quhile still the firmament it proves.
>
> And syne it's like a wab in which the warld
> Squats like a spider, quhile the mune and me
> Are taigled in an endless corner o't
> Tyauvin' fecklessly ... (79, *CP* 151)

The thistle has become too much for MacDiarmid's efforts, which
seem puny by comparison. He and Dostoevski are homeless in the
world, their voices lost in wind, as the thistle obscures everything, its
leaves like a dense snowstorm.

> And still – its leafs like snaw, its growth like wund –
> The thistle rises and forever will! (79, *CP* 152)

His being-in-the-world involves so much that, made an object of
surveillance, it has acquired an impersonal quality and become a sort
of objective condition of which he partakes. Thus a little later he says,

> Nae mair I see
> As aince I saw
> Mysel' in the thistle
> Harth and haw! (81, *CP* 153)

It is now the "michty thistle in wha's bonds I rove," and (with
acknowledgements to Dante) "the scattered leaves of all the universe;
substance and accidents and their relations, as though together
fused," not in a synthesis in this case but in a problem of universal
scope and dimensions (82, *CP* 154). He abandons himself to
determinism:

The wee reliefs we ha'e in booze
Or wun at times in carnal states,
May hide frae us but canna cheenge
The silly horrors o' oor fates. (83, *CP* 155)

He carries this to an extreme so that his existence becomes merely a
collection of bones for the dog truth to chew on (83, *CP* 155).
This description seems rather too melodramatic, and the poet
recovers his poise with a passage which sums up his predicament as he
now sees it, and which recaptures the controlled intensity of the
earlier sections of the poem with a rich display of Lallans at its most
effective. He is a helpless prisoner aboard the ship of heaven, and the
thistle is the rigging which fills the sky (84, *CP* 155-6). But even bound
hand and foot as he is, hardly the captain of his soul, the possibility of
enlightenment, although remote, refuses to fade. Even at this ex-
tremity, he cannot give up hope, and this leads to an affirmation of
the thistle's power, after the implicit reassertion of his own active role:

Grugous thistle, to my een
Your widdifow ramel evince
Sibness to snakes wha's coils
Rin coonter airts at yince,
And fain I'd follow each
Gin you the trick'll teach. (84, *CP* 156)

The transition from prisoner to disciple is easily made, and one
senses that his delight in the thistle which follows is in fact a delight in
the potential that seems to be wakening within him. His existence
bears "sibness to snakes," and he suggests therefore the possibility of
winning through to the sea-serpent after all and learning anew from
his projected situation – an astonishing return of confidence, but one
which is not altogether unpredictable. MacDiarmid is not one to
remain passive in the grip of circumstances for long, or give in to
despair, and his attitude towards the world is more than of a Byron
than a Keats. After attacking England with the old vigour, he makes a
wry comment which seems to refer to what he has achieved:

Hauf his soul a Scot maun use
Indulgin' in illusions,
And hauf in gettin' rid o' them
And comin' to conclusions
Wi' the demoralisin' dearth
O' onything worth while on Earth. (85, *CP* 157)

Having failed to reach understanding, MacDiarmid at last brings the poem to a close, first of all with a long passage dealing with the theoretical goal for which he has striven, and which here becomes the general goal of mankind. An intellectual construction replaces former vision, as he conceives of a great wheel, unimaginably huge, which contains all there is, and which will either whirl all men along, "pent / In adequate enlightenment," or else shrink and "birl in time inside oor heids / Till we can thraw oot conscious gleids / That draw an answer to oor needs." Poetry is to have the function, he states explicitly, of bringing about the unity of man and the cosmos. This passage as a whole seems rather contrived, and the third and last intrusion of the poet as poet rather than drunk man, which ends with his inner voice telling him that a Scottish poet must die to break the "livin' tomb" of his fellow countrymen, suggests that a pose is being struck, and that MacDiarmid is trying to impose a conclusion upon his poem (86ff, *CP* 158ff).

Whether or not this is the case, the poet does not end with this passage but with two short lyrics which carry much more conviction. He feels a great emptiness after his endeavours, and the thistle now fills the universe, drawing its sustenance from him. His problem of being has drained him in his attempt to solve it, and this "sterile growth" has turned his life into a great void. His search for certainty has left him worse off than before, for the vast scope of his task has now been revealed, together with the knowledge that vision, at least in his case, does not mean revelation. The last passage, however, is a simple and powerful statement of renewal, which in effect cancels all unsuccessful efforts to achieve understanding and leaves the poet composed and prepared for the future. As the poet began, so he ends, with silence. But this is no retreat into silence, like that of Wittgenstein. And this silence, which envelops him, which is his absence of certainty, the fundamental condition of his existence which he has struggled to overcome, is at the same time infinite possibility and total freedom. For MacDiarmid it is the silence of genius, the inexhaustible potential of the human spirit which is particularly realized in such lonely strivings as his own, which has "deed owre often and has seen owre much" but is constantly renewed. The ending of this passage is a joke:

O I hae Silence left,

  – "And weel ye micht,"
Sae Jean'll say, "efter sic a nicht!" (95-6, *CP* 167)

It is hard to imagine a more satisfactory ending for the poem; here is the nervous laughter which follows a long period of tension, or, alternatively, the good-humoured return to the real world of a man outwardly unchanged but inwardly transformed.[7]

Drunk Man is not, therefore, an "open-ended" poem like so many modern long poems. The last two passages signify that this adventure, at least, is over. There can be no further rhapsodies on a hillside. It is curious that the preceding section on the Great Wheel, which is not in itself successful, does set off the last section in a highly effective manner. The contrast between an ideal which has proved (for the moment) beyond him, and which is only capable of an unsatisfactory intellectual formulation, and the poet's actual state focuses the attention necessarily upon the latter. The reader is left with a sense of expectation as the poet, without any blustering or pyrotechnics, recognizes the enormity of his predicament and at the same time reveals a calm self-confidence. His failure to solve his problem, however, is emphasized in the last few lines as well, and his realization of this failure (to some extent implied in the comic ending) is a resolution which excludes further meddling with the thistle as such.

J.M. Reid has written that *Drunk Man* "deals with the twentieth century 'situation' more effectively than anything else in Scots verse."[8] It is in fact one of the most effective treatments of the modern dilemma in the wider context of English and American verse of the age. MacDiarmid's powerful creative energy and craftsmanship are brought to bear explicitly and directly upon this theme as has been shown, in a manner which makes this poem in many ways an aesthetic formulation of the idea of the modern. Despite David Daiches's assertion that it has more in common with mediaeval and Renaissance poetry than with contemporary writing, MacDiarmid's way of seeing as revealed in *Drunk Man* makes him very much a man of his time.[9] If his bawdry, flyting, and gusto are characteristic of Goliardic verse, mediaeval Scots poetry, and Milton, his obsessive self-consciousness, nervousness, and uncertainty leading frequently to despair, far more important aspects of the poem, are strongly characteristic of his own period. He may or may not have derived his idiom from the grab-bag of "ancestors" which Daiches invites us to examine, but whatever his sources and traditions, he has bent them all to a peculiarly contemporary sensibility. His ribaldry only highlights his spiritual desperation, and his polemics play a subsidiary role in what is in fact a drama of the modern self. His blustery assertiveness masks a profound disquiet which may indeed be discovered in the poetry of Villon (also an outsider) but which is hardly typical of Chaucer, Dunbar, or the Goliards. And this continual sense of unease becomes the very focus of his poem, leaving Villon far behind; in his direct confrontation with it, MacDiarmid has much in common with Kafka, Eliot, Beckett, and so on, much more so than with the representatives, or even the *bêtes noires*, of past ages.

MacDiarmid, not Scotland past or present, is the theme of *Drunk Man*, and if he looks to the past it is only to throw the present into relief. Scotland, as Kenneth Buthlay rightly points out, is to him an "idea," and "the 'genius' of his people, their psychological 'quiddity,' became merged with the creative principle in himself, by virtue of which he was always 'speaking of Scotland' as he understood it."[10] But it is not the nature of the creative process which is the theme of the poem, as Buthlay suggests, but the nature of existence in a world without handrails (and why should he provide them for his poem when he had none himself?),[11] an existence, moreover, as a poet and through poetry. *Drunk Man* is desperately atheistic, Christian imagery being used to suit the strategic purpose of a man who knows he is fundamentally on his own, is anguished by that knowledge, and struggles fiercely to escape this state of isolation. The continual explicit emphasis upon his plight, which, despite invocations, remains his own to resolve, is the very essence of the modern condition.

Two aspects of the poem which characterize it as contemporary are the basic uncertainty of stance, a continual and marked shifting of ground which is less unique to Scotland than suggested by the phenomenon of Smith's Caledonian antisyzygy, and the frequent borrowings from the work of other poets. The first is revealed rather obviously by the wild zigzags and contrasts in tone and imagery as passage succeeds passage, and by a self-division into conflicting voices which often presents the spectacle of the poet in dialogue with himself as line succeeds line. The theory of the Caledonian antisyzygy provides a rationale for modern perception even more than it gives a local habitation and a name to the creative process, although the latter, suggested by Buthlay, is partly the case.[12] The violent juxtapositions, which are supposedly characteristic of the Scottish perception, are part of the modern consciousness. Anything which seems solid or certain can be negated, nothing seems to be immune to its opposite. *The Waste Land* has contrasts in tone and imagery as violent as anything in *Drunk Man*, for example, and one could cite many more instances. Frequently recurring and intense clashes of extremes characterize modern culture; this atmosphere of confrontation and contention permeates modern art. *Finnegans Wake* is founded upon such contrasts, the novels of Kafka are constructed out of sudden, unpredictable shifts of situation, the plays of Pirandello revolve aound surprising transformations from "reality" to illusion and back again; see *Cosi è – se vi pare*, for example. More recently one thinks of the black humorists such as Joseph Heller and Thomas Pynchon, the grotesqueries of the camp movement, or the seesawing from innocence to cynicism and from tenderness to obscenity in so much of the activity and production of the counterculture of the 1960s. The dispassionate, almost delicate treatment of human butchery in Truman Capote's *In Cold Blood* presents a contrast between content and expression so appallingly profound that MacDiarmid's juxtaposition of "the homely and the fantastic, the popular and the learned, the reverent and the blasphemous, the tender and the cruel" in *Drunk Man* seems mild in comparison (104). The latter work carries the reader along on its turbulent course, the former tears us apart by eliciting wildly contradictory aesthetic, emotional, and moral responses. In fact, the polarities which one encounters in *Drunk Man* are, within the modern context, distinctive only insofar as they are presented explicitly as polarities. MacDiarmid's self-consciousness illuminates not the Caledonian antisyzygy but the modern environment, and it is this which pervades *Drunk Man* and underlies the polemics and Goliardic ribaldry which Daiches observes. MacDiarmid, here and in his work as a whole, oscillates continually between extremes, defined in this case by the juxtaposition of a spiritually unsatisfying present and an ideal future. His despair, disgust, revolutionary enthusiasm, hatred, love, exultation, bitterness, and joy, emphasized often to the point of exaggeration, are all educed from his powerful sense of having no "sure ground for his feet," accentuating and accentuated by the tantalizing, ever-elusive solution to his problem, which dangles before him as an ever-present possibility no matter where he turns.

The practice of borrowing material from other writers, which T.S. Eliot endeavoured to make respectable, is part of the modern aesthetic as well; what in past ages has amounted to an imitation of manner now becomes an appropriation of substance. Quotation in the body of a poem is a commonplace even where it has not been given the status of the poetic method as in the work of Eliot, Pound, Jones, and MacDiarmid. In MacDiarmid's case the integration of this material into new contexts usually justifies the act, at least on artistic grounds. In *Drunk Man* several of the lyrical passages, "from the Russian of Alexander Blok" and so on, are Lallans adaptations of English translations of these poems, as Buthlay has noted, rather than direct adaptations as suggested by the poet's footnotes.[13] What he has done, in fact, is to give poems from a variety of countries a Scottish locus, and at the same time invest his fighting Scottish persona with some academic authority. The poems, so transformed, are expressions of the Scottish essence; as crystallized intensity and order they are at MacDiarmid's service in his struggle, and he makes them his own. (A carpenter, to use an analogy, employs tools he has not made himself.) There are possibly deeper reasons for this practice as well, which will be discussed in later chapters; as will be shown, both inflated claims and the liberal use of quotation, adapted and not adapted, acknowledged and not acknowledged, are endemic in his work well after "Scotticization" has been abandoned and Lallans has almost ceased to be a viable medium for the poet.[14]

Drunk Man, in short, reflects the age in which it is written both thematically and structurally. It represents MacDiarmid's attempt to resolve his existential dilemma through intuition alone; in other words, to cure the modern disease with old-fashioned remedies, to achieve revelation through such well-worn tactics as invoking the muse. But the thistle, as has been indicated, does not allow passivity. MacDiarmid does not wait for the truth to be visited upon him but actively strives for it. *Drunk Man* is not the poem of a visionary but of a man who would have visions and has no intention of merely letting them come of their own accord. The poet pushes intuition to the limit here, prods it and chivvies it, twists and turns in gigantic efforts to meet the answer half-way. To do this he imbues himself with the Scottish essence, employing a rich Scots vocabulary and giving an emblematic shape to his struggle. The incantatory nature of the Lallans words has been seen in a Scottish context, and this, tenuous as it may be, provides the necessary framework within which his inspiration, fragmentary or not, can manifest itself.

In the above examination of the poem, greater attention has been paid to the first half of the poem than to the second. David Craig is too harsh when he writes, "I feel that the poem as an organization of feelings with real interrelations beneath all their shifts ... lasts no further than the passage with the refrain 'Yank oot your orra boughs, my hert!'" but that passage, or the one on lust and law which precedes it, does represent a turning point in the poem.[15] The single-minded intensity of the first part of the poem gives way to a rambling discourse which lacks much of the control so evident in the former. His struggle dissipates iself in too much thought, in abstract speculation, which seems a response to the hard fact that he has failed to solve the puzzle of the thistle. Yet the interrelations remain, for all that, and *Drunk Man* does not suddenly fail as a poem less than halfway through, as Craig suggests. The reflective or meditative posture which MacDiarmid adopts is an alternative, if less aesthetically satisfying, approach to his quandary, but he never loses sight of his object, and his symbolic scenery does not vanish in a welter of philosophizing. There are moments, as indicated above, where the powerful directness of the early part of the poem recurs later on, but even setting this aside, the poet's attention to what he is about is clearly in evidence throughout the poem, which remains an unfolding process no matter how diffuse his expression becomes. This being said, it must still be pointed out that most of the latter part of the poem, the extended apostrophe to Dostoevski, for example, intrinsically linked to the poem as a whole, is of considerably less interest in itself than much of the earlier section.

Drunk Man is a qualified success; it is uneven, possessing great power but manifesting weaknesses that one observes in later work. In it one finds superb craftsmanship, energy, and fertile imagination on the one hand, and a tendency to talk too much, to give too much scope to an undisciplined intellect, on the other. As in the later poetry, but here kept to a minimum, purely aesthetic ends on occasion seem to be sacrificed to the immediacy of his self-concern. But the poem remains organized and a consistent whole. The theme of drunkenness has been pounced on by critics eager to prove the opposite, but in fact the poet's inebriation is not an aesthetic refuge at all; far from an excuse or a bluff to legitimize supposed incoherence, it functions as a brilliant device by means of which both the poet's imagination and his uncertain state of existence are allowed full expression in a credible symbolic guise.[16] *Drunk Man* has in fact been given rather cursory treatment by commentators, which has frequently meant unjustified attacks upon a poem which, as Roderick Watson aptly puts it, "tends to swallow critics."[17] The confusion, one feels, or most of it at any rate, lies not in the poem but in the uncomprehending reader. John Weston is quite right in saying that "most of the poem proceeds by linked references, repetitions, and associations,"[18] and this does not seem an "external arrangement," as Peter Thirlby maintains (a charge which is more suitably levelled against some later work, as will be demonstrated), but on the whole reflects a consistent and self-sufficient internal logic.[19]

In *Drunk Man* the poet has relied upon intuition to give him the understanding he wants, and he has failed to achieve it. The problem of existence looms larger than ever. The Scottish muse has not given herself to him, and succeeding poetry reveals a widening approach to his predicament in which revelation is sought through less traditionally "poetic" means; committed to poetry, MacDiarmid redefines his art, which is eventually transformed radically, becoming the controversial poetry of facts. The work which follows, *To Circumjack Cencrastus, or the Curly Snake*, is precisely what the title suggests, a statement of MacDiarmid's problem and a consideration of how it might be solved. Cencrastus, the one in the many, is to be "circumjacked" by the poet – that is, he is to make himself circumjacent to it, thus knowing it and possessing it. The problem is both existential and aesthetic, for he ponders how to accomplish the task through poetry.

Cencrastus is, therefore, a poem about the question of approach, not an approach itself. In this it is quite unlike *Drunk Man* and indeed it represents a turning point in MacDiarmid's poetic development in several respects. In it he returns to the discursive style of early poems such as "Sea-Serpent" (even the rambling later section of *Drunk Man* retains an intensity and nervousness which are all but lacking in *Cencrastus*), the Scots is noticeably less rich, the writing is often flat and prosaic, and the overall construction gives the earliest clear indication of the technique of serial collage which becomes an important aspect of subsequent work, a technique which involves the arrangement of organically unrelated bits and pieces in a single poem. Such methods have been attributed to the poet in the creation of *Drunk Man*, but where it is clearly untrue of that poem, one finds it more difficult to absolve its successor with its undigested lyrical and satirical inserts and obviously contrived ending. *Cencrastus* barely hangs together; at the same time there is a main thread of discourse, if frequently interrupted, so that one observes here a stage in the development of the collage method rather than an outright collage such as "Cornish Heroic Song" or *In Memoriam James Joyce*. Separate passages, which are absorbed in the process of *Drunk Man*, merge less easily into the body of *Cencrastus*, so that one sees that the construction of the latter is a development arising out of an earlier technique but at the same time qualitatively different.

The central symbol of the poem is Cencrastus, the sea-serpent, but unlike the thistle, the snake remains an abstraction (of necessity, since it is uncircumjacked) rather than an image. Its chief quality is elusiveness. It is introduced at the beginning of the poem, and here the idea of acquiring knowledge, foreshadowing the poetry of facts, is given approval by MacDiarmid; Cencrastus, says the poet, gave Eve "soond advice" in the garden of Eden (1, *CP* 181). A little further on he writes, "Come let us face the facts. We ken that there's / Nae invocation that's no' fause but this" (3, *CP* 182). The facts are more certain than moonlight, it would seem, and are certainly preferable to maudlin sentiment so far as poetry is concerned; the following passage indicates that MacDiarmid's conception of poetry has been transformed owing to his inability to achieve transcendence:

> And gin we canna thraw aff the warld
> Let's hear o' nae 'Auld grey Mither' ava,
> But o' Middle Torridonian Arkose

Wi' local breccias,
Or the pillow lavas at Loch Awe. (148, *CP* 261)

The geological theme assumes major importance in later work as stone comes to symbolize the certainty he is trying to attain. The poet, no longer outstretched on a hillside wrestling with a recalcitrant inspiration, turns his attention to the world, and thus to knowledge of the world; circumjacking Cencrastus inescapably involves awareness of the facts, he realizes.

The serpent contains no contradictions in its coils, for contradictions reflect an imperfect understanding. It is omnipresent, and cuts "a' airts at aince" (7, *CP* 184). The poet goes on and on explaining, largely by means of an extended description of the snake's qualities, the difficulties which face him in accomplishing his task, expressing as he does so his restlessness and uncertainty, his sense of imperfection, and his recurring confidence that the seemingly impossible can be achieved. From the resigned statement "snails may dream that they'll be eagles yet," he proceeds to an affirmation which makes explicit the fundamental importance he gives to his craft:

> The consciousness that maitter has entrapped
> In minerals, plants and beasts is strugglin' yet
> In men's minds only, seekin' to win free,
> As poet's ideas, in the fecht wi' words. (12, *CP* 187)

But he has already made it clear that his concept of poetry has changed. In a criticism of his fellow men he has turned his back on the kind of poetry *Drunk Man* represents; men, he says, "hate poems dry and hard and needs / Maun hae them fozy wi' infinity" (10, *CP* 186). Dryness and hardness become qualities to strive for in poetry which is at least potentially capable of embodying the Truth; the "poet's hame is in the serpent's mooth" – that is, he is its tongue and voice, or should be (11, *CP* 186).

MacDiarmid deals with the possibility that his idea of Cencrastus is an illusion, the mere wriggling of man's divided vertebrae, as he puts it, and quickly rejects it (14-15, *CP* 188). After considering questions of human achievement (embodied in Napoleon) and ignorance (in a witty satirical insert in which the darkening of the sky during Christ's crucifixion gives rise to this comment from hunters on a Scottish hill: "Isn't that juist like oor Scottish weather!"), MacDiarmid falls victim to fresh doubts (15-16, *CP* 189). How does he know he is not merely duplicating some poor German song? He becomes aware that he must read a great deal, even to eliminate the possibility that he is going over old ground. Heringer, Heym, Zech, Benn, Kasach, Loerke, Mell, Billinger, "and mair than I need tell" are mentioned, and then the philosopher Husserl who perhaps has anticipated him as well (16-17, CP 189-90). Taking heart for a moment, he suggests that a poet's perception is enough to enable him to circumjack the serpent, but he soon despairs that life is too short for him to sing the songs he should. The snake has become a stream trapped in shadows (18, CP 190). This section of the poem ends, therefore, with the poet none the wiser.

The next section of *Cencrastus* consists of two shorter poems and a series of epitaphs. The first of the poem, "The Mavis of Pabal," emphasizes the poet's plight. Lacking a "wee thing in strength and skill" to resolve it, he is

> A pool cut off trae the sea,
> A tree withoot roots that stands
> On the ground unsteadily ...
>
> For poetry's no' made in a lifetime
> And I lack a livin' past;
> I stand on the tap o' the hill
> – But the miracle canna last! (20-1, CP 191-2)

Having introduced the idea of the Scottish Waste Land, he develops it in the second poem, "The Parrot Cry," and in the epitaphs, the voices of Scotland's dead (22ff, CP 192ff). The despairing voices seem in fact to echo MacDiarmid's own fears.

The digression ends, and the Cencrastus theme is resumed. The poet once more expresses his widening concept of poetry, stressing the importance of consciousness and rejecting the fool's approach to the problem the snake poses, which consists of a pious hope that it might disappear and leave a "gowden warld" without crinkles (30-1, CP 197). MacDiarmid has no interest in deluding himself in this manner by waiting for his problem to go away. A lengthy translation, in pure English, of Rilke's "Requiem – Für eine Freundin" follows (a thoroughly aroused critical caution forbids the automatic crediting of this to the poet) in which, in the new context, Rilke, much admired by MacDiarmid, acually appears to partake of the same myth which the latter has been establishing (31ff, CP 197ff).[20] The idea of the elusive Cencrastus seems to pervade the passage, in phrases such as "The saps within you mounting in a life / That climbed and circled," and "Are you still here, unseen?" and in the general sense of longing and separation which the poem evokes (36, 40, CP 200, 202). The language and style, startlingly different from the rest of Cencrastus, in contrast to thematic similarities, seem to emphasize that, despite divergent forms of expression, certain other poets share MacDiarmid's understanding of what is missing and what must be struggled for. By introducing something analogous to a "guest editorial", the poet establishes a kinship of poets seeking the truth, and thus legitimizes his own poetic stance, the direct opposite to that of the fool whose romanticism, unlike Rilke's, is utterly false.

The Scottish question is now reintroduced in some short poems, and the usual denunciations and promises are made (41ff, *CP* 203ff). Aware at length that he is becoming mired in opinions, ideas, and speculations (for the work suffers a continuing loss of clarity as it proceeds), MacDiarmid says, in that curious mixture of uncertainty and defiance which one finds throughout his writing, "Wrang-heidit? Mm. *But heidit*! *That's the thing*" (47, *CP* 206). This is an important clue to his poetry as a whole; he is never one to wait for outside forces to act of their own accord, as a comparison of his energetic drunk persona in the preceding work with Keats's swooning knight-at-arms on another hillside convincingly shows. Without understanding, he might well be wrong in his poetic endeavours, might be far from circumjacking the one in the many, but to do nothing would avail him nothing.

The idea which may underlie the choice of the Rilke passage becomes explicit as he says that he has found co-workers, "In whom I see the licht / O' wills like mine / Increasin' shine / – In a'e shape to unite." And no doubt in others still unknown to him, "The spirit's at work / – And it may lurk / Unkent in neist to a'body, / Unkent to a' eternity." Scotland, or the Scottish idea, becomes submerged in a more fundamental, non-national concern; he wants the "shape o' Scotland's purpose" to be revealed, but "Scotland's purpose to the world's [is] / A comparison to me / As 'twere a bonny dear / To the serpent at her ear," and Scotland under scrutiny, in fact, becomes a concept rendered empty by over-generalizing (47-9, *CP* 206-7). Lermentov, Wergeland, Byron, Kant, Satie, Jean Rictus, Chopin, and Stendhal are all Scottish or possess Scottish connections, in MacDiarmid's view (50-1, *CP* 208). But Scotland nevertheless remains a starting point for him, a source of raw material as it were: "Praisin' Morag or dispraisin', / What does a poet care? / Sugar Brook's tune, sea's diapason, / A's grist that's there." In this passage he seeks kinship with the Gaelic poet Alasdair MacMhaighstir Alasdair, in whose brain "as in God's ain / A'thing's ane again!" (57, 56, *CP* 210).

Cencrastus becomes the theme once more, and MacDiarmid begins to wonder if, after all, he is the only one to have guessed its presence.

Having mentioned another host of figures, including Moses and Melville, he asks, "Is there nae man amang them that has seen / In yon unsullied stream the symbol o' / The unity frae which a' movement springs ..." (59, CP 212)? Plunging into Scottish history brings him no nearer his goal, and even the vague intuition which is all the serpent has amounted to so far now fades. "O I hae tint you," the poet says, and the whole quest seems fruitless: "in the middle o' the nicht what guarantee / Has ony man, tho' day's lang followed nicht, / It'll dae't again, or Truth keep growing clearer / To human consciousness? Clearer? Or's ever kythed / To ony man's mind at a'" (62-3, CP 214)? But he has decided his course, for all of that. If thought is "no' the e'e to see it wi'" he will nevertheless continue with it, as he finds it challenging. Cencrastus becomes error rather than truth, and feeds on "a' the rays o' Licht," as MacDiarmid ascribes his failure to increase his understanding to the serpent itself (63-4, CP 215).

Language itself becomes of central concern. The Scots language, he says, is not big enough to embody the snake, for even English, French, and German, highly developed languages, "haena circum-jacked you yet" (65, CP 215). Further on, in a passage called in the Collected Poems "Tyutchev was Right," largely a collection of philo-sophical speculations and criticisms of MacDiarmid's contemporaries which have by now become commonplace and almost ritualistic, the limitations of language once again are seen as an obstacle to progress: "The trouble is that words / Are a' but useless noo / To span the gulf atween / The human and 'highbrow' view." With language in such an embryonic state, silence as he says may well be the only way, for speech at the moment "squares aye less wi' fact." But this is instantly qualified:

> Silence – like Chaos ere the Word
> That gar'd the Play enact
> That sune to conscious thocht
> Maun seem a foolish dream.
> Nae Word has yet been said,
> Nae Licht's begun to gleam. (70, CP 218-19)

MacDiarmid intends no retreat into silence, but is speaking of a difficulty which is to be temporary, although, as In Memoriam James Joyce shows, this very problem was obsessing him two-and-a-half decades later. Here is one of the earliest examples of the projection of an ideal poetry, the kind of poetry he wants, as remote as Cencrastus himself; he seeks to say that word himself.

The idea of progress, expressed in evolutionary terms, is now given the quality of inevitability: "Naething can backward turn," he says, in the stream of consciousness, which "rids us o' vain dreams / And thraws us back upon / Oorsels'" (71, *CP* 219-20). But this condition of existence, if preferable to illusion, is precisely what MacDiarmid wants to overcome. Ceaseless change which pervades everything and destroys all imagined absolutes is a state which would be transcended if the wily snake could be circumjacked. The poet is at once grateful for his freedom and anxious to lose it. He wants to be liberated from the pell-mell of existence, to know the underlying unity he feels must be there. "A sideless, bottomless, endless sea / Is no' for me," he insists, a "waesome jobble, nae skyline seen, / Nae land ..." He wants the necessary "coign o' vantage" (78, *CP* 223).

The Scottish essence, or the idea of it, continues to haunt MacDiarmid, and the sea becomes the actual sea around Scotland, giving rise to a great fog (78, *CP* 223). The mystical bride appears, but in an account of a past encounter rather than as the words are being written as in *Drunk Man*. Her hair, "plaited / Like the generations o' men" (this passage, incidentally, reappears in pure English in *James Joyce*) is the serpent in another guise;she herself, even as a memory rather than a presence, is the victim of the poet's doubt, as he makes explicit the uncertainty underlying *Drunk Man* and clearly implies the remedy, wider knowledge:

> But tho' I'm blinded in her licht
> The hardy doot's still rife
> That aiblins I am sair beginked
> Thro' sma' experience o' life,
> And favoured here wi' nae King's dochter,
> But juist ... a minister's rinawa wife ... (80-4, *CP* 224, 226)

Following this, as though to boost his confidence, he engages in what by now have become tiresome attacks upon his fellow human beings, fellow Scots in particular, the state of Scots culture, and so on (85ff, *CP* 226ff).

When Cencrastus once more is the theme, MacDiarmid complains that he once had a purer view of it; this seems a comment upon the progress of the poem itself, in which the snake disappears in a jumble of crude philosophical speculations, cruder polemics, and unabsorbed inserts (91, *CP* 230). He attempts to win back to that purity of awareness, if not of actual vision, in a long passage entitled "Frae Anither Window in Thrums." The poet is in darkness, the only light coming from a window which becomes the serpent's eye holding him transfixed. The snake itself has faded to a shadow. But despite some powerful lines in which he evokes his sense of uncertainty, being "in the daurk, while like a frozen / Scurl on Life's plumm the lozen / Skimmers," and not knowing what poetry he will produce ("Seed in my womb, I ken nae mair / Than ony wife what bairn I'll bear / – Christ or a village idiot there / A thronèd king, or corpse i' the air?"), MacDiarmid falls victim once more to disorder. "Back at the start whaur a' began" he seems unable to do more than repeat himself. Even his muse has now lost her identity, he discovers. He feels polluted, he says in a short lyrical insert, like water fouled with clay and dead leaves, his ideas, perhaps, which merely accumulate in him, or the demands of everyday life which are utterly at variance with his poetic ambitions; for this passage is followed by one in which he attacks his boss. Instead of working he has been staring out of a window while sitting in a dark room, and when discovered must be polite and apologetic in order to keep a job which bores him. This latter-day person from Porlock represents not only his class, but most men, says MacDiarmid, who does not suffer fools gladly, whether they are bourgeois or proletarian; the scattered political ideas in the book are derived from his impatience with any barriers in the way of self-realization rather than from general sympathy with the oppressed and exploited. If the boss is a fool, the workers are guilty of "mob cowardice" as well.[21]

MacDiarmid turns his attention to his poetry. If, as a poet, his home is in the mouth of Cencrastus, as he claimed at the beginning of the poem, his double tongue is crippling his efforts to achieve authentic expression: "Curse on my dooble life and dooble tongue, / – Guid Scots wi' English a' hamstrung – / Speakin' o' Scotland in English words / As it were Beethoven chirpt by birds" (103, CP 236). But besides this obstacle preventing the full expression of the Scottish essence, there is a more general problem which seems to have afflicted the development of this poem: "this curst infirmity o' will / That hauds me bletherin' this way still / On things that like a midge-swarm pass / Sub specie aeternatatis [sic]" (103, CP 237).[22] His "loose and gallus tongue" is clarifying very little. His predicament remains, and he is no closer to knowing how to circumjack Cencrastus. Thought, which had seemed more promising than intuition, has offered him few clues, and he is still lost:

> Yirdit in this plight alive
> A' in vain I shout and strive ... (104, CP 237)

He knows that he is increasing his own confusion as he goes on in helpless despair: "Hell tak this improvisin' / That leads a' airts and nane; / A kind o' anti-poetry / That is true poetry's bane" (105, *CP* 238).

He has dreamed of his muse, but wakened to "toom nicht." The "cruel licht o' day," paradoxically, is equated to this empty darkness, for it makes his "poet's moods" look as silly as trying to grasp a ghost. "And ilka sang is like a moon / That hings, a bonny aught, at noon," he writes (105-6, *CP* 238). The moon is no longer mysterious at noon, but looks slightly ridiculous against the sun. But thought or knowledge have not fulfilled their promise either. MacDiarmid is now "weary o' the shapes mere chance can thraw / In this technique and that; and [seeks] that law / To pit the maitter on a proper basis." "A' this is juist provisional," he avers, and will become "something rich and Scots" when he wins "back to the true language o' [his] thoughts" (106-7, *CP* 238-9). But the problem remains, and knowledge becomes a possible source of illusion as well: "O Knowlege, wha can tell / That o' ye ilka bit is / No' juist a dodge to hide faur mair" (110, *CP* 240)? In what is plain wishful thinking, he claims his muse is disciplining him:

> "There's owre mony yads in the fire,"
> Cries my Muse, and her taengs hae taen
> A'thing but Godheid and Scottishness
> Oot o' my sang again! (110, *CP* 240)

His "ditherin' motion" continues (114, *CP* 242). He is a poet, and must write, but committed to an existence free of illusions he seems unable to pursue any one course for long.

"Sisyphus anew begins his climb." MacDiarmid wants to open the "grave o' the universe" in order to free the serpent which is "wa'd up in life." He looks towards his future achievements. "Suddenly my verse'll give men / Glisks o' the serpent wallopin'" (115, 117-18, *CP* 243, 244-5). He sees (if a little self-deprecatingly) his ideal, triumphant self, at least in outline: "Noo in synoptic lines / A Scot becomes a God / – A God in Murray tartan" (121, *CP* 246).[23] This is in marked contrast to his actual state. "There's naething that a man can be / That's mair than imbecile to me / In the licht o' totality," and he has not come close to attaining totality:

> Hoo can I sing lest I begink
> Mysel' wi' a sang less mine than I think
> Or some short-circuit o' a kink? (121-2, *CP* 247)

The reason for his aesthetic stuttering now becomes explicit. He is threatened with existential paralysis – that is, being unable to choose for fear of making the wrong choice. His insistent faith in a hidden, external scheme of things, which Sartre would call "bad faith," is having serious aesthetic consequences, for it is robbing him of confidence; this accounts for his "ditherin'." He is unable to tell if he is circumjacking the snake or not, and is unwilling to sing falsely.

MacDiarmid presses on, clarifies nothing, and cries despairingly to the snake, "Lead thou me on – to stil mair leadin' on; / There is nae goal, for any goal 'ud be / A lauch to last for a' Eternity." He tries to laugh at himself, but this leads only to bitterness: "Lauchter's nae lauchin' maitter." He remains "aneth the sea" (126-7, CP 249-50). At this point Cencrastus himself seems to mock his efforts to clarify his conception of it, saying to MacDiarmid, "There's owre mony killyw-imples in your singin'" and, continuing, "your sang's faurer frae me" than the sun is from the earth (128, CP 250). This voice, the voice of the poet's uncertainty, haunts him throughout his career. MacDiar-mid's whole life is "built on shiftin' sand," he feels, grit which grinds into his brain's "maist delicate windin'" (131, CP 252). But having realized the enormity and seriousness of this task, he is unable to aim any lower. In his passage on "hokum" he is not stating his unwilling-ness to write rubbish, but his inability to do so (132-5, CP 253-4). He is free only to pursue Cencrastus.

But he has become hopelessly muddled:

> The brilliance o' form nae langer shines
> Upon the subject-maitter o' my poem
> I've let owre muckle in't no' needfu' to
> The licht that su'd ha'e been my a'e concern
> Dulled and debauched my work ...
> O I hae tint you (gin e'er I saw)
> You that can ne'er be tint. (135-6, CP 254)

Even this cannot be asserted without a second voice breaking in and disagreeing, although admitting that his "leid is scarcely Scots." In all this uncertainty he might at least make "a better joke in politics and art / Than the Engish yet – and damn consistency!" (137-8, CP 255). But humour is seldom MacDiarmid's strong point, and his attention returns to the serpent. "I ha'ena seen you haill, Cencrastus, and never may," he says, having made yet another beginning ("I'm back to my original stanza noo") as he tries to improve on his distressingly vague idea of the one in the many, aware as he does that he is just as susceptible as previously to shifts of attitude and direction: "A' men are changelings owre and owre again" (138, 140, CP 256).

The sea of chaos remains, giving up only its dead, or "apprentice deid," as the poet sardonically remarks. If anything is to come of his empty command "To wark, then, wumman! Let the bairn be born!" he must find a way out of this ever more complicated maze. Involvement with facts is one alternative, and he contrasts the sentimentality of popular Scottish songs with knowledge of the "relation o' John Davidson's thocht / To Nietzsche's," and of geological formations (145, 147, 148, *CP* 259, 261). A return to lyricism, which, in the light of what has been said up to now, would constitute a retreat, is another alternative, and MacDiarmid proceeds to sing twenty songs "of true Scottish pride." These are a series of exhibits, far from exceptional in quality despite the poet's claim that they are "in mair than diamond cast," in which he merely succeeds in reiterating his plight and his ambitions. His emphasis on poetry over all other concerns is aptly expressed in one of these poems: "Better a'e gowden lyric / Than a social problem solved," he claims, and then, "Better a'e gowden lyric / Than anything else ava" (156-7, *CP* 265-6). He seems here to have turned his back on a great deal, but is careful to follow such a sentiment with a poem which seems addressed to Cencrastus, and ends:

> Oh there's teasin' and there's teasin',
> But your cruelty shows nae easin'
> And in fact it's aye increasin'
>   And has come to sic a pass
> That I'm contemplatin' treason
>   – Equally in vain alas! (158-9, *CP* 267)

Driving the point home, this is followed by a resumption of the main discourse which provides a long coda to "Treason." He writes of the "only road," which is endless, which is silence, which is "dark withoot a whistle." "There's nae road," he continues, "unless we mak' it – gin it can be made." Clearly he is considering no return to "wee bit sangs"; he concludes the passage by affirming the role of science in enriching our mental lives (161, *CP* 267-8). He far prefers being engaged in a task which he deliberately seems to make sound as depressing as possible.

He continues with his anthology nevertheless, including "The Wild Beast Show," which is a lesser variant of Yeats's "The Circus Animals' Desertion," and the exceptionally fine "North of the Tweed." In "The Lion Rampant" the mocking voice of doubt recurs: "You'll fine nae way oot. / Its spell is no' to brak'." He ends the series with his early poem "A Moment in Eternity," which could represent to him the closest he has come to resolving his plight in the lyric mode (175ff, *CP*

269ff). But the lyric alternative is barely considered here, as the interruption part way through indicates.

In context, these short poems provide a surprising contrast with the rest of *Cencrastus*, and one senses that the poet is caught in a cleft stick. Even though the long poem triumphs as the mode he adopts, the lyrics are an uncomfortable presence, not merely a negative point of reference or a series of straw figures. He could, of course, be merely asserting that lyricism has a place in the circumjacking he plans.

The rest of the poem amounts to a summing-up. The primacy of language is asserted, as the point is made that amid the desolation of the poet's Waste Land, "language rises / And towers abune the ruins and music wi't." Poetry is "the movement that the mind invents / For its expression" (184, *CP* 281). MacDiarmid is saying, in fact, that he has language left. He accepts his burden of despair: "To hell wi' happiness!" His approach is "the only road. / The beaten track is *beaten* frae the stert" (186, *CP* 282). As for Cencrastus, he is "an eternal solution and eternal problem" (188, *CP* 283). MacDiarmid, on his own, confronts "the impassive eternal universe / Wi' the states o' his restless hert" (188, *CP* 283). And, foregoing the lyrical enjoyment of the past, he pins his "faith to Thocht," realizing as he does so its "accidental character, weakness, and limits" and that "If he wins he wins alane. / It lies wi' himsel" (190-1, *CP* 284-5).

He expresses his confidence in winning by saying "your coils are no' / Mair numerous than the plies o' my brain" (194, *CP* 286). The motif of Scottishness remains as well, suggesting the ever-present possibility of a Scottish channel to the truth, but this is by now an intellectual concept amid a host of others. If the faintest gleam of Cencrastus "kyths" in his work, he exclaims, the whole revelation might be next; but this is not confined to national boundaries:

> If there is ocht in Scotland that's worth ha'en
> There is nae distance to which it's unattached
> – Nae height, nae depth, nae breadth, and I am fain
> To see it frae the hamely and the earthly snatched. (198, *CP* 289)

The ending of the poem is a matter of convenience, a contrived passage which is an adaptation of a piece of prose in *The New Age* called "The Great Sea-Serpent," as Roderick Watson discovered.[24] Two symbols are contrasted here, the sea (not chaos in this context, but false calm, living in ideals as through they were realized) and the serpent. One calms and soothes, swallowing humanity up in an unruffled infinity and relieving us of responsibility, and the other forces us to create ourselves. There are those for whom the writings of the serpent cease, for they have grasped it, have seen the ineffable in "serene fury" (203, *CP* 292). This is plainly what MacDiarmid hopes to do.

It is almost impossible to evaluate this strategic poem. John Berryman called it "a complete failure,"[25] and Iain Crichton Smith termed it, with some reason, "a ragbag of ideas."[26] As a plan of action, a study of approach, it succeeds as a sort of existential *What Is To Be Done*; in it MacDiarmid plunges resolutely into chaos, which happens to be his environment, in order to evolve an idea of how to tackle his plight which he expresses as alienation from a truth. But this is not without its aesthetic dangers, too many of which the poet fails to avoid.

It is certainly the case, for example, that much of *Cencrastus* drags the reader behind what is often a poor, dull, prosaic diction. Moreover, the frequently uninteresting, far from rigorous philosophizing one finds in the poem often satisfies neither as poetry nor as philosophy, being too undisciplined for the requirements of either; the poet's curious relationship with ideas, which becomes more clearly defined in later poetry, can quite frequently lead to a tiresome, repetitious parade of them, although this is certainly not to state that philosophy has no place in poetry. Thought does provide a continuing basis for MacDiarmid's activity where intuition comes only in flashes, and, as chapter 4 will show, some remarkably effective poetry can result, but the pitfalls of this approach are more than evident in *Cencrastus*. Perhaps the most serious flaw in the poem derives, as Kurt Wittig points out, from the fact that the serpent is "not visualised so concretely as the Thistle."[27] In fact it is not really an image at all, and for that reason MacDiarmid is focusing his attention upon what amounts to an all but empty concept; the result is a poem which can logically be about nearly anything he pleases, and often seems to be just that.

But he has made a decision, to concentrate not upon his uncertain powers of inspiration but instead to look outwards to the world, to involve himself in thought and knowledge, to deal with the hard and the dry and eschew mysticism. He has become more interested in substance, and less in form, as the prosaic nature of much of *Cencrastus* indicates, and one sees in his glide into a watered-down Lallans a clear indication that he is changing, or indeed has changed, poetic direction.[28] An examination of subsequent work reveals the dramatic extent and results of this change.

CHAPTER FOUR

The Poetry of Particulars

After *Cencrastus*, MacDiarmid's poetry undergoes, for the most part, a series of transformations rendered less startling by clear indications in that poem that he had broken forever from the *"Drunk Man* line," together with implicit and explicit suggestions of future trends. Thus Scots gradually gives way to English, lyricism becomes secondary, the material of the world comes under exhaustive scrutiny, knowledge takes precedence over intuition, and ideas predominate over immediate sensations. The centrifugal force which threatened to burst *Cencrastus* apart succeeds in preventing the coalescence of the planned "Clann Albann" and "Mature Art," and no poem approaching the length of *Cencrastus* (with the perhaps allowable exception of the crypto-poem *Lucky Poet*) appears until the publication of *In Memoriam James Joyce* in 1955. The obtrusive self-consciousness of the poet, which in *Cencrastus* became focused upon his poetic activity, slowly but surely leads in this later work to a self-distancing from that activity, and indeed from his very medium. *James Joyce*, the culmination of this process, will be considered in chapter 5.

MacDiarmid did not choose to modulate into English; it was forced upon him. In the Scots verse of *Sangschaw*, *Penny Wheep*, and *Drunk Man*, the use of Scots *per se* was an overriding concern. This is less evident in the linguistic halfway house of *Cencrastus*; and, with some notable exceptions such as "In the Caledonian Forest," the poet reveals no equivalent interest in the medium of English itself during his later career. *Cencrastus* marks the point at which MacDiarmid began to be more concerned with what he was saying rather than the colour of saying itself. And what he wanted to say involved the vast array of materials which he attempted to transform into poetry after that, and which were well beyond the resources of the most plastic of "plastic Scots." In the post-*Cencrastus* work, therefore, thin Scots gives way by 1935 almost exclusively to English and an increasingly vast breadth of subject matter. The poet's deftness in lyric never deserted him entirely – there is a smattering of accomplished lyrics throughout this period, in English and thin Scots, such as "Of John Davidson" and "At My Father's Grave" – but the landmarks in this terrain are the wide-ranging discursive poems such as "The Kind of Poetry I Want," for which lyricism would have been inappropriate and Lallans inadequate.

The development which has been traced through the earlier work continues, but it is much more difficult to follow for two reasons. First of all, MacDiarmid became more diversified after *Cencrastus*, and the individual poems spin off in all directions, seeming to offer no clear line of development. Added to that is the lack of a chronology; in his particular case, manuscripts have a habit of appearing much later than when they were written. To cite only one of numerous examples, a passage from a poem on the Spanish Civil War, "Fascists, You Have Killed My Comrades," published in 1946, appears two years later in a completely new context, in "To Those of My Old School Who Fell in the Second World War," and nine years after that as part of *The Battle Continues.*[1] To seek an unfolding pattern in this work seems a dangerous undertaking. There are critics who see his later work as Marxist, for example, but this is to impose a pattern; David Craig has pointed out a few poems which he considers to be Marxist, but concludes that this vein, in the context of his work as a whole, is "too much an evocation of only the *attitude* of seriousness and militancy" and this is in fact quite clearly the case.[2] The poetry of this period is composed of several such veins.

Nevertheless, besides the more obvious movement from Scots to English and from a lyric craftsmanship to a very often prosaic discursiveness, it can be demonstrated that development does take place in two other major respects. First of all, there is a growing emphasis upon longer poems as time goes on, and Edwin Morgan is correct in suggesting that the later poetry, such as *James Joyce*, seems part of "one megatherial unpublished work."[3] MacDiarmid attempts continually to achieve the coherence of statement suggested in his logically constructed outlines for unwritten long poems. This is structural evidence of the poet's single-minded synthetic approach, an approach which has ensured that most of his poems are related to the central concerns which have been discussed previously. The second aspect of his development, which has been referred to already, is the increasing gap between the practice and theory as regards his poetic activity itself, typified by the poem "The Kind of Poetry I Want." This, as will be indicated, is a consequence of the self-preoccupation which characterizes MacDiarmid's poetry in general.

This development unfolds as the poet continues to concern himself with the existential problems which have been plaguing him, and as he comes to grips with aesthetic problems adumbrated in *Cencrastus*. The curly snake remains uncircumjacked. How to accomplish this goal as a poet is a question which obsesses MacDiarmid. As a modern man, he seeks an all-embracing unity which is denied him, expressing his continually thwarted desire thus:

> O ease my spirit increasingly of the load
> Of my personal limitations and the riddling differences
> Between man and man with a more constant insight
> Into the fundamental similarity of all activities.
>
> And quicken me to the gloriously and terribly illuminating
> Integration of the physical and the spiritual till I feel how easily
> I could put my hand gently on the whole round world
> As on my sweetheart's head and draw it to me.[4]

This modern prayer, addressed one supposes to whatever gods that be, expresses MacDiarmid's ultimate aim of certainty and rest. His goal is Being, oneness with the world, and this poem makes it explicit. But it is as a poet that this ideal is to be achieved, and as suggested in *Cencrastus* the world must be confronted in all its chaos and particularity by the poet. This of course results in formidable aesthetic problems. "The Point of Honour" reveals the conflicting poetic tendencies in him.

This poem begins as an English counterpart of his Scots poem "Water Music," a pure delight in sound and an exultation over the endless variety of movements of water to which he is "wedding words" and which, he affirms, must still be "reined by unseen / And ubiquitous disciplines" for all its "apparent freedom." Seemingly fluid, it is in reality "cut water"; could he but grasp these disciplines the water would appear as a hard, many-faceted, changeless gem. As it is, he can joy in its

> Pride of play in a flourish of eddies,
> Bravura of blowballs, and silver digressions, [as]
> Ringing and glittering she swirls and steadies,
> And moulds each ripple with secret suppressions.

Abruptly he stops playing with sounds and a tough new voice and form emerge: "No more of mere sound, the least part!" He begins to worry about the "engagement / 'Twixt man and being" and other questions which are avoided by mere word-play. Discovering the architecture of the water is to reveal the pattern of his own being, but his muse "lacks ... the right temper." The water has an integrity but the poet still searches on: "Where is the reach-point (it exists I've known long / Waiting for me) of this integrity?"

> Found I shall know it like a turned lock's click
> But I fumble and juggle again and again.
> Your every least move does the trick
> But I watch your quick tumblers in vain.

Clearly such problems are avoided by what now seems a well-nigh irresponsible lyricism. Yet the poem ends upon a nostalgic note; the poet looks back on younger days when he was not out of sympathy, as he now claims he is, with "nature, sheer sensual force, / Lust of light and colour, the frequent note / Of free enthusiasm in its course." He suggests strongly in this poem that his shift from the lyrical celebration, typified by "Water Music," is due not to a willing choice but to recognition of crucial problems which must, regretfully, be tackled – this is his "point of honour."[5]

The conflict within him between the free enthusiasm of lyrical impulse and the sense of duty leading to the "grim business of documentation" which is so characteristic of his later work is also expressed clearly in these lines from "Ode To All Rebels":

> I used to write sic bonny sangs
> A'body wi' pleasure and profit could read ...
> Why dae I turn my back on a' that
> And write this horrible rubbish instead?
> – Sustain me spirit o' God, that I pay
> These seductive voices nae heed![6]

Perhaps the most comprehensive statement of the existential and aesthetic problems facing MacDiarmid at this time is contained in the poem "Whuchulls." The setting of this poem is Whitshiels Wood, near the poet's birthplace of Langholm. It is somewhat atypical of later work in that it is written in a fairly rich Scots, but it could almost serve as a prologue to the post-*Cencrastus* poetry. Here awareness of a vast world of particulars is expressed, along with an explicit recognition of the problems this poses. The wood serves as a microcosm, and the poem does seem an implicit illustration of what it means to be unable to see the wood for the trees. The poem's theme is progress, and for once, as the rubric from Baudelaire indicates, it is the progress of the self which is being dealt with, not that of mankind or Scotland. It reads, "Il ne peut y avoir du progrès (vrai, c'est-à-dire moral), que dans l'individu et par l'individu lui-même."

"Gie ower your coontin'," begins the poet, saying that a complete inventory of the contents of the wood is impossible. Against the backdrop of this microcosm the drama of human conflict is enacted in MacDiarmid's mind. The poet's ballooning perspective recurs here as he speaks of "triflin' distinctions" between wise men and fools, continents, and centuries, against the totality of "a' that is," a contrast made explicitly in *Cencrastus*. Satisfaction with the present is the deepest of sins, he continues, because it denies the vast progress which the self holds in reserve. The itemization of particulars is "aside the mark," for

> The poet hauds nae brief for ony kind,
> Age, place, or range o' sense, and no' confined
> To ony nature can share Creation's instead.

To itemize is to restrict one's view to the few particulars which are noted, and thus to ignore the plenitude of Being. "Then cite nae mair this, that, or onything," he reiterates to himself. "To nae belief or preference I cling," he goes on; for to do so would mean to negate the others. Thus he insists "I'll no' toy wi' the fragments o't I ken," and yet, paradoxically, this is just what is happening:

> Yet here's a poem takin' shape again,
> Inevitable shape ...

The process of choice is already taking place, through the very activity of poetry. The wood, symbolizing the many "airts" of life, is already being given the shape of a poem; the poet himself is taking shape through his word struggle, much as he would like to avoid the "freedom constrainin' [him]" which forces something so unsatisfactory upon him, a process "impredictable, relentless, thriddin' the rabble / O' themes and aspects in this thrawart scene," a progress which seems to supplant the progress he really wants.

He is missing the total grasp of the wood that he seeks – "Clearlier it comes. I winna ha'e it." But he sees an alternative open to him in trying to realize this goal, the very one he was at pains to reject earlier:

> ... gie me tutors in aboriculture then.
> Let me plunge where the undergrowth's mair thick.

Experts in forestry, botany – a' that ken
Mair that I dae o' onything that's here.
I ken sae little it easily works its will.
Fence me frae its design wi' endless lear.
Pile up the facts and let me faurer ben.
Multiply my vocabulary ten times ten.
Let me range owre a' prosody again.
Mak' yon a lammergeir, no' juist a wren.

The way of knowledge thus appears to be just another blind alley, confusing matters, keeping the poet at a remove from the wood in itself. The last line refers to the inevitable loss of a sense of proportion which follows the minutely detailed study he here outlines. One other alternative is posed (and implicitly rejected since the poem continues): "Is he in silence safer frae attacks?"

Having resolved nothing, the poet reiterates the original problem:

Yet wha can thole to see it [the poetic process itself]
                    cavalierly choose
In God's green wud – tak' this and that refuse?

In his search for totality he continues, "Gar memory gie the place fower seasons at aince." The unsatisfactory process of selection is once more attacked, as the poet argues with himself:

Is that Creation's nature you evince,
Sma-bookin' Whuchulls to a rice or twa
Sae arbitrarily picked, and voidin' a'
The lave as gin it wasna worth a jot?

He comes up against two equally unsatisfactory alternatives, expressed in terms of relationships with women. If there are differences between them, and resemblances as well, "whatna freak / Thinks, frae the latter, ony ane'll dae / Or, frae the former, fain 'ud sair them a'?" So, in Whitshiels Wood, is he to adopt a generalizing or a particularizing approach? They seem mutually exclusive and yet both are necessary. Not only that, but creation is of a nature which seems to be beyond any approach: it "disna live frae hand to mooth / Juist improvisin' as it gangs, forsooth," but MacDiarmid, with his constraining freedom, is able only to improvise, not having the certainty which would allow him to do otherwise, as the struggles in this poem, illustrated by the poet's conflicting voices, indicate in particular. He might be more interested in the "deep constituent principles" rather than "fleetin' shapes," but he as yet has won no approach to either. The poem does move towards a resolution, however. Whether, as one of the voices has it, the wood is only "temporarily triumphant against control," or whether, as another voice insists to the first,

> Hauf saurian-emeritus, hauf prentice spook
> You'll never see the plantin' for the trees,
> This Eden where Adam comes fu' circle yet.

MacDiarmid is still left with the many as he was at the beginning. But he is Adam; and the wood is Eden could he but recognize it. Instead of struggling to find an approach, he will simply continue to write:

> There is nae ither way. For weel or woe
> It is attained. Tho' idle side-winds blow
> In on me still and inferior questions thraw
> Their crockets up, a' doots and torments cease.
> The road is clear. I gang in perfect peace,
> And my idea spreids and shines and lures me on,
> O lyric licht auld chaos canna dam!

He has, temporarily, delivered himself from "the need o' trauchlin'" with this "blainy blanderin'," his poem with all its struggles and posed alternatives. "Lyric licht" is not the "gowden lyric" but the power of poetic creation. His "idea" is progress (in poetry). He will continue to create, secure in his poetic gift, "for weel or woe." This is the resolution of the poem, and a convincing one too. The progress he embodies contains within itself the promise of a deeper resolution, as the light-imagery would indicate. Having come full circle, back to the plenitude of the wood, he has resolved the inherent difficulties of his situation by an affirmation of faith in his own poetic talent. Even if, as he says in *Cencrastus*, the only road is endless, Whuchulls *is* Eden, and, as Adam, MacDiarmid can at least struggle to find his way back to it. The confusion which marks the present situation is clearly presented in terms of a fall: and a fall implies possible redemption.[7]

This poem indicates MacDiarmid's essential uncertainty as to how to proceed, for intuition fails to give him the grasp of totality he seeks, and knowledge of particulars as a method is an unsatisfactory approach as well. But the poet is far too concerned with what he is doing merely to let things fall into place almost of their own accord, and the choice, here deferred, is made in his later poetry after all. Although never rejecting intuition, he refuses to depend upon it – it has tricked him too often in the past – and so he chooses the method of itemization in later work, despite the pitfalls he knows are in store for him. Faced with a world of particulars, and highly conscious of this fragmentation, MacDiarmid is unable to let them alone.

This is not to say that the later work is a monolithic treatment of these fragments. Several of his shorter poems have little to do with his poetry of facts, and, as has already been indicated, it is grim determination, not joyful exuberance, which tends to characterize his sorties into the Waste Land. On occasion he reacts consciously against his choice:

> Between two European journeys of Neville Chamberlain's
> And two important speeches of Herr Hitler's
> I return to the Taliesin and Llywarch Hen poems,
> Full of hiraeth, of angry revolt
> Against the tyranny of fact ...[8]

But Romantic escapism of this kind is the exception that proves the rule. So single-minded is MacDiarmid, and so dogged in his confrontation with the intractable outside world, that he is unable to let his poetry stray off the stern course he has set it for very long. His later work, on the whole, concerns the sea of particulars in which he finds himself adrift, and consists of his attempts to come to terms with it.

What sets MacDiarmid's later poetry apart from the pre-*Cencrastus* verse, then, is an abrupt widening of scope, not from the particular to the general but almost vice versa. The minute particulars of the "concrete world of existents" became a preoccupation of the poet, not as an abstract category (as in *Drunk Man, Cencrastus*, and earlier lyrics in which MacDiarmid seemed more concerned with a possible standpoint from which all could be viewed), but in themselves, as facts, opinions, ideas, and so on. The poet's emphasis shifts from *being* (the experience of himself in various states) to *knowing*: intuition, having proved undependable in the past, is to be held in reserve while the poet gathers material for it to feed on. If poetic inspiration proves to be illusory, in that truth is not attained, then perhaps the exterior world, a mass of data, offers a channel to it; so in order to synthesize the inner and outer realms, that is, remove the gulf the self feels separates it from Being, MacDiarmid now concentrates upon the latter. If the self eludes all questioning, the facts are felt to be above question. Having established the foundation, the poet hopes the self will eventually come to rest. As he says in "Water of Life," "Happy wha feels there's solid ground beneath / His feet at ony time – if ony does" (echoing a statement made as early as *Annals of the Five Senses*), and, pursuing this, he comes up against the raw particulars of the outside world.[9]

It is important to note that facts for MacDiarmid are little absolutes, pieces of truth which, like axioms, are never questioned. They are, in fact, the limits of his near-ceaseless questioning, for the poet's view of scientific enquiry is utterly erroneous. He mistakes the probabilities established by the scientific method for certainties, the discovery of which has nothing to do with the aims of science. Objectively speaking, this matters not at all as far as the free play of the poet's imagination is concerned – no more so than a belief in God, for example – but it may help to account for the intensity with which the poet seizes upon facts, sometimes showing more interest in these as such rather than in bending them to his poetic will. (If facts too might be illusory, how could MacDiarmid conduct his search for certainty? Neither inner nor outer realms could then offer any vantage point from which to carry out his poetic activity.)

Perhaps the clearest illustration of his poetry of facts at its most factual is provided by the small volume *Poems to Paintings by William Johnstone 1933* (1963). Here the facts are of the purely scientific variety. In "Wedding of the Winds," MacDiarmid writes of the possible synthesis of soil science and ductless gland research, of sexual selection being directed by the need to economize iodine, and so on.[10] In "Composition," Scotland is held to be a polyhedron in the brain with all sides visible at once, a polyhedron "of knowledge drawn from every field of life." "Polyhedrons everywhere!" he exclaims. And "he must find yet" how to combine them.[11] He is tired of mystery and moonlight; as he puts it in "Knight," people are afraid of facts, wanting fact to be "a bubble floating on the surface of Mystery," but he implies strongly that he will reverse the situation.[12] Yet his assertion that value is a concomitant of fact underscores the essential need felt by the poet to place his existence at the centre of the world of facts. Detached as he seems to strive to be, MacDiarmid is never willing to make his own existence a fact like all the others.

In a chapter of *Lucky Poet*, "The Ideas Behind My Work," which is a poem in itself, MacDiarmid outlines his attitude towards the world of particulars. His ever-present sense of potential is related to the acquisition of data: "All men are ripe for the highest any man knows." The actual/ideal polarity which pervades his work is expressed on this level as well: "All the facts which are known should be collated / And available for immediate practical use." He mentions the highly complex popular poetry of the Icelanders, and elsewhere he notes the complicated bardic poetry mastered, he would have it, by Welsh policemen and farmers. A poetry which contains the intricate world of particulars should therefore, he implies, be possible (320, 329, 353, *CP* 655).

Using the symbol of Byzantium, MacDiarmid suggests that the collation of data is not all that he wants:

> ... These things are merely
> The elements which combine to form
> A stupendous life pregnant with symbolism. (322, *CP* 1004)

Facts are the tools by which understanding might be won, as he indicates in another passage:

> ... [T]hought is reality ...
> And must absorb *all* the materials – [the] goal
> The mastery by the spirit of all the facts than can be known.[13]

So when he takes "the whole world of knowledge for [his] province," he is at least theoretically interested in using this material, embodying it in an understanding which finds its focus in the supreme fact of his own existence (322). In lines which are of great importance because they epitomize his attitude towards the universe of particulars, MacDiarmid writes:

> We do not know a mosaic
> By adding up the stones.
> On the contrary,
> The picture comes before the stones,
> Without which the picture means nothing. (315, *CP* 642)

The facts, "this string of pearls, which in themselves / Are single and loose," do not comprise "the final form" he is after:

> The Supreme ...
> No empty abstraction, but the life
> Which can never be grasped,
> That is transcendent.
> And no bridge carries us
> From "Word" to "trans,"
> Even as no bridge, but a leap,
> Carries us from the plane to the cube,
> From shallows to the bodily likeness. (316, *CP* 644)

It is plainly this "leap" which MacDiarmid hopes will occur after enough stones of the mosaic have been pieced together. The "picture" will come into focus of its own accord. Of course one

problem with this is that putting the "stones" in place presupposes
some awareness of the order he hopes will be revealed to him. The
pieces of the mosaic are actually (as will be indicated) fitted together
rather loosely in his poetry of facts, sometimes in a haphazard
fashion. A concomitant problem is suggested by these lines, quoted
from Thoreau:

> I see that if my facts
> Were sufficiently vital, and significant,
> Perhaps transmuted more
> Into the substance of the human mind,
> I should need but one book of poetry
> To contain them all! (327, *CP* 653)

How is the poet able to decide what makes a given fact "vital and
significant?"

Moreover, for all his determination and energy, the world of
particulars presents problems in itself. Even the slightest things seem
impossibly complex and beyond the reach of language in this passage
from "The Divided Bird":

> What speculative grammar, what pot-hooks of thought,
> What three and three-quarter millions of words,
> ... are these in my mind as I look
> At one turn of the flight and think of the bird's
> Automatism of feathers altering their angles
> Closing and opening the airspaces between them
> As wind and weather require?[14]

And how does one seize the thing-in-itself which, as Sartre points out,
overflows the knowledge one has of it? MacDiarmid is clearly aware of
this difficulty, which casts a shadow over his new-found source of
certainty, as demonstrated by this passage from his short prose
pamphlet *Five Bits of Miller* (1934): "I have only these five somewhat
analogous bits of Miller left – mucus, phlegm, wax, horn, and the
parasitic worm – five unrelated and essentially unrepresentative bits
of the jig-saw puzzle that I used to flatter myself I could put together
with blasphemous expertise. All the rest are irretrievably lost."
Knowledge is inexhaustible. MacDiarmid cannot win through to
Miller, possessing as he does a few meagre bits of him at the most: the
contrast suggested here is heightened by the fact that these bits are
not really part of Miller at all, but excretions. So the world of
particulars may prove troubled ground, for any ones which are

chosen may bear the same tenuous relationship to the whole as the "bits of Miller" to Miller himself. And they are all "somewhat analogous," for nothing establishes any one of them as more important or essential than the others.

But the poet, despite the dangers and difficulties, has determined his course. As he expresses it in a passage from "The Ideas Behind My Work:"

> I am at one with the New Writers who waste no words
> On manifestos but are getting down
> To the grim business of documentation
> Not seeking a short cut to the universal
> But with all their energies concentrated
> On gaining access to the particular.[15]

These particulars are not merely facts in the scientific sense; as his poetry illustrates, ideas, opinions, quotations, book titles, information of all kinds, even words themselves, are all included. *Poems to Paintings* is only one aspect of a type of poetry which emphasizes the fragments which make up his poetic environment. His own term, the "poetry of facts," is thus somewhat misleading – "poetry of particulars" would be more accurate – but if it is kept in mind that a "fact" to MacDiarmid is a piece of reality, not merely a linguistic construct representing an observation which has a high probablility of being correct, then "poetry of facts" does serve as a description of the post-*Cencrastus* work in general.

When particulars are being dealt with by MacDiarmid, his language tends to become almost prosaic, losing the tight, controlled quality so characteristic of his lyric work (and so admired). Facts and opinions are given first importance in themselves, and this of course cannot be done if the poet devotes too much time to the "how" of expression. As Roderick Watson puts it, "It is the 'facts' that must attract us and not their expression, and so MacDiarmid uses a spare prose-like diction – an approximation to the language of the text-book." "The 'fact,'" he says, "is used rather like the found object in art, its context is changed, but itself must remain intrinsically unchanged except through association with its context; any otherwise and it loses its identity."[16] If one tries to imagine the General Theory of Relativity or a speech by Winston Churchill put into *terza rima*, one can understand more clearly that MacDiarmid's so-called "chopped-up prose" is well suited to his subject matter, and that he is steering a difficult course between retaining the integrity of his material and his integrity as a poet. The craftsmanlike, evocative quality of other parts of the poetry of facts, notably the passages of natural description, where the poet seems to surface for a moment from the sea of data in order to respond more imaginatively to the immediate world of the senses, helps give the lie to assertions about his so-called decline in poetic power.[17] The truth would appear more likely to be that he is forced by his determination to confront particulars, most of which have no emotional or imaginative connotations, to keep this power in reserve.

The poet's gaze has become concentrated upon a universe of fundamentals, but his explicit Scottish concerns do not disappear, although they assume an almost ritual quality in their presentation. The Scottish essence is reaffirmed, for example, in his prose biographies of *Scottish Eccentrics* (1936), in which, in a passage which could readily be taken as self-descriptive, he writes that eccentricity is typical of the Scottish psychology, "extraordinary contradictions of character ... lightning-like zig-zags of temper" illustrating the Caledonian antisyzygy.[18] In *The Islands of Scotland: Hebrides, Orkneys, and Shetlands* (1939) he weds his world-theme to the idea of the Scottish essence as well. Besides poetry, including the fine "Island Funeral," there are fascinating prose comments; after reading L.A. Waddell's *British Edda*, for instance, he writes, "the original impetus to civilization was an Ur-Gaelic initiative."[19] This, as one can see from "Poems of the East-West Synthesis," is actually a series of symbols: civilization is order, infused with the Scottish essence by means of this grasping for dubious historical straws, and through such means MacDiarmid is able to conceive of a great synthesis of culture, reflecting the synthesis of understanding he is after, originating in the East which comes to symbolize the unity he seeks.[20] Not only does communism (personified in Stalin) originate in Georgia, that doctrine being a unifying force of great potential to a poet continually enamoured of a synthesis, but the East in general is the lost integrity which MacDiarmid strives for. The dispersal which has replaced the pure wellspring of Ur-Gaeldom is a sort of fall. This concept unites the Scottish essence with the idea of a former unity, pure Scottishness at the source, undegraded and unsuppressed which, could the poet but recreate it, would burst into bloom.

MacDiarmid chooses the Scottish islands as material for a book since "Above all, [islands] are useful nowadays because an island is an almost startlingly entire thing, in these days of the subdivision, of the atomisation, of life."[21] And the abilities of the Scottish islanders show him what the mind can be capable of: "In the Shetlands of old ... not only the animals but all the elements of nature – every breath of wind and movement of water – was known and named in like fashion." He continues, "The finest example of similar intimacy I know is in my friend, Father John MacMillan, of Barra, who has a marvellous knowledge of all the different ways water is accustomed to break over rocks and can discuss in completest detail the various shapes they take and their precise colouration under varying conditions with that old precision of discrimination which is so rarely encountered today and seems, indeed, to have been almost wholly blurred and swallowed up in that general omnitude of today which is indeed 'without form and void.'"[22] Once again the concept of a fall is implied, the idea of unity being given a historical context similar in many respects to the Golden Age in Confucian doctrine. The volume is laced with catalogues: types of wind, birds, sea-names and so on, the poet indulging in what is a common practice in later work, both prose and poetry. Seeking unity, MacDiarmid, like William Blake, rejects the blurring generalization, and at the same time brings particulars together in ordered arrays. In this book and elsewhere he suggests that such an approach is inherent in the Scottish character.

The poet's concern with things Scottish recurs in his self-styled autobiography, *Lucky Poet*. Here he reiterates assertions about "Scottish psychology," Scots decadence, and the Scots language (which, considering that his work is by this time predominantly in English, goes to show that it is the ideal rather than the reality which interests him – be bemoans the fact that this book is not written in Scots, for example).[23] But one senses from the tone and phraseology that much of the freshness of the Scottish idea has left him. Nevertheless, in this passage from "The Ideas Behind My Work," the poet's search for understanding is given a cleanly worked Scottish context, even if one is forced to take the claim of the second section with a large grain of salt:

> It requires great love of it deeply to read
> The configuration of a land,
> Gradually grow conscious of fine shadings,
> Of great meanings in slight symbols,
> Hear at last the great voice that speaks softly,
> See the swell and fall upon the flank
> Of a statue carved out in a whole country's marble,
> Be like Spring, like a hand in a window
> Moving New and Old things carefully to and fro,
> Moving a fraction of flower here,
> Placing an inch of air there,
> And without breaking anything.
>
> So I have gathered unto myself
> All the loose ends of Scotland,

And by naming them and accepting them,
Loving them and identifying myself with them,
Attempt to express the whole.[24]

Here his self-comparison with a Creator is very evident, as is the faith
in a Scottish noumenon which reveals itself as human-shaped. Of
course the universal problem of existence facing the poet is implied
here, for the "whole" is not merely Scotland but everything to which it
is attached, just as Blake's Albion was not merely England.

Even the problem noted earlier of rendering all experience by means
of language is dealt with in "Scots Unbound" by having the Scottish
language substitute for "ocht in the world ootby there."[25] But despite
this and the near-plagiarized "Little White Rose,"[26] the pessimistic
sentiments in "Towards a New Scotland," echoed by the funereal tone
of "Lament for the Great Music" and "Island Funeral," seem to
express the overriding uncertainty which close and deliberate scrutiny of "Scottishness" inevitably induces in MacDiarmid:

The time isna ripe yet and in vain I hae tried
To separate the base elements you ne'er could accept
Frae sic faint forerinners o' your comin' dawn
    As whiles I thocht within me leapt.

And he writes as well, "I've been hailly wrang, / Mista'en bog-fires for
your true licht at last."[27]

MacDiarmid's emphasis upon the Scottish essence, then, as sure
ground for his feet, is for the most part displaced by this faith in the
facts, facts which include ideas, as noted earlier. Actually his central
concerns are overspread with a patina of such ideas. Thus in *Lucky
Poet* communism and Social Credit both are mentioned with approval, as are the ideas of Chestov and Korzybski.[28] A reference to *The
Protocols of the Learned Elders of Zion* appears in the same volume as
references to Lenin.[29] The following passage is not surprising either:
"If I were asked to frame a test paper for literary aspirants, I would
ask: (1) A poem on the fact that what is known as the Lorentz
transformation looks like the Einstein transformation. When manip-
ulated numerically both give equal numerical results, yet the meanings, and the semantic aspects are different. Although Lorentz
produced the "Lorentz transformation," he did not, and *could not*,
have produced the revolutionary Einstein theory. (2) A short paper
discussing the fact that the semantic aspects of practically all
important mathematical works by different authors often involve
individual semantic presuppositions concerning fundamentals."[30] This

shows Korzybski's influence, but that aside, one sees right away that it is an ideal MacDiarmid, not the actual one, who is setting this examination. The actual MacDiarmid's poetry never strays quite so far from his essential preoccupations. The actual MacDiarmid does not "possess" these ideas; in fact, this passage emphasizes the idea of *having* ideas, rather than the particular ideas themselves. For all the poet's emphasis upon particulars, it would seem from the evidence of much of his poetry of facts that he is too busy gathering them to make them his, whereas the balance was splendidly kept in his Lallans poetry. Actual ideas, facts, and so on which appear in the poetry indicate the poet's awareness of this vast environment to which he has committed himself, but are hardly stones carefully placed in the mosaic of truth. His looser arrangement results in a collage effect as the poet surrounds the central "I" with material of potential usefulness. One notices a curious floating of ideas over the poet, which is explained only by the fact that they too are fragments, elements in a collage, things rather than beliefs. The basis of selection seems to be the poet's own preconceptions. Korzybski's "childishly simple" "structural metaphysics and semantic components," for example, which would supposedly enable all of us to come to grips with the real world, is attractive to MacDiarmid because it suggests the possibility of accomplishing what he has been wanting to accomplish all along. But the Korzybski theory is only one datum among many, and MacDiarmid does not become a disciple. In fact, Korzybski derives much of his authority in this context from his implicit assent to MacDiarmid's own feelings. In general, one finds no dialectic of ideas in MacDiarmid's poetry, nor in his prose for that matter. They are rarely allowed to clash with each other, being related only to MacDiarmid himself, as an orbiting series of bits which he has attracted in the course of his reading.

Perhaps the clearest example of the poet's relationship to an idea is given by his longstanding adherence to "Marxism." His career in the Communist party was an uncertain one – he joined in 1934, was expelled in 1937, was reinstated, then was re-expelled in 1938 for national deviationism, and then rejoined in 1957 – and his comrades never really knew what to make of him. This is not at all surprising. The Marxist critic David Craig, after establishing that it is "surely in his poetry, and nowhere else, that his Marxism lies," demonstrates very clearly indeed the true extent of MacDiarmid's "Marxism"; in life-work perspective, Craig concludes, the few poems in the Marxist vein are only a foretaste of something never actually achieved.[31] Moreover, Craig's itemization of poems which he does consider to contain sound Marxism may be somewhat overgenerous. Such poems as "Another Epitaph for an Army of Mercenaries" and even "The Skeleton of the Future" allow other than Marxist interpretations. (Perhaps well-advisedly he does not include the laughable "Girl on the Vertical Capstan Lathe" in his shortlist, an unconscious parody that might serve to discredit MacDiarmid not only as a Marxist but as a poet as well!)[32] The truth of the matter is that communism for MacDiarmid has an intense personal significance, but scarcely remains communism *per se* in his hands. Craig has performed a valuable service in examining the evidence (the poetry) for MacDiarmid's self-styled Marxism rather than taking the poet at his word as so many others have done, and has revealed that, as might be expected after all, his poetry bears little trace of a developed socialist sensibility.

What does Marxism-Leninism mean to MacDiarmid, then? Firstly, Marx doesn't come into the picture at all – there is little evidence that the poet ever read Marx. His admiration is for Lenin, and on occasion for Stalin as well. In *First Hymn to Lenin and Other Poems* (1931) he reveals a poet's response to something of symbolic potential, and the "promise of Lenin" is a particular case, in this context, of the promise the poet feels in himself. Lenin, in fact, becomes quite clearly an alter ego, described in "First Hymn" as a "descendent o' the unkent Bards." He seems to embody the superhuman potential which MacDiarmid claims, and they become partners:

> What maitters 't wha we kill
> To lessen that foulest murder that deprives
> Maist men o' real lives!

Lenin's secret, as he says, is his own as well, something far above "the majority will" and "the crood."[33] Lenin, not the masses, is MacDiarmid's concern; for the latter he nearly always shows an aristocatic contempt. In "The Burning Passion," the actual state of his poetic struggles ("A line, a word – and emptiness again!") is implicitly contrasted with the "full floo'er o' Lenin."[34] In this poem, similar to his expressed wish in *Drunk Man* to take humanity to the heights and cast it into the depths, he asserts his desire to make the masses suffer the torments of genius, another example of drawing humanity-in-abstract into what remains his own essentially lonely struggle.

The title poem of *Second Hymn to Lenin and Other Poems* (1935) establishes even more clearly the true significance of communism in MacDiarmid's poetry. After a gesture or two, saying, for example, that his poems must be spoken in factories, fields, and the streets, or else he is failing in his duty, he settles into the theme of the great poet and his tasks. Lenin appears as an ideal, but MacDiarmid insists that poetry is ultimately of far greater importance that politics. After solving the "breid-and-butter problems," the masses can get on with the spiritual struggle which he is engaged in:

> Poetry like politics maun cut
> The cackle and pursue real ends
> Unerringly as Lenin, and to that
> Its nature better tends ...

> Your knowledge in your ain sphere
> Was exact and complete
> But your sphere's elementary and sune by
> As a poet maun see it.

The poet's position is a tricky one:

> He daurna turn awa' frae ocht
> For a single act o' neglect
> And straucht he may fa' frae grace
> And be void o' effect ...

> Freend, foe; past, present, future;
> Success, failure; joy, fear;
> Life, Death; and a'thing else,
> For us, are equal here.

Poetry must synthesize the world:

> The sailor gangs owre the curve o' the sea,
> The hoosewife's thrang in the wash-tub,
> And whatna rhyme can I find but hub,
> And what else can poetry be? ...

> Unremittin', relentless,
> Organized to the last degree,
> Ah, Lenin, politics is bairns' play
> To what this maun be! (298ff, CP 323ff)

MacDiarmid wants the "haill art," and the task is enormous as he sees it, but it can be completed. The "real ends" of his poetry consist of his struggle for understanding, not revolutionary socialism. Yet Lenin provides an exemplar; the revolutionary type, hard, organized, eyes ever fixed upon his goal, is what MacDiarmid wishes to be on the poetic plane. By "Third Hymn to Lenin" the bolshevik revolutionary has become practically indistinguishable from the ideal Scottish one.[35]

On the whole, Marxism remains a doubtful aspect of his poetry. And, as Watson notes, the poems to Lenin "seldom expound any Leninist doctrine."[36] One is not, or should not, be led astray by assertions such as "Above all, my poetry is Marxist"; this line, for example, from "The Kind of Poetry I Want," is followed by indications that this "Marxist poetry" too is what he wants rather than what he writes.[37] Further on, in a superb example of the disparity between theory and practice which every consistent Marxist supposedly eschews, he attacks the English poets of the left for not giving the working class "comfort and strength," not finding "common ground with them, and themselves [deriving] strengthened faith and reinforced resolution from the experience," goes on to say that he himself is striving to reach workers through his poetry, and gives, as illustration of this, a long passage, in French, on the thought of Martin Buber, a passage which, as evidenced by quotation marks, is not even of his authorship.[38] Perhaps the best indication of this reluctance to ally himself with the working class, a position demanded by the Marxism-Leninism which he supposedly adopted, is given in a rather distasteful passage from the original "Etika Preobrazhennavo Erosa," bowdlerized in the *Collected Poems* version. Seeming to bewail his separation from the masses, he writes:

> O remorseless spirit that guides me
> The way seems infinite;
> What endless distance divides me
> From the people yet!

The pose of despair is immediately followed by lines carrying the appalling sincerity of 'gut reaction':

> It is next to impossible still
> For me to bear any other man close – for deep
> As what hinders a white man to sleep
> With a nigger, the unspeakable smell

prevents his identification with the people. When socialism threatens to become more than a concept symbolizing the poet's personal sense of potential, he shies away from it, betraying as he does so a streak of inhumanity so profound that two lines which follow, "All the distinctions that divide / Man from man must be swept aside" become the emptiest of gestures, a pious abstraction.[39]

This is not to say, however, that MacDiarmid has written no poetry of merit which could be called Marxist. "Lo! A Child is Born," which Craig rightly praises but which he says "could be just humanist" rather than socialist, contains, as he notes, the word "strategic," upon which, in fact, the whole poem seems to hinge, and this suggests Leninist strategy;[40] the world is like a pregnant woman suffering a bad birth, but the poet sees the possibility of a child with a "strategic mind" choosing how best to be born.[41] The past out of which such an event might arise, however, is still in the future. This can certainly be applied to the concept of world revolution, and "the great end in view" could be interpreted to mean communism. But in the context of MacDiarmid's work as a whole, one can view this poem as a personal statement as well, at once a reflection of the poet's present state where "the great end in view" seems remote and unconnected to any past achievements, and a powerful evocation of the ideal he is seeking to realize. The poem admits of both interpretations. There is a fine blending of the personal and the social/political elements here, and the latter truly become his whilst retaining their own integrity, refusing to become merely allegorical. But this poem is the exception – the rare exception – which proves the rule.

"The Seamless Garment" is a poem which perhaps best sums up all that has just been discussed. It is supposedly addressed to a millworker cousin, and it traces a unity among several types of human activity, Lenin's on one plane, Rilke's on another, the cousin's on a third, and MacDiarmid's on yet another. Machinery is linked to the poet's recurrent theme of evolution: "Machinery in a week mak's greater advances / Than Man's nature twixt Adam and this." A sort of spiritual kinship is thus established between MacDiarmid and his cousin. The relation between weaver and machine, second nature to cousin Wullie, becomes a symbol of the perfect relation to the world that MacDiarmid seeks. The seamless garment, the ideal, which the poet wishes to achieve, is compared to the cloth which the weaver produced:

As for me in my fricative work
    I ken fu' weel
Sic an integrity's what I maun ha'e,
    Indivisible, real,
Woven owre close for the point o' a pin
    Onywhere to win in.

Complete knowledge in one's sphere results in such an integrity in the product of one's activity, whether it is Lenin's oneness with the working class that produced revolutionary socialism; Rilke's understanding of emotions which give rise to his poetry; Wullie's knowledge of his machine which produced high quality cloth; or MacDiarmid's being completely at home in his sphere, the universe itself, which, when achieved, is to result in the seamless garment of an ideal poetry.

Ending as it does with the above stanza, "The Seamless Garment" makes it clear that the demands of poetry, not of the revolution, are the most immediate and fundamental concern of MacDiarmid. Lenin, Rilke, and his cousin are used as illustrations of what he himself is about. The placing of that stanza at the end puts the Marxist-Leninist message in wider perspective. The poet's method of bringing his cousin around to a Marxist understanding by extrapolating from the lessons of Wullie's immediate experience, coaxing him into a wider view of the world, is in accordance with revolutionary practice, but at the end all this proves merely to have been leading up, not to a call to arms and party, but to a clarification of MacDiarmid's own poetic aims. The poem, an accomplished piece of work, contains Marxist concepts (such as the alienation of the worker: "Mony a loom mair alive than the weaver seems") but it is by no means a Marxist poem. Here, unlike "Lo! A Child is Born," but like the other poems on political topics which have been mentioned, the Marxism is at once more explicit and less important in its own right than is its usefulness as an analogy of MacDiarmid's more personal preoccupations.[42]

Unlike most of the poet's other ideas, Marxism is to some extent actually used in his poetry rather than merely being included. At the same time, however, MacDiarmid's poetry is seldom if ever Marxist. Like Korzybski's General Semantics or Douglas's Social Credit, Marxism embodies certain concepts which the poet finds attractive for reasons of his own, and is thus used for poetic ends (therefore losing any real meaning in itself, since Marxism so used is no longer Marxism but an aesthetic plaything). The doctrine, then, floats over the poet just as surely as the ideas he merely takes note of, for although he borrows aspects of it to make poems, the doctrine as a whole escapes him.

The impression may have been given, by this time, that MacDiarmid's post-*Cencrastus* poetry consists for the most part of particulars floating about in a free state which have come into the poet's gravitational field, as it were, and that the imagination has been placed in abeyance. This is far from being the case. Despite the poet's increasing self-consciousness, manifested among other ways by his identifying the ideal he seeks with poetry itself, as seen in "The Seamless Garment," the poetry of particulars can have a powerful evocative quality, especially in physical description, and the literal can give way to the symbolic.

Two of the most important symbols which recur in this poetry are those of water and stone. Although water occasionally signifies the essence of life, it is more often its behaviour which is emphasized, representing the chaos which everywhere surrounds him, and thus, more particularly, the chaos of his own being, the very problem of existence itself. For water, like his being-in-the-world, is a mass of ceaseless, innumerable, and apparently random changes, without any system being available to explain them; it is shapeless, fluid, enigmatic. Stone, in contrast, possesses the qualities of hardness, impassiveness, and stillness, and, by giving the impression of rest and permanence amid the continual flurry of ephemera which the poet experiences, is used to symbolize the certainty MacDiarmid is looking for, the solution to his problem. A quotation from Paul Claudel's *La Mystique des Pierres Précieuses*, which MacDiarmid uses as a rubric for "Once in a Cornish Garden," illustrates this quality. Claudel compares the formation of precious stones with "le philosophe qui, par le brassage d'une multitude de faits, arrive à un concept, au joyau abstrait d'une définition irréprochable." MacDiarmid also quotes a passage of poetry in which a perfect spiritual state is to be seen "in terms / Of Cornish geology."[43] Stone possesses above all else that "massive" quality which Sartre attributes to non-conscious being in general and to which, in his view, conscious beings aspire.[44] Individual stones, as in "On a Raised Beach," symbolize hard and unchanging bits of truth, parts of a mosaic as has already been seen. The two symbols, stone and water, recur throughout the later work, often in antithetical relation.

While in "Water of Life" and "The Glass of Pure Water" it is the essence of life which is emphasized, in "The Point of Honour" it is the plight of existence which is symbolized. The solution to the problem is there given as "cut water," the hardening or crystallizing of this chaotic stream into the still certainty of stone, an understanding which MacDiarmid wants to achieve but which remains theoretical. In "Water Music" a river serves as the vehicle for onomatopoeic Scots words, the poet wedding these words to her waves, as he puts it later in "The Point of Honour" (which is probably a sequel to this poem), naming various movements of the water.[45] The poem is a delightful exuberant exercise in pure sound, but there is much more to "Water Music" than that. As has been indicated throughout this study, MacDiarmid has chosen the activity of poetry with which to bear down on his problem, and the poem epitomizes this concern. By naming the water movements he is demonstrating his control over the water, and so affirming the potential of the Scots language in particular, and of language and poetry in general, for resolving his plight. It should be noted, however, that only the illusion of mastery is provided here, for the same reason as the poet himself gives in "The Point of Honour."

Land takes over the symbolic attributes of stone in "Larking Dallier," where he says that it has been tricked from the sea. It is an empty promise, for no more will come. The sun, which is the larking dallier, as explicitly stated in "On a Raised Beach," once bade the land to rise; it also makes larks soar and sing, but slips away before hearing the birds out. Man's thoughts outsoar the larks, but night obscures any profit unless the larks belong to the sun.[46] The most plausible interpretation is that the sun is the paradoxically present unrealized understanding which haunts MacDiarmid, and the guidance of which, as always in the poet's experience whether he looks inward or outwards, proves deceitful. The role of the sun seems to be the one formerly ascribed to the moon, an interesting transition noted by George Bruce: the powers of inspiration, once emphasized, are now shrouded in mystery, but for the facts the poet needs the bright light of day. Some degree of certainty seems to have been reached, perhaps the facts he has gathered, but only a tantalizingly small amount of it. Any soaring and singing is soon wrapped in darkness – the poet finds uncertainty all around him even after a seeming glimpse of the as-yet-unrealized truth which has inspired him to start writing. His thoughts may well outstrip these achievements, but if the latter prove to be based utterly on illusion, having nothing to do with the sun, the thoughts are worthless. At any rate the poet is left with little land and much water.

In "Direadh III" occurs perhaps the clearest illustration of the water-stone antithesis. The poem contains several well-wrought passages of physical description, distinguished by vividness and precision and conveying a wonderful sense of freshness and aware- ness. Evidently the things immediate to the senses, which are subject as any other particulars to the poet's precise and observant gaze, allow the imagination more scope than do those he isolates from his reading, for there is a depth and quality of emotive response in such writings which one doesn't usually find in his "scientific" or "philos- ophical" poetry. MacDiarmid's physical environment acquires in his poetry a harmonious unity of scene, and the detailed elements of it, through the poet's profound identification with them, acquire symbolic attributes. Here the poet is responding to the stark environment of Skye, a "simple place of clean rock and crystal water, / With something of the cold purity of ice in its appearance." The whole place is utterly still. MacDiarmid sets eyes on a stream and plants which grow in it, water-crowfoot which, he says, can remain rooted during "the raging winter torrents." He chooses to identify with the plants rather than the water, and comparison is made between them and the "treasures of the Gaelic genius" surviving the overwhelming historical chaos of the "cataracting centuries." MacDiarmid, surrounded by chaos, affirms his ability to withstand it and flourish just as the treasures of the Gaelic genius have done.

The image of clean rock and crystal water given earlier, and the sense of utter stillness, give the impression that the whole tableau has frozen, the poet and his surroundings locked in a perfect harmony. This suggestion is enhanced by the all-pervading "intensity of light" which indeed is compared to the water in which the water-crowfoot grows. The water is "crystal" in a scene which is compared to the "cold purity of ice," so that it seems to have taken on the quality of the rock. It is pure and motionless as the sunlight. Then comes the passage described above, about the plants keeping their roots in violent torrents – the water now is in turmoil, the promise of the opening lines seem negated. But abruptly the poet returns to the original sense of stillness:

> I am possessed by this purity here
> As in a welling of stainless water
> Trembling and pure like a body of light
> Are the webs of feathery weeds all waving
> Which it traverses with its deep threads of clearness
> Like the chalcedony in moss agate
> Starred here and there with grenouillette.

The promise is fulfilled. The water has turned to stone; the whole scene has fused into changeless perfection.

And yet the poem continues, belying the permanence of this resolution; it too is revealed as only a passing ecstasy after all. The rest of the poem, while there are fine descriptions including one of quake grass, does not retain an overall coherence, but consists of a series of eddies and cross-currents. It is a good example of the kind of associationism which has become a marked structural characteristic of much of the poetry in this period – problems of language, exemplified by exhibits of Gaelic words, are pieced together with historical references, references to love, communism, the Scottish muse, and so on. This is a grand sweeping gesture, an accretion of concerns which indicate, but do not comprise, the synthesis he seeks. The web of associations he provides is only a promise, the links between the elements only a substitute for the pattern he wants to discover. "The inaccessible Pinnacle is not inaccessible," says Mac-Diarmid, but he has yet to scale it.[47]

The goal is once again superbly evoked in the quatrain "The Skeleton of the Future (at Lenin's Tomb)":

> Red granite and black diorite, with the blue
> Of the labradorite crystals gleaming like precious stones
> In the light reflected from the snow; and behind them
> The eternal lightning of Lenin's bones.[48]

On one level this appears almost as socialist realism, with the promise and example of Lenin, the outline of the future, seen against the hard backdrop of the material world. It is no doubt this interpretation which leads David Craig to call the poem Marxist. But there seems no reason for excluding wider interpretations, and in fact, given MacDiarmid's personal view of Marxism, one should suspect that this poem goes beyond the merely political.

As a man, Lenin surmounted history, personified progress, and in general was a poet in concrete who deployed people and material as MacDiarmid would like to deploy words, driving relentlessly and single-mindedly towards a certain goal. World communism to the poet is allied with his more personal ideal of understanding, for they are both final, both realizations of potential, both order born of, embodying, and transcending chaos, the former in a historical and the latter in a personal sense. As a monument, Lenin becomes a symbol of everything he has stood for, and as such seems to sum up the whole process of transition from actual to ideal. Since this is MacDiarmid's main preoccupation, Lenin's tomb comes quite readily to hand as a symbol.

It is a symbol, in fact, of the future the poet wants. As poetry, particulars while retaining their separate identities have fused into the unity of vision, something yet to be achieved in the poetry of facts. The precision and clarity of the description are not dissipated but enhanced by the attention to detail. The focus of the vision is the skeleton, symbolizing the underlying pattern felt to be present in the confusion and chaos of human existence-in-the-world, as indicated in "The Dead Harlot" story, and in poems such as "Krang" and the borrowed "Perfect," a pattern to be revealed in the future: "eternal lightning" is the revelation for which the poet strives. This skeleton lies in a matrix of stone and crystallized water. All is immobile, solid, fused, and bathed in light.

As "Lynch-Pin" indicates, however, the pattern remains evasive; the poet always seems to be lacking something:

Here where I sit assembling in the sun
The salient features o' my structure o' banes
I feel that somewhere there's a missing one
That mak's a dish o' whummle o' my pains.
Sma' but the clue to a' the rest, and no'
In ony woman hidden nor on this earth,
And if there's ony ither world, hoo it's got there,
If 't has, I ken nae mair than hoo I ken my dearth
That yet fills my haill life wi' the effort
To embody a' creation – and find this ort.[49]

The use of the East, Ur-Gaeldom, and so on as symbols has already been touched upon. Socialist ideas and Scottish concerns are linked to the poet's more fundamental preoccupations by a tenuous, pseudo-historical method. Thus, in "Direadh III": "Georgia, / Stalin's native country, was also the first home of the Scots." In the first poem of the "East-West Synthesis," "The Fingers of Baal Contract in the Communist Salute," he calls Stalin a Gael. In "Ceol Mor," the second of these poems, the Greeks and Romans are held to be of Celtic origin too, and a huge Celtic empire of the distant past is recalled. He continues,

> ... And remembering how urgently civilization to-day
> Needs, like its quintessential element (the stone
> The builders have neglected) the Gaelic genius,
> To renew itself at its original springs!
> Lift every voice!

Of course one can readily substitute "MacDiarmid" for "civilization" in this passage. His personal sense of a fall is exteriorized as the dissipation of the Gael genius through history; his personal hope for redemption is similarly exteriorized as the communist mass movement led by Stalin the Gael.

The last of these poems, "Tristan and Iseult," is entirely in French, and is an attempt to establish another link between East and West by means of the universal quality of this myth. Not surprisingly, MacDiarmid tries to prove by means of a little etymology that the legend originated in the Caucasus, his Ur-Gaeldom. The poem is supposed to be part of the "Cornish Heroic Song for Valda Trevlyn," presumably through the linkage MacDiarmid: Valda:: Tristan: Iseult. Thus MacDiarmid's relationship with Valda would be linked through this poem to the Scottish essence, to history, myth, and communism![50]

The "East-West Synthesis" is conceived, but not made. It is a disguise for the universal synthesis the poet wants. It is an objective embodiment of social and cultural concerns in pseudo-history almost akin to myth and related to myth directly in the last of the poems. The constructive principle in these poems is not the more usual simile but a tenuous causal network, through which the present situation of the poet as communist, ideas man, lover, cultural ideologue, and Scot is seen to have a single basis which unifies these fragmentary selves. The kind of symbolism evinced in these poems is, as George Bruce puts it, a means of exposition primarily, evocation being secondary. But by no means, as has been seen, is this the case throughout the later work as he maintains.[51]

It is in "Island Funeral" that fact and symbol become blended in one statement, in which the poet's concerns are lucidly expressed. The setting of the poem is one of the Hebridean Islands, where a funeral is taking place. But the funeral at which MacDiarmid mourns is that of the Gaelic essence which this island has possessed but which has worn away by attrition. There is a similar theme in "Lament for the Great Music," where identification is clearly suggested between the poetry MacDiarmid wants and the vanished purity of Gaeldom. The island itself will soon be dead, and the poet seems to be writing the sermon he has prepared for that eventuality.

The physical description here is, as one has come to expect, clear and controlled. The dominant images are of stone and water. The island seems almost a slab of stone. The water is the sea, against which the fishermen struggle all their lives. Much of the island is deserted; the qualities of the people who lived there are those which MacDiarmid would realize in himself. Possessed by the purity and strength of the Gaelic essence, they were "sure of every thought they had." Certainty was theirs. The poet contrasts this explicitly with "the chaos of the modern world."

The stone possesses a permanence which seems to belie the process of death. As it contrasts with the sea, as a haven for the returning fishermen, so too it contrasts implicitly with what appears to be the gradual disappearance of the Gaelic spirit. Then the power of the islanders' language is compared to that of Bix Beiderbecke's cornet playing, both of which reflect a perfection which MacDiarmid wants to attain. It seems inconceivable that such perfection could die: there is too much affirmation in the poet's tone as he describes the various manifestations of it. And so we are told at last that "Materialism promises something / Hardly to be distinguished from eternal life." MacDiarmid expounds a curious materialist theory of resurrection, and, expressing his faith in the facts, writes,

It is quite unimportant whether we call
Our ultimate reality matter, electric charge
Ψ-waves, mind-stuff, neural stuff, or what not,
Provided it obeys laws which can, in principle,
Be formulated mathematically.[52]

A certainty underlying even the Gaelic essence (since it is the foundation upon which it rests) is materialism, which finds expression in the realm of knowledge, in the facts. It is factually demonstrable that the souls of the islanders will develop throughout the future in "all possible environments" and will be able to "express themselves / In all the ways possible to them." In other words, the complete realization of the potential of the Scottish spirit is guaranteed by materialist laws, which are discoverable. The images of the Gaelic past, of stone and of water with their symbolic overtones, give way finally to this affirmation of literal, factual truth, the bedrock, as it were, upon which MacDiarmid founds his present poetry as a whole.

Such an attitude towards the world of particulars can frequently lead to a prosaic use of language, as illustrated, for example, by the passage just quoted. But the poetry of facts is distinguished by several characteristics other than the type of language used. There are several structural aspects to this poetry which can be shown to be fundamentally related to this confrontation with particulars as well.

One such aspect is an associationism where images and ideas and so on come together in a poem almost incidentally. The trouble with the world of particulars, of course, is that its constituents are single and discrete, profoundly related neither to each other nor to anything beyond themselves other than to the poet's own fragmented perception. His intuition or imagination seems less and less capable of fusing this endless profusion of details, so that very often their association in a poem seems more or less contrived. In "Once in a Cornish Garden" it is primarily colour which binds things together, besides the categorization or listing which is another related structural characteristic; in this poem, flowers, stones, and Gaelic words are so treated. Thus his wife brings together the colours of hair, possessions, and make-up; these are related to the flowers, and so on. The poem does seem to be about synthesis, in a sense: MacDiarmid and Valda, his wife, are linked; the Scottish and Cornish essences are linked; stones, flowers, and vocabulary are linked.[53] But the poem itself rests upon little more than these obvious and superficial connections, and thus, despite the clarity of the descriptions, is a failure. The same can be said of the web of associations already noted in "Direadh III," or the endless examples of "the kind of poetry" MacDiarmid wants which are linked only by their relation to the poet, or the segments of "Cornish Heroic Song" and so on. Once in a while, however, the poet produces a more successful fusion, as in "Edinburgh." Here the connecting principle is the image of smoke, which carries some symbolic weight, as an obscurer of light. The poem is concerned with a fall – we have lost control over the world, he says, we cannot control the smoke as the cave-woman controlled the smoke from her campfire. "Auld Reekie," or Edinburgh, is the world in microcosm; we are all surrounded by smoke, and the poet prays that dormant creative powers might burst through the "scum of swinish filth of bourgeois society." Thus the realm of politics assumes importance, for it is "the social corpse, the dead class" which prevents the self-knowlege of humanity from realization. Edinburgh stands in her own light yet, the poet concludes.[54] In such a poem MacDiarmid's powerful sense of his own situation pervades the imagery, and the elements of the poem gel. But in most of the longer poems the reverse, unfortunately, seems to be the case.

The use of lists in "Once in a Cornish Garden" has already been mentioned, to which numerous other examples can be added, not the least of which is the vast series of such lists in *In Memoriam James Joyce*. Before that time they may be found in such poems as "Stony Limits" (geological formations), "On a Raised Beach" (stones, Norn words), "The Progress of Poetry" (writers and their achievements), and even, in capsule form, in "The Skeleton of the Future" (the types of stone in Lenin's tomb). Listing is a technique found in Homer and Walt Whitman, and generally serves a number of purposes, such as creation of atmosphere, establishment of the poet's credibility as observer, and the revelation (see Whitman's "Song of Myself," for example) of an underlying essence by means of an itemization of particulars which share it. Given MacDiarmid's elemental view of the world, the technique in this case perhaps has an additional and more fundamental purpose, namely to bring together particulars in a world whose elements, in general, refuse to cohere. His emphasis upon, and sometimes exaggerated use of this device seems to suggest this interpretation.

The use of simile is a marked feature of this poetry as well. To Craig, this analogy method is an "essentially chaotic practice," a "helpless intellectual free-association," and certainly examples can be found of both. The technique, of interest in itself, however, can lead to good results, as in "The Bobbin-Winder" and "To a Friend and Fellow-Poet," which illustrates as well that simile in MacDiarmid's hands becomes an involved and intricate device.[55] To the poet it is usually more than an explanatory or illustrative means of expression;

it becomes yet another way of forging links between things, and the two terms of the simile tend to remain of equal authority, in that one is not used to illustrate the other with the latter being the poet's real concern. Sometimes the poet even seems to be setting up identities in the algebraic sense, so that one thing becomes equivalent to another, exactly like it in every respect. By so doing, of course, the poet hints at a unity underlying all seemingly discrete particulars. The following are some examples of MacDiarmid's wide-ranging use of this device.

"The Bobbin-Winder" is constructed out of a comparison which, it is explicitly stated, is less than exact. Nevertheless, the two terms are of equivalent weight. Lace threads converge on a woman who winds the bobbins in a lace factory; this cannot quite compare with the perfection of a water-lily's bowl from which fine threads extend into the depths of the water.[56] This simile, or near-simile (the word "like" is not used to bring the two images into relation), has a profound *thematic* significance here. One image is from the world of humanity, and one is from the natural world. The human activity cannot quite become the same as the natural process, so that the latter becomes an ideal. But the similarities are there, and both reflect, by implication, the poet's own activity. Just as the water-lily sends out threads for sustenance, and the bobbin-winder is the focus of as-yet-unwoven threads, so the poet himself is the focus of an activity which reaches into the outside world, many threads (his "wide range of interests," or the various types of expertise outlined in "The Kind of Poetry I Want" are examples which spring to mind) converging, spiritual material out of which he hopes to weave his seamless garment. The actual poet is more like the bobbin-winder; one thinks of his comparison with Wullie the weaver in "The Seamless Garment," or his phrases "I have gathered unto myself / All the loose ends of Scotland" and "Have I failed in my braid-binding?" It is the ideal poet who has achieved the serenity of the water-lily, floating above the current and naturally imbibing his nourishment rather than having to act to do so. The haunting double image of focus in this poem, and the comparison involved, thus serve to define the difference between actual and ideal existence for MacDiarmid as poet.

"Crystals Like Blood" is a more contrived use of this technique. An exhaustive description of cinnebar processing, the changing of the red crystals to mercury, is given a personal correlation:

So I remember how mercury is got
When I contrast my living memory of you
And your dear body rotting here in the clay
– And feel once again released in me

The bright torrents of felicity, naturalness, and faith
My treadmill memory draws from you yet.[57]

Here the facts of the exterior world are used to give shape to an interior fact, so that an identity is established between the poet and his world. Actually, a synthesis is suggested, as the detailed nature of the description of cinnebar processing would help to indicate – its whole essence, it is implied, has been joined to the essence of the poet's feelings on remembering a loved one, and the result is fusion of the two. The last line, where his memory has become a treadmill, strongly reinforces this suggestion. Two other examples of this fusion come from "The Kulturkampf." MacDiarmid relates the struggle of his ideal figure in the "theatre of intellect" to phenomena in the physical world:

> What a progress that was – the unfolding of his thought,
> The brilliant and incalculable profusion with which he threw
> > new ideas off,
> Suggests nothing so much as a psychic analogue
> Of the mutant-bearing *Cenethera Lamarckiana*
> Or, at times even, the sudden simultaneous appearance
> Of one specimen of each of the different varieties
> Of *Drosophila melanogaster*, for which, as we know,
> There is not enough matter in all the known heavenly bodies
> And probably not in the universe.[58]

The last example relates MacDiarmid's felt potential, here "realized" in this ideal, to the natural world in terms of a realization which transcends both his actual self and the world, indicating a synthesis almost in the classical Hegelian sense, one which transcends thesis and antithesis (here, self and not-self) and embodies them both. Such identity or synthesis of self and not-self, of course, would be when achieved the solution to the problem of being-in-the-world which the poet has been seeking. MacDiarmid does seem to be suggesting just this in his referring of exterior being to the self in this way, for nothing of the exterior (as seen by the meticulous use of detail in many instances) is sacrificed; it is not merely used to illustrate, thus losing some of its essential character, but retains its independence of being. One observes that any synthesis in the examples just given is only theoretical, however: the drawing of these identities is overly intellectual and contrived so that no real interiorization of fact takes place, even on the level of an imaginative or metaphorical identification.

"Cornish Heroic Song for Valda Trevlyn" depends heavily upon a continual comparison of one thing with another; in general, the poet's relation to Valda becomes an aesthetic excuse for the bringing together of numerous ideas, images, facts, and so on, and the word "like" is everywhere in evidence. Once again MacDiarmid is adumbrating a synthesis, by intimating his sense of a fundamental unity underlying things. The poet himself, of course, is the focal point. Images from the natural world, which allow the reader to respond imaginatively to the ideas with which they are compared, may reflect the poet's attempt to react to particulars of all kinds in the same evocative and immediate way he demonstrates when the world of the senses captures his attention directly – it is as though he were trying to transfer his freshness of response from that realm to the "theatre of the intellect." At times he comes close to achieving this, as when he compares English cultural depredations in Scotland to a killer whale rending out the tongue of a white whale, or when religion in Cornwall is compared to "fairy rings" which kill trees.[59] In such instances, then, simile seems to have the added function of imbuing intellectual concerns with imaginative force.

As has been suggested in some of the examples given above, one very common use of the simile is to relate the personal and the impersonal, indicating a synthesis of the sort which has been discussed. "The Kind of Poetry I Want" carries this to an extreme. The poem is an extended simile of potentially infinite length which consists for the most part of comparisons between an ideal poetry which MacDiarmid wants and various human activities and achievements which reflect the certainty of expertise, and so are themselves implicitly idealized. Each expert, named or implied through his activity, is or was absolutely at home in his (sub) universe, just as the weaver in "The Seamless Garment" is one with his loom. MacDiarmid's gun-handler, one feels, never misses, his bridge-player never loses a trick in error, his pool-player sinks the ball every time. There is no hint in his examples of error and uncertainty. One sees only the splendid results of certain, perfect skills, over which a mantle of infallibility seems to shimmer. Each illustration is thus a bit of truth, just like a fact, or so the poet indicates.[60]

As a poet, MacDiarmid is concerned with the whole universe, and the poetry he wants is one which establishes an absolute relation between himself and the world, just as his experts possess such a relation to their spheres of activity as their perfection of skill and accomplishment seems to indicate. At the same time, every example in itself is *like* the poetry he wants, in that he wants the latter to embody the essence of the former. This goes for the few comparisons he makes with actual things in the exterior world as well. Otherwise, of course, one example would have sufficed. All human occupations of this kind must be transformed into this ideal poetry; more profoundly, it is implied that the outside world, in itself and as revealed and seized in this expert human activity, must be embodied in MacDiarmid's poetic practice, through a mysterious transmutation that will leave all these essences intact, if his ideal is to be achieved. In all this complexity it is interesting to note that the simile assumes thematic importance; far from being a mere method of construction, it is in many ways what the poem is about.

The result of the construction methods outlined above is a kind of poem which we have called serial collage, in which fragments of language are juxtaposed without any real fusion of the parts into an organic whole. In many cases there seems to be presented only a collection of found objects, although it must be pointed out that very often these objects are highly interesting in themselves and in their relation, stated or implied, to the poet's predominant concern with being-in-the-world. It has been noted that elements of this collage work are in evidence as early as the prose *Annals of the Five Senses*, and can be traced through *Drunk Man*, where a balance is struck between the integrity of the parts and of the whole, to *Cencrastus*, where the whole tends to vanish in multaneity, and which provides, to an extent at least, the first manifestation of serial collage proper. When the unifying influence of intuitive vision is displaced by an obsessive concern with the particulars of which MacDiarmid's environment is composed, this tends to be the result. The "grim business of documentation" is put forward as a poetic technique; MacDiarmid gathers material and waits for the blueprints to arrive. The piecing together of this material, in the meantime as it were, is all too frequently a haphazard affair.

"The Kind of Poetry I Want," made of quotations, facts, and examples of expertise, is held together only by repeated reference to an ideal poetry, a concept which is itself aesthetically nugatory because, like *Cencrastus*, it cannot be imagined. "Cornish Heroic Song," another example of serial collage, does not possess even this elementary continuity. Any flow it might have is disrupted by what seems a capricious insertion, from time to time, of huge parenthetical afterthoughts. The poem is an incoherent mixture of fulsome praise for Valda Trevlyn's hair, nationalist comments, and so on. Certain sections are clear and powerful, others are fuzzy philosophical reflections sometimes appearing as blocks of exotic English vocabulary. Despite the perennial simile which links many of the disparate elements of the poem (something is nearly always being compared to something else), "Cornish Heroic Song" still consists, in the final analysis, of large chunks with only the most tenuous of interrelations. As a poem (or part of a poem; MacDiarmid claims there is much more) it must be judged a failure.[62]

"Ode to All Rebels" is yet another example of this type of poem. It brings together shorter poems such as "A Pair of Sea-Green Eyes" and "With a Lifting of the Head," and miscellaneous material such as ruminations on sex, a passage on underclothes (sandwiched between two short verses, the first of which concerns speaking brokenly of trifles, and the second concerning "idiot incoherence," supposedly the only language that "wi' God can deal"), and several more sections in a thin Scots which are to reappear, Englished, in *Second Hymn to Lenin*. It is not enough, one feels, for MacDiarmid to cry, "trace the connections / In a' directions / And you'll aiblins ken what I'm aboot." Merely presenting the fragments for others to knit together is a gesture of helplessness, and it is this he seems to be doing, for his veiled suggestion that he has constructed an interrrelated whole that we might discern if we applied ourselves diligently is less than convincing. The kind of poetry he wants is still an ideal:

> We are like somebody wha hears
> A wonderfu' language and mak's up his mind
> To write poetry in it – but ah!
> It's impossible to learn it, we find,
> Tho' we'll never ha'e ony use again
> For ither language o' any kind.[62]

The serial collage reflects the poetic environment and the fragmented perception of MacDiarmid. As poetry it is not a successful form. Often the pieces have little in common but authorship, and even this is not guaranteed, as parts of "The Kind of Poetry I Want" and of that supreme example of serial collage, *James Joyce*, bear out. The selection and rough arrangement of these particulars reflect the absence of a unifying revelation which MacDiarmid can believe in, the material thus achieving cohesion only through a series of analogies or by referring each bit to the author himself or to some general concern of his. When the latter is the case, as it often is, the unadaptability of the collage method to poetry reveals itself.

Poetry must be read in a certain manner which is intrinsic to this art-form, namely from left to right, line by successive line, from the beginning to the end. A poem is not one of McLuhan's "fields" where a complex message is presented in a flash, but instead shares in the legacy of Gutenberg. This may not have all the dread consequences that McLuhan imagines, but it has considerable consequences never-theless, in both the creation and the appreciation of poetry. Such a question is well beyond the scope of this study, but some general observations can be made. A true collage is a visual experience in which all elements are seen at once; they do not have a temporal relationship to each other. To add a serial structure to this, setting up a progression in time from one to another, is to impose, willy-nilly, an order upon the material, an arrangement in time which characterizes any serial art, such as literature, music, film, or dance. Any example of such art implies process, continuity, unfolding, because this is its most essential structure. But the elements in a collage are discrete. One does not succeed another in an organically unfolding continu-um. To place them in such a continuum is to impose a succession upon them, a succession which is not the result of an internal logic or movement but a mere consequence of that imposition.

Serial collage, then, contains at its heart a serious flaw. Collage as a method does not lend itself to poetry. There is much evidence to suggest, however, that in his pursuit of long poems, which in essence reflect a triumph over the discrete particulars of his world, MacDiar-mid is forced to rely upon this flawed form. The planned "Clann Albann" appeared as a series of single poems, indicating the difficulty the poet was finding in achieving the "unfolding" of a long poem, a difficulty clearly prefigured by much of *Cencrastus*.[63] "Ode to All Rebels" falls into pieces, many of which appear separately in *Second Hymn to Lenin*. (The suppression of the former by the publishers is not enough by itself to explain this dispersion, for it leaves an essential question unanswered: Why was the breaking-up of the poem so easy to accomplish? The *Second Hymn* poems do not look like excerpts from a longer poem.) The parenthetical insertions in "Cornish Heroic Song" have no demonstrable thread of continuity with the lines which precede and follow them. Mere suggestions will not do, for although two passages can be so linked, such links are incidental to the poem as a whole, and to each other. One finds in such a poem no unity of atmosphere, since unity is sustained by an unfolding which one in this case seeks in vain. The endless examples of "The Kind of Poetry I Want" are unsubtly strung together and have only a incidental relationship to each other. The poem, moreover, seems to be altered in size at will, and appears in large pieces in *Lucky Poet*, in a somewhat shorter version (but in one piece) in a booklet, in fragments in periodicals such as *Voice of Scotland* and in *A Kist of Whistles*, and in a much shorter version in *Collected Poems*. What is more, we are told that the poem is itself only a part of his planned "Mature Art."[64] No other author modern or ancient has treated his poems like this. Clearly,

"The Kind of Poetry I Want" consists of counters to be moved about at will. All the above examples indicate very strongly that MacDiarmid has adopted serial collage as a form in the absence of a creative sense of progression, which would have transformed particulars from counters to integral parts of a whole.

A study of the *Lucky Poet* volume, and the two related poems "Stony Limits" and "On a Raised Beach," provides an adequate summing-up of what has been examined in this chapter so far. *Lucky Poet* is a crypto-poem, a work largely written in prose but with a poetic underpinning, where blocks of prose (quotations, lists, paragraphs on various topics) substitute for images in a kind of latter-day "Song of Myself." This "self-study" features an ideal protagonist, a larger-than-life figure who resembles the one in "The Kulturkampf," and is a composite illustration in words of who and what he is. The rhetoric and "argument" of which much of this book is composed are the verbal outlines of this figure. There is no prose narrative here, but yet another example of serial collage.

The distinction between prose and poetry in MacDiarmid's work began to blur as early as *Cencrastus* where, for example, the passage on the Gaelic idea and the "parallelogram o' forces" appear elsewhere fundamentally unchanged as prose passages.[65] If it is asserted that much later work is "chopped-up prose," it can perhaps be equally asserted that much of his prose is a special type of poetry. One curious passage on the Esk River, in *Lucky Poet*, indicates how fundamentally unimportant this distinction seems to be to MacDiarmid: "the quick changes in the Esk that in a little stretch would far outrun all the divers thoughts of Man since Time began." This passage easily becomes the first four lines of a "Habbie stanza":

> Quick changes in the Esk that in
> A little stretch would far outrun
> All the divers thoughts of Man
> Since Time began ...[66]

Admittedly this is purely circumstantial in itself, but in the light of the structure of the book as a whole it is a highly interesting occurrence.

It has been noted earlier that lists, similes, and a loose kind of associationism are pronounced characteristics of much of the poetry of this period, and they certainly feature prominently in *Lucky Poet*. Catalogues of enemies, flowers, Scottish places, capitalist vices, authors, oriental saints, and many other such groups occur in this book. A fine example of simile which occurs in the prose part of the text is the following:

It is true, that the matters with which I am most concerned are for the most part like snipe chicks. One moment they are in evidence, piping in subdued tones, or contentedly pecking about. Then, as one's advance under cover of boulders or ling can no longer be disguised, the parents resort to clamorous flight and in the same instant the spot where the family has been becomes to all appearance as destitute of life as though the grass had never bent beneath any weight more perceptible than that of a dragonfly. Over it the bog-cotton waves, the clouds cast their reflections, but the tiny chicks have melted into the friendly heath, which so kindly lends its colours, like a screen, to shelter the young life which through the long course of the centuries it has produced and fostered (307).

The book as a whole is a series of particulars in a free association, including the above, but consisting primarily of ideas, the relationship of the poet to what has been dealt with earlier. It should not surprise us that this volume too is supposedly only one part of a larger unwritten work.

To look for a coherent philosophy in this hodge-podge of ideas is utterly futile. MacDiarmid claims at various points throughout that he is an anarchist, a communist, and a follower of Vedantic philosophy (67, xxi, 408). Some further examples of the sort of content one finds in *Lucky Poet* illustrate the poet's non-intellectual approach towards what might be supposed to be subject only to intellectual activity, and reveal also the projecting of his ideal, which can partly be seen to be his playing the role of MacDiarmid to its fullest.

Thus, when he quotes Prince Mirsky's praise of him for fine translations from the Russian, which were not translations at all but relied upon extant English translations, as Kenneth Buthlay has shown, what he is really indicating is an emphasis upon learning itself. The MacDiarmid figure in *Lucky Poet* is polyglot; it is immaterial whether the actual poet knows foreign languages or not. This is equally true of his claim to have read 12,000 books as a boy, or of this statement: "I have never met anyone who has read anything like as much as I have, though I have known most of our great bookmen; and it is a common experience of mine to have professors and other specialists in this or that language or literature, or in subjects ranging from geology to cerebral localization or the physiological conditions of originality of thought, admit that I am far better read even in their own particular subject than they are themselves. The range in all my books bears this out." This need not be taken seriously as a statement of fact, but only as indicative of a concern with the potential of the mind in handling these fields, a concept of knowing rather than any particular knowledge in itself. The MacDiarmid of *Lucky Poet* is a "realization" to some extent of the potential he feels he has. If the book is "the record of a man whose mind has always been on the track of something which required an awareness that was integral and continuous, and, no matter how small the detail of life he was observing, always strove to relate it to something more inclusive, to make it part of a whole," then the central character in it can be said to have travelled much further in this direction than MacDiarmid the author (13, vii). It is only this ideal who has "the knack of dealing with facts as a puffin with fish"; one sees no "artful tessellation of commonplaces" in *Lucky Poet* or in the poetry of this period in general (128, 120, *CP* 606, 1013).

None of this means that the facts and ideas presented are purely incidental. It is the case, however, that MacDiarmid does not often stop to examine and make his own any one particular, so quickly does he move from one to the next. It is as though he were too fearful of possible disillusionment to give an undue amount of importance to one over another. If, as he says, his subject matter races to him from all directions, it seems also to race past him, for there is often no "unfolding" in his poems, the glance just moving from one thing to another with no picture becoming visible. To become aware of as much as the poet has, it would seem that real knowledge would in many cases have to be sacrificed; to be a scholar of Russian, or a geologist, for example, would be a full-time occupation in itself, and to MacDiarmid such areas of knowledge are themselves only particulars drawn from an inexhaustible supply. Yet at the same time he is aware that merely having these resources in his vicinity does not lead to the kind of poetry he wants. They must be possessed, not merely noted. Thus, particular essences as such are stressed, and often detailed in a way which shows they are allowed to retain an importance in their own right. At the same time, MacDiarmid's thoughts outstrip his achievements, his ideal projection emerges, and a continual emphasis upon "knowing" in the abstract is revealed as a major preoccupation anterior to the recording of any one fragment of his world.

The poet's attitude to the world of facts is emphasized in the book. He quotes Lenin: the communist must work "over in his consciousness the whole inheritance of human knowledge ... [make] his own, and [work] over anew, all that was of value in the more than two thousand years of development of human thought" (xxi). And Whitman: "To conform with and build on the concrete realities and theories of the universe furnished by science, and henceforth the only irrefragable basis for anything, verse included," is the kind of poetry he wanted, at least at the point when he made this statement, although the discrepancy with "Song of Myself" is very great (xxii). The facts to MacDiarmid are these "concrete realities," irrefragable, the limits of his enquiry, which are to be the sustenance for his wayward intuition. "I am of course aware," he writes, "that most of the matters perhaps with which as human beings we must be chiefly concerned can no more be effectively illuminated by any knowledge of their constituent facts than the apprehension or the sensation, if it be such, of a concord between two musical notes implies in any sense any apprehension of the vibrations which are its physical cause"(58-9). Illumination is not inherent in the physical world, but depends upon it. The phrase "constituent facts" is of great interest, for facts are clearly given ontological status here; they are not "about" a thing, but, *in toto*, the thing in itself.

These pieces of reality, then, are to provide the substance of the "hard and dry" poetry MacDiarmid wants. His ideal for poetry is a stone-like quality, as this passage on Rimbaud demonstrates:

> He walked in granite within and without,
> And perhaps only his poetry had not found
> ... A method of being which was, for him,
> What he desired, perdurable as the granite. (152, *CP* 615)

Allied to this is a God-like perspective, that of his ideal, suggesting that he has brought the whole universe into range:

> Is poetry done for? Wars, the Robot Age, the collapse of civilization,
> These things are distracting and annoying, it is true
> – But merely as to an angler a moorhen's splashing flight
> That only puts down a rising fish for a minute or two! (341, *CP* 657)

The most obvious characteristic of the book, other than its lack of continuity, is the exaggerated reliance upon quotation, which reflects even more clearly than the above the poet's attitude towards the particulars of his environment. MacDiarmid speaks with the voices of others very often indeed in this work, which is full of such phrases as "I agree with Ouspensky's contention," "My cry has always been Liam O'Flaherty's," "I agree with ... Ezra Pound," "I echo," "I quote," "I am at one with," and so on. This practice, which sheds some light upon the poet's plagiarism, exemplifies his concern with identity in the sense used earlier. The quotations are not merely similar to views of his own, they are those views (so he says), word for word. As objects which he has picked up because he liked the look of them, they have been made his by his making them part of his own utterance. Even if one doubts the literal truth of this amazing coincidence of views and ideas, the implication, at least, is clear.

It is "Stony Limits" and "On a Raised Beach" which provide the most cogent expression of MacDiarmid's concerns in this period. Here the dominant image is stone – or stones, rather, pieces of truth like the poet's facts. The identification between the two is more than implicit, as two examples from other poems show. In "The Kind of Poetry I Want," the ideal poetry is said to need stones, a list of which is provided. The only possible interpretation of this is that the stones symbolize the particulars upon which the kind of poetry the poet wants is to be founded, and of which it is to be made. Even clearer is a passage which MacDiarmid uses to head "Once in a Cornish Garden":

> Even as St. John could not depict
> The glories of the New Jerusalem without
> Recourse to gold and precious stones, so we
> Our spirits' perfect state in terms
> Of Cornish geology.

The poem, in the *Lap of Honour* version, contains a long list of stones. Taking these together, one sees that the identification is explicitly made here (52, 56-8, *CP* 1102, 1106-9).

"Stony Limits" is only a promise of what is to come in the often brilliant long poem "On a Raised Beach," a preamble which familiarizes one with the material, the hard, unyielding stones. The poet, in his pursuit of Being, is aware that the truth he wants is neither purely in himself nor in the exterior world, but embodies both:

> Nor in vain mimicry of the powers
> That lifted up the mountains shall we raise
> A stone less of nature's shaping than of ours ...

The truth which resides in the stones dwarfs the actual state of man: "ultra-basic xenoliths ... make man look midges." The comparison here is one of durability, not size, so that Edwin Morgan's criticism of it in his *Festschrift* essay is made on a false assumption.

MacDiarmid is a poet; how can he deal with the stones?

> The poem that would praise you must be
> Like the glass of some rock, sleek brown, crowded
> With dark incipient crystal growths, we see ...[67]

The poetry must transmute the hardness, the clarity, the very "stone-ness" of the stones themselves. The poem is entitled "Stony Limits," it is plain, because the stones symbolize MacDiarmid's poetic elements, which cannot be broken down any further. It is of these elements (concrete particulars) that his ideal poetry is to be composed.

This all becomes much clearer in "On a Raised Beach," a hymn of affirmation which is one of the most accomplished poems MacDiarmid wrote at any time.[68] There is none of the haphazard arrangement of serial collage in this work. The myriad of tenuously related ideas, facts, opinions, and so on, of which other poems of this period are composed, here undergoes a *reductio*; all particulars achieve the discrete, solid, flawless nature of stones on a raised beach. Image thus replaces intellectual datum with a consequent appeal which is lacking in much of the contents of *Lucky Poet*, for example. The literal and the symbolic come together in one movement (for the stones are not only symbols, but themselves as well, giving the poem a kind of objective authority), an intense and coherent statement seldom excelled by MacDiarmid, its occasional flaws such as forced rhyme notwithstanding.

The movement of the poem derives from the poet's attempt to be one with the stones, an objective he himself is finally willing to admit might be beyond him even though he can intuitively grasp what it must be like to have achieved it. Here, with the stones at his feet, the solution to this life problem seems in his very grasp, for it is the elements of truth which lie there. Nothing on the beach is misleading, or a false clue. All is at its most basic here: "There are no twirly bits on this ground bass." The stones are the fruit of the forbidden tree of knowledge, avers MacDiarmid, unmistakeably linking them to the world of facts. As he says a little later on, "Truth has no trouble in knowing itself. / This is it. The hard fact. The inoppugnable reality, / Here is something for you to digest." This latter suggestion, which he is really making to himself, indicates the task of transmuting the stones into personal substance of which his ideal poetry is to consist.

The poem opens with the stone panorama, and the first verse-paragraph is an exhibit of vocabulary in itself, the building stones of the poet, here a list of particular qualities the stones possess. Words too are particulars; and identification is made in this poem between vocabulary and the stuff of the exterior world. The possibility of embodying truth in poetry is thus affirmed. But naming qualities has availed the poet nothing. He ends this paragraph with a series of questions, realizing that he has "brought [his] aesthesia in vain to bear" and the stones are still at a remove from him. These questions are concerned with the purpose or meaning the stones are felt to indicate. He asks what rebound-shot (bricole) has piled them there, what artist has placed them, "What Cabirian song from this cantasta comes?" He has not achieved the certainty the stones seem to promise. As he says later in the poem, the severance between object and image is "still wrongly [felt] 'twixt this storm beach and [himself]." In this opening passage he is scratching at the surface of the stones, noting qualities and textures, but their quiddity is denied him. The "Cabirian song" is yet to arise from the stones. (The reference to music here links poetry to the stones explicitly.) As to how they came to be there, MacDiarmid does not pursue this line of questioning, as the certainty takes hold in the poem that truth is the stones themselves, which are thus their own "cause."

The morning in which the poem is set is utterly still except for one bird, which is contrasted to the stones. The "secret of its song" lies in the fact that its "inward gates" are always open. Ours are not. But those of the stones are eternally open. The obscurity here might be resolved if this openness is taken to mean that the bird and the stones, unvexed by uncertainty, are repositories of truth. The bird is ephemeral in comparison to the stones, so that even if MacDiarmid seizes it he shall "only have gone a little way to go back again / And be like a fleeting deceit of development." It is with the stones that he "must begin ... as the world began." The stones "have dismissed / All but all of evolution": they are the realized process from potential to actual which has been MacDiarmid's concern from the beginning.

Abruptly a verse-paragraph appears which deals with life, in this case animal life. The contrast between this life and the stones is an intense one. Its "flashing fragments we are seeing" allow "no general principle [to] be guessed." These glimpses are "foam-bells on the hidden currents of being." (The image of water appears: the problem of existence is restated.) The animals can be described factually, yet "their purposive function is another question." This purpose is hidden just as many of the colours of animals go unseen. But

> Varied forms and functions though life may seem to have shown
> They all come back to the likeness of stone,
> So to the intervening stages we can best find a clue
> In what we all came from and return to.

It is not simply death which is being referred to here; the passage is not merely equivalent to "Ashes to ashes and dust to dust." MacDiarmid is questioning the mystery of life as a phenomenon; how it mysteriously arises out of matter and returns to it. That this is all part of one Being is assumed, but it is in the stones that the ultimate answer is to be found, since they precede and succeed life, and thus seem to be anterior to it.

The poem turns to a description of the truth of the stones, again in concept only, for MacDiarmid is still on the outside. "These stones are one with the stars." They are indivisible, elemental: "There are plenty of ruined buildings in the world but no ruined stones." Any attempt to build with the stones has resulted in failure. Their essence still remains hidden. "It is a paltry business to try to drag down / The arduous furor of the stones to the futile imaginings of men." They must be understood as they are.

It is eternity the poet is after, for which "hot blood is no use." The feelings, quick and random, must be "chilled," for an "emotion chilled is an emotion controlled; / This is the road leading to certainty." So MacDiarmid strives for "detachment," which suggests the poet's unwillingness to commit himself, lacking the authority of understanding as he does. He writes of letting his mind become a battleground of ideas, in which the "strongest and most universal" wins, which might almost be taken as an implicit reference to *Lucky Poet*, where the ideas certainly are left to themselves. By bringing the particulars together, the poet suggests that he can let them sort themselves out. But this attitude does not win out, for it is not merely detachment but passivity, something foreign to MacDiarmid's nature. Detachment from misleading feelings does not preclude an attempt to involve himself in the whole of Being.

Thus the next paragraph begins, "I must get into this stone world now." But, yet again, his labours result only in a series of descriptions:

> Ratchel, striae, relationships of tesserae,
>   Innumerable shades of grey,
>   Innumerable shapes,
> And beneath them all a stupendous unity,
> Infinite movement ...

This is only an affirmation of what has yet to be achieved. The "stupendous unity" of stone-ness, the sum of all movement, just as the sun in "The Glass of Pure Water" is compared to truth which has "a monopoly of movement," remains a concept.

The poem continues, as MacDiarmid looks at his problem from all angles. The "inerrable" stones are "no heap of broken images." They "go through Man, straight to God, if there is one." But this is theoretical. They came "out of the water," but halted. They do not move. They do not come the rest of the way to the poet, and, he says, partly in hope and partly in despair, that "These stones will reach us long before we reach them." Non-being, uncertainty, afflicts him with fancies and threatens an illusory understanding which is the logic of death rather than life. The certainty of the stones does not seem capable of being transmitted to MacDiarmid's self, which is so near and yet so far from truth. If we "must reconcile ourselves to the stones," "shed the encumbrances that muffle / Contact with elemental things," get into the stone world, the very concept of which fills the poet "with a sense of perfect form," there just seems no conceivable means of doing this. The poem leaves us only with "musts" and "shoulds." The goal which is sought remains an abstraction: it is "Alpha and Omega," or, in terms of the poetry MacDiarmid wants, it is "the Omnific Word." "These stones have the silence of supreme creative power," says the poet, but this seems almost an apology for their dumbness which has left everything to him. The stones remain on the beach, wholly inscrutable.

MacDiarmid returns to the age he lives in, no longer giving his attention solely to the raised beach which has seemed to epitomize all his poetic and existential concerns. "It is a frenzied and chaotic age, / Like a growth of weeds on the site of a demolished building. / How shall we set ourselves against it ... / With a constant centre, / With a single inspiration, foundations firm and invariable?" How can he "Be [himself] without interruption, / Adamantine and inexorable?" For "The truth we seek is as free / From all yet thought as a stone from humanity." "All human culture," he continues, "is a Goliath to fall / To the least of these pebbles withal." He will have "nothing interposed / Between [his] sensitiveness and the barren but beautiful reality." But as Sartre points out, it is precisely this "nothing" which is interposed between consciousness and Being, thus preventing MacDiarmid from achieving the understanding he wants.

Speaking of himself and his age, he writes,

> We have lost the grounds of our being,
> We have not built on rock.

Here are the grounds of Being at his very feet:

> These bare stones bring me straight back to reality.
> I grasp one of them and I have in my grip
> The beginning and the end of the world,
> My own self ...

But the stones are still opaque, entire of themselves. The poet, to use the marvellous image from Neil Young's song, is like a blind man with an answer in his hand: truth is literally in his grasp, but utterly inaccessible.

The poem moves inexorably towards a resolution. Life (the poet's life) remains a mystery, but it might well be bound up in death. The earlier passage in which animal life is contrasted to the stones seems to be recalled, only this time it is MacDiarmid's life which is concerned:

> I lift a stone; it is the meaning of life I clasp
> Which is death, for that is the meaning of death;
> How else does any man yet become
> Sufficiently at one with creation, sufficiently alone,
> Till as the stone that covers him he lies dumb
> And the stone at the mouth of his grave is not overthrown?

There is no Christian resurrection, in other words, for any such thing would render the truth of the stones illusory. Since men have "lost all approach to" the stones, one can be with them and like them only in death. "And in death – unlike life – we lose nothing that is truly ours."

But MacDiarmid is not finished yet. It is as a poet that he confronts the problem of the stones, and he must bring his struggle with them back into the realm of poetry. To do this he applies words for types of script and rhetorical terms to the exterior world, implying by so doing that language can embody the hard reality he has been dealing with since it now appears the world is language. (The identification was suggested earlier, where the stones were described in words which, owing to their unfamiliarity, appear as discrete objects themselves; the same is true of a subsequent well-placed list of Norn words.) The stones are the "diallage of the world's debate." Perhaps the most erudite pun of all time, "diallage" is a rhetorical device by which arguments, having been looked at from various angles, are all focused upon one point, and it is also a kind of mineral. The word sums up in one image the flurry of particulars of which MacDiarmid's world is composed. All the problems and preoccupations which he has come down to this stark confrontation between a solitary man and the stones of a raised beach. The hyperbole ("auxesis") of the world ends here in the simple, unexaggerated truth. The poet suggests that it would be easier to check Pegasus with a rein than to have any effect upon these stones. Even if his struggle has been in vain, however, he prefers them to all other forms of nature. They are demotic characters, the runic alphabet which spells the ideal he seeks ("the future," that is, the poetry he wants), as opposed to the rest of the world which is composed, it seems, of hieroglyphs, an esoteric script understandable only to one of the initiated.

MacDiarmid's poetic gift, song, sudddenly becomes fully realized as his ideal poetry in a flash of vision. As an apprentice to the stones, it tries to become one with them. In a brilliantly apposite image it is seen as a crinoid becoming a fossil, achieving life-in-death, stone-ness, synthesis. It acquires universal range, seeming "to sweep / The Heavens" just before the solidification takes place. At that point it "closes / Earth's vast epanadiplosis" with "the same word that began it." (Epanadiplosis is a rhetorical figure by which a sentence is made to begin and end with the same word.) The omnific word, timeless and all-creating, is attained as all the potential in the universe is completely realized. This is the final synthesis that MacDiarmid wants; nothing less will satisfy him. It is this which he has failed to achieve in this grappling with the stones; the stones themselves, as characters, must be arranged through his inspiration in order to make that word which is his ideal poetry. He cannot even read the individual letters, for the essence of each stone escapes him. Yet the final vision does seem, somehow, to qualify the pessimism immediately preceding it.

The clearly outlined situation of the poet in "On a Raised Beach" might be taken almost as an emblem of his situation as expressed, explicitly or implicitly, in the poetry of facts as a whole. Here are the particulars, the poet who surveys them, the frustration of the actual and the glimpse of the ideal. It is a poem which provides valuable insight into MacDiarmid's emphasis upon particulars, but perhaps more importantly it reveals his concern with poetry, something that has itself become an ideal and for the writing of which he seems to be preparing by this accumulation of material in the post-*Cencrastus* work. Transcending this activity for a short time, struggling with material rather than collecting it, MacDiarmid has produced a superb poem; engaged in it, he produces the flawed serial collages which have been discussed.

The poetry of facts exposes the constant gap betwen actual and ideal which has been the poet's concern throughout the earlier work as well. "On a Raised Beach" captures all the passionate intensity of MacDiarmid's desire to close it through his struggle with particulars. The particulars remain particulars. Nevertheless, his faith in them as a means by which the ideal might be achieved never wavers.[69] The conclusion of this chapter will be a consideration of the effects of his awareness of his situation, and his determined attitude towards the facts, upon his poetic development.

MacDiarmid's poems are almost entirely about himself. While this is true in a theoretical sense of any poet, however objective, it is explicitly so in this poet's work, early and late. The first person is seldom absent from his poems, and usually occupies the centre of the stage; he rarely sees himself as only an observer of something greater, as Dante Alighieri did, but stands dazzled in the glare of his own spotlight, unsure whether he is to be interrogated or merely expected to perform, but never failing to rise to the occasion. It is through his poetry that he exists. For of one thing he has no doubt whatsoever: he is a poet. The word does not merely describe his occupation, but his very essence. Having so defined himself, he has defined his mode of being-in-the-world. His problem of existence is therefore a problem of poetry, and the ideal solution is the aim of poetic activity.

In the poetry of facts the world itself, a series of fragments, becomes his only hope of an existential foundation, since intuition alone has failed to provide it. The intuition is to be informed. Piece by piece the world is to be made available to it so that, partaking thus of reality, it can no longer be subject to doubt; lacking the power of revelation, it is to be given material upon which to feed. Poetry is to be factual, in short, because to MacDiarmid the facts are not open to question.

The world of particulars becomes available to MacDiarmid through the medium of language. But language for the poet has, from the days of synthetic Scots onwards, been more than a series of signs. As Lallans it seemed to embody the Scottish essence. In later work it is not simply a means by which the exterior world is confronted; it embodies the exterior world. The particulars of the world become part of their names, in other words, and by dealing with language the poet is dealing with things:

> In this depth that I dare not leave
> I who am no dilettante of chaos and find
> No bitter gratification in the contemplation of ultimate
> > Incoherence
> Know that the world is at any given moment anything it
> > may be called
> And ever more difficult to group round any central character,
> Yet it is out of this aimless dispersion, all these
> > zigzagging efforts,
> All this disorderly growth, that the ideal of an epoch ends
> By disentangling itself.[70]

He is the "central character" around which he is trying to group the particulars in order that an ultimate pattern be established. He is writing of the world here, not of words, feelings, and associations.

MacDiarmid's awareness of his situation, his self-consciousness, often leads to a reification of language, since his very mode of being, poetic activity, becomes an object of scrutiny. This allows us to glimpse his conception of the nature of language, and the assertion made in the preceding paragraph is borne out. In "On a Raised Beach" the whole world actually becomes language in his vision at the end. In "Water Music" the poet clearly indicates his sense of being able to capture "waterness" in language. Here water can be harnessed and controlled by language, each of its movements mapped, frozen, and transcended in the word which names it. The symbolic aspect of this poem was mentioned earlier, but whether the water is taken on the symbolic or the literal plane, the emphasis upon the primacy of language is plain to see. In "Lament for the Great Music," MacDiarmid writes, "Amid the desolation language rises, and towers / Above the ruins; and with language, music," so that this primacy is explicitly stated.[71] Through language he can be at once in the world and "above" it.

The ideal poetry he wants is identified with the essences of the exterior world as well. His persona in "The Kulturkampf" writes that poetry in a style

> ... like the country he described
> Flowing like the great moors and fertile straths,
> And often strong and staccato
> Like the Highland hills.[72]

A closer identification has already been noted in "The Kind of Poetry I Want," and in the passage from a chapter of *Lucky Poet* about gathering up the loose ends of Scotland, in which

> ... by naming them and accepting them,
> Loving them and identifying [himself] with them,
> [He attempts] to express the whole. (324, *CP* 652)

Just previous to these lines MacDiarmid has imagined himself as a God-like arranger, not of words but of things: "Moving a fraction of flower here, / ... an inch of air there, / And without breaking anything." It is through language that he is able to seize things in order to arrange them and create what he called in *Drunk Man* a "concrete abstraction."

With the poet giving so much power to language, one might expect that, as in the Lallans poetry, he has given himself a mandate to produce a continual stream of major poetry. The actual work, as has been indicated, is severely flawed, even though some of MacDiarmid's finest poetry can be found in this period. The deficiences of serial collage have already been pointed out. Added to this is the coming into being of idealized conceptions of poetry and language, the latter reaching its culmination in *James Joyce*, which tend to absorb the poet's attention to the detriment of the actual work he is producing. Much of the latter is an accumulation of material, aesthetic tools which are not used but merely itemized. "The Kind of Poetry I Want," for example, is an inventory and little more, a series of found objects placed in no new context, only a promised one. His widespread tendency to list particulars rather than come to grips with them is the most serious defect in the later poetry. The result is often tedious repetition, clumsy and obscure phrasing, and a presentation of material which makes little appeal to the intellect and none to the imagination. The contrast of this type of poetry with poems such as "On a Raised Beach" is startling. The former is proto-poetry, an unfulfilled promise, a series of elements which refuse to become a whole; it seems to be, as W.S. Merwin said of *James Joyce*, "a series of notes for a poem" which has become an ideal. "On a Raised Beach," in contrast, is an active confrontation with material, and a failure to achieve the ideal thus becomes the theme of one of MacDiarmid's most successful poems.

The rule in the poetry of particulars, however, seems to be that the particulars retain their particularity, and the poems remain inchoate. Even the language material itself takes on the appearance of a series of particulars on occasion. The numerous foreign tags, the synthetic English experiments such as "In the Caledonian Forest," "Ephyphatha"[sic], "The Sense of Smell," and parts of "Cornish Heroic Song" and "On a Raised Beach," and the catalogue effect of the Scots vocabulary in "Scots Unbound," "Water Music," and "Balefire Loch" are all a presentation of vocabulary itself as found objects.[73] Although in some cases, notably "On a Raised Beach" and "Water Music," this quality of "object" is both retained and has an active use as well, such parading of resources is not generally successful. The unreadable "In the Caledonian Forest," for example, seems, as evidenced by a suspicious amount of alliteration, a mere syntactical framework for unfamiliar words taken from a restricted portion of a dictionary.

This unique and extreme attitude towards words indicates just how far removed MacDiarmid can be from the actual practice of poetry. Having made poetry an ideal as this chapter has indicated, and to some extent language as well, much of the work of this period seems to be scarcely more than a declaration of resources. The poet's collection of fragments does not fuse, although he continues to imply his hope by the simple fact that he does not abandon his craft and keep a journal of particulars as Thoreau did instead. Simple juxtaposition at worst and analogy at best, not a synthesis ideal or actual, are the usual ways in which MacDiarmid treats the particulars, but this often leaves them almost untouched. The tragic truth is that he is not writing the poetry he wants to write, but only a preamble. His determination to face the facts is matched only by his uncertainty as to where to proceed from there.

Three major factors have undoubtedly played their parts in contributing to this development. The first and most important is the poet's exaggerated self-consciousness. MacDiarmid is unable to accept his own authority amd responsibility for his activity. He invariably seeks a sanction from without, whether revelation or the facts. His mode of being-in-the-world is therefore constantly subject to questioning because it lacks justification. Aware of himself, he is aware of himself as poet; having committed himself to that mode of being, he conceives an ideal poetry free of the doubts which plague his present work. Aware of himself as a user of language, that language is not beyond question. Eventually he conceives an ideal language as well.

The second factor is paralysis of the intuition. By providing himself with so much material (the particulars), the imagination is unable to act. Far from laying the groundwork for revelation, MacDiarmid has ensured that even the mistrusted inspiration of earlier work is able to return only occasionally. The more material he gathers, the more helpless is the imagination to deal with it and thus the more self-consciously contrived the relations among the elements. Allied to this glut is the third factor: much of the material MacDiarmid has brought into his ambit is resistant to the imagination. Even if ideas are treated as things, for example, the poet is unable to make them appeal to his imagination – for one thing, an idea casts no image. Moreover, treated as a thing it cannot appeal to the wit or the intellect either. The effect of these two factors is to impede poetic activity, and thus to reinforce the emphasis upon ideal poetry.

It can be seen that in fact a mutual reinforcement is set up between the ideal and the actual poetry. The conception of the former contributes to the character of the latter, and the reverse is equally true. It could also be argued that self-consciousness contributes directly to the paralysis of the intuition, and so on: the interrelation of the three factors, and the aspects of the poet's development which have been discussed, is a highly complex and non-linear one. But it is MacDiarmid's self-consciousness, his awareness of his situation, which is anterior to all else and provides a stream of continuity throughout his work as a whole.

As has been suggested, language too becomes idealized. This is not so much the result of dissatisfaction with actual language as such, which is expressed in "The Divided Bird," "The Sense of Smell," and "Scots Unbound," for example, as almost a logical sequel to the development of the concept of ideal poetry. MacDiarmid, turning his attention to the very substance of his craft, transforms that too into a goal in his book-length poem *In Memoriam James Joyce*.

CHAPTER FIVE

Speaking in Tongues:
The Final Statements

In Memoriam James Joyce: From a Vision of World Language is the practical culmination of MacDiarmid's poetic career. After its publication in 1955, he confined himself almost entirely to editorial functions, bringing out such collections as *A Lap of Honour, A Clyack-Sheaf,* and *Collected Poems.* The latter does contain a section, "Impavidi Progrediamur," which is supposed to be from an unfinished part of "Mature Art," and a few new poems appeared from time to time, such as the one addressed to Danny Cohn-Bendit in *A Clyack-Sheaf,* but by and large nothing more on the scale of *James Joyce* was to be forthcoming.

There is one exception: the book-length poem *The Battle Continues,* published in 1957. This is concerned with the Spanish Civil War and the fascist poet Roy Campbell, and its publication occurred the year MacDiarmid rejoined the Communist party. It can thus be taken, perhaps, as a renewed pledge of loyalty to communist ideals. As a poem, it is hardly worthy of attention. As an attack upon Campbell, its subtlety can be gauged by the fact that it was originally going to be called "Anus Mundi."[1] It is a jejune mixture of crude insult and incoherent anger, in which, for once, the poet seems almost at a loss for words as he struggles to express his hatred and contempt for the South African satirist, who was the only poet of any stature to have fought on Franco's side in Spain. The poem is a culmination of MacDiarmid's political concerns, and it comes closer to socialist realism of the Stalinist variety than anything else he has produced, with the exception of a few short lyrics in *Second Hymn to Lenin,* such as "Reflections in an Ironworks," and of course the later risible "Girl on the Vertical Capstan Lathe." One can observe how flat his supposed political concerns reveal themselves to be when he tries to make them his directly, rather than using them to indicate deeper concerns, examples of which were given in the last chapter. There is a curious emptiness, showing more than ever how peripheral the poet's "Marxism" is to his poetry as a whole. There is no real passion here, only a series of gestures for the most part, although in the last section the tone softens somewhat and the writing improves, as he turns from hatred of Campbell to admiration for the Spanish people.[2]

But *James Joyce* is altogether different in quality and concern. It is a summing-up of many of the preoccupations of the post-*Cencrastus* period, and represents also the epitome of the serial collage form used previously: borrowings, tough prosaic diction, fine clear descriptive passages, lists, exotic vocabulary, facts, and ideas come together in the longest non-lyric poem of MacDiarmid's career, which itself is supposedly a mere fragment of a much larger poem. The water and stone symbolism is all but absent here, for the theme of this poem is not so much the problem of existence itself as the means by which the poet must come to grips with it, namely language. "World language," as was mentioned earlier, does not mean a mélange of words from various languages but an ideal language which captures and transcends the world in all its multifariousness and complexity, which can crystallize all the essences of the external world and spell Being.[3] A resolution of the problem of being-in-the-world, that precarious and uncertain state, might be the swallowing of the world by the self, the transmutation of the world into self-ness. MacDiarmid's ideal poetry, written in an ideal language, is to achieve just this synthesis of the self and not-self.

The poem is not simply a random collection of bits and pieces but a serial collage which embodies at the same time a general movement in the direction of an outline of what the poet means by world language and what he wants to do with it. As will be indicated, this movement is not a subtle interplay of forces, not an orchestration, but a far simpler, almost logical unfolding of ideas around the central conflict between the ideal and the actual: the poem, despite the almost endless details, is in fact an exposition of MacDiarmid's central theme of potential, at its clearest and most explicit. The poem will therefore be examined as it progresses in order to demonstrate this theme, and the chapter will be concluded with an evaluation of its poetic method.

The first section of the poem sets the theme and tone of the ensuing ones, and takes the title of the whole work. It begins with a series of quotations, including Rabindranath Tagore's motto "When the whole world meets in one place," which can easily be assumed to refer, in this context, to MacDiarmid himself as the nexus of phenomena (20-1, *CP* 737). But it is the poet's own medium, language, which is established as the theme of the poem from the first line, so that the motto implies the relationship between the world and language which characterized MacDiarmid's approach throughout his earlier poetry.

After rejecting the suggestion that English could ever be the universal language, MacDiarmid makes a series of allusions and quotations referring to writers who have sought out rare words of power, and praises Doughty for "Making language at once more rich and more precise, / And passionate for naming particular things / And particular parts of things" (21-3, *CP* 740). It must be remembered at the outset that the poet's line-up is composed of those who reflect his own strivings, so that Doughty's achievements reflect the greater heights to which he aspires. Doughty's preoccupation with the word, examined in an essay by MacDiarmid entitled "Charles Doughty and the Need for Heroic Poetry," mirrors that of MacDiarmid.[4] To capture all the essences of the world it is necessary to name them; it is the exemplifying of this practice for which Doughty is valuable to him.

After an interjected passage concerned with the author himself, a "funny one" distinct from the mass, a prophet, that is, whom people think mad, the thread is picked up again (24, *CP* 741). What sort of words does MacDiarmid want? "Words like the fortune-telling table" of scientific prediction, for example the periodic table, in which undiscovered elements "exist" as an abstract set of properties, so that a system may be discovered which can express the whole even when only the part is known; this reflects MacDiarmid's continual hope that the mosaic will leap into focus when he has accumulated and pieced together enough "stones." He wants words which have the power that the sacred name of God has in the *Imyaslavtsy* cult (24, *CP* 742).

A cautionary passage follows, in which he rejects the possibility or desirability of "total speech," neatly comparing it to the equally unwanted possibility of silence as a goal (25, *CP* 742). Total speech as a concept evidently refers to the lump sum of human discourse, the aggregate of words and statements both trivial and profound. This accumulation "could transmit no light." The language MacDiarmid wants is that of enlightenment itself. This goal is not easily won; the poet goes on to list grammars, books on linguistics, and so on as an indication of the complexities to be mastered in the world of language (25, *CP* 742-3). The user of language, too, must bring to the medium a life lived to the hilt. MacDiarmid's ideal author has lived, knocked around in the world, had adventures, explored all manner of realms. These are

... men who, when they sat down to write,
Had merely to let their pens run freely,

So great was the pressure of memory
And the weight of the thousand living images
That dwelt with them. (26, *CP* 743-4)

Continuing, MacDiarmid suggests that

There is much to be said today for reviving
The poetical method of Jalal ud-Din Rumi
Who made use of every kind of anecdote
And allowed his pen to run on unchecked
With every idea, every fancy, every play on words
Which suggested themselves to him ... (26, *CP* 744)

(It might be suggested that *Lucky Poet* revives this method!) The synthesis of language and experience on the outside, and of language and cerebration on the inside, has the potential of an ideal poetry which would have the power of a barometer, of prediction, since of course it would transcend present, past, and future in the timeless certainty of understanding.

After a teasing riddle ("And all this here, everything I write, of course / Is an extended metaphor for something I never mention") suggesting Christ's pronouncement that His parables were made deliberately obscure in order that the vulgar could not too readily penetrate to the truth and by doing so, supposedly, dismiss it as readily, MacDiarmid continues to list grammars, ending with a reference to Stalin and all the "languages and literatures of the U.S.S.R." presumably united in the Marxist framework and pointing therefore in the direction of the world language he wants (27, *CP* 745-6). He has always insisted that the concern for learning and thought is essentially a communist concern, and here he as usual connects politics with his own fundamentally lonely quest.

The realm of speech is dealt with next. Espousing, in his maddeningly whimsical assertive fashion, the theory that a person makes sounds not with the vocal cords but with the sinuses, he goes on to list a series of singers such as Jenny Lind (28-9, *CP* 748). No aspect of language, plainly, is to remain unexplored. The poem concerns itself with almost every conceivable way of looking at words, as a matter of fact. He then expresses a concern with different types of speech, failing to distinguish between speech and language even though he had earlier praised one of his authorities for doing so (25, *CP* 743), and lists as examples *welt literatur* [sic], the faux pas, wisecracks, and Vogule (about which, as Edwin Morgan points out, he is misinformed).[5] He goes on to "examine" linguistic structure, providing lists of terms such as "phonemes" (29-30, *CP* 749). Once again we observe that the closest MacDiarmid ever seems to come to a real examination of realms of knowledge is to list them or to talk about their possibilities vis-à-vis his own aims.

If human history interests him, it is "in the fertile sense /... not the history of the human species / But the story of the universe of experience" (31, *CP* 750). The universe of experience, or more exactly his universe of experience, is open to the possibility of being dealt with in poetry, but this depends upon the power of language to transmute the phenomena of the world. Thus he introduces a passage concerned with the kind of poetry he wants, a series of examples of expertise followed by a description of the ideal:

> – An exacting intellectual undertaking,
> The expression to a far greater extent
> Of thought and reason than of emotion,
> And fully understanding
> The sources of its emotions and ideas,
> – Trying to see the whole of life reasonably,
> Adopting a detachment whence I can judge
> Man with unbiased, personal calm ... (31, *CP* 750)

The potential for this is bound up in language, he feels, so he quotes a writer who claims that workers and peasants use more words than Shakespeare did: if these people can master language, of what heights is MacDiamid not capable?

> For it is in literature as it is in mountaineering
> Inevitable when once all the great ridges and faces
> Have been conquered by "fair means"
> New piton techniques must be evolved
> For the creation and solution
> Of new climbing problems. (32, *CP* 752)

An aesthetic mountaineer, MacDiarmid expresses the faith that reality, the world of experience, can be conquered by language.

Any sort of speech, says the poet, may "become the corner stone of a miracle of expression" (32, *CP* 752). The use of the word "stone" is not incidental, for the problem of being-in-the-world can be solved through language alone if language possesses an ontological priority as is suggested in this important passage:

> For in the aesthetic experience
> Instead of language meaning the material of experience
> – Things, ideas, emotions, feelings –
> This material means language. (33, *CP* 752)

It is precisely this point which we attempted to show as an underlying conception in much of the post-*Cencrastus* poetry of the 1930s and 1940s. Here is an explicit affirmation of the primacy of langage and of the subsuming of all else into it.

But affirmations are not enough, and once again the breach between the ideal and the actual is made clear. The poet is reduced to listing topics to be dealt with by language, such as "The ethics of dictatorship" and "The white grapes of Thomery" (35, *CP* 755). He seems continually concerned with mapping out more areas to cover, rather than covering the ones of which he is already aware. He insists upon more intellectual effort, and gives this very poem as an example of what must be done and of what he is trying to do. But it can be seen that his description of this poem is more the description of the ideal than of the actual:

> ... this *hapax legomenon* of a poem, this exercise
> In schlabone, bordatini, and prolonged scordattura [sic],
> This *divertissement philologique*,
> This wort-spiel, this torch symphony,
> This "liberal education," this collection of *fonds de tiroir*,
> This – even more than Kierkegaard's
> "Frygt og Baeven" – "dialectical lyric,"
> This rag-bag, this Loch Ness monster, this impact
> Of the whole range of *welt literatur* [sic] on one man's brain,
> In short, this "friar's job" as they say in Spain
> Going back in kind
> To the Eddic "Converse of Thor and the All-Wise Dwarf"
> (Al-viss Mal, "Edda die lieden des Codex Regius," 120,lf)
> Existing in its present MS form
> Over five centuries before Shakespeare.
> You remember it? (35, *CP* 755-6)

At the most, only a few of these comparisons hold true; it is not, for example, symphonic, nor is there anything here like the "impact / Of the whole range of *welt literatur* on one man's brain," for the simple reason that MacDiarmid has not, nor could have had, experienced such an impact, despite the mischievous question at the end implying vast learning. (He could of course be referring to an imagined impact.) To some extent the poet seems to be laughing at himself, as though suddenly aware that he has been a little pretentious. What does become clearly evident in this passage is the poet's concept of struggle which is present in so much of his work, a struggle for the ultimate fluency and craft of the ideal poet. In this poem the struggle itself is only a concept. And although we may agree that MacDiarmid has in a sense deliberately mistuned an instrument to create special effects (*scordatura*, misspelled in the text of the above passage), the problem as outlined in the poem is in fact the problem of finding one. In this passage the comparisons, coming quickly and explosively, seem almost like invective as the poet, surveying his labours, points to them and says "this -" as though to praise and damn at once. Detaching himself from his work as he does here, it is clear from his tone that he is not entirely satisfied with it, for he has turned it into an object separate from himself, a curious specimen not above a few pokes and prods. For all this emphasis upon the word, and the poetry made of his world language which is to come, he has succeeded in fact in producing a monster, in the original meaning of the term. This passage, however, summing up what has come before, is a sort of climax; the world of books has led to this conclusion. It is immediately, and significantly, followed by the fine lyrical passage beginning, "Let the only consistency / In the course of my poetry / Be like that of the hawthorn tree."

A startling contrast arises here between the lyric intensity of this passage and the garrulous and almost matter-of-fact discourse which precedes it. It is a tight, controlled handling of language, replete with crisp, clear imagery, and as a whole is a symbol of the ideal poetry MacDiarmid seeks, a clever transmutation of the concerns reflected in the tone and substance of the passage just quoted into a quiet, reflective, focused lyric. Any consistency in his poetry is to be a natural consistency like the life of the hawthorn,

> Which in early Spring breaks
> Fresh emerald, then by nature's law
> Darkens and deepens and takes
> Tints of purple-maroon, rose-madder and straw. (35, *CP* 756)

The poet's life, and his poetry which is that life, is to be organic, of the world, and underlain by "nature's law." As in the quotation from "The Kind of Poetry I Want" in the previous chapter, he expresses once more the feeling that a pattern exists to be discovered in his own life, that the understanding which he seeks can be revealed in the confusion which surrounds him. The simplicity and seeming harmony expressed in this natural description contrasts with the disharmonious complexity of his environment as a whole.

After making this initial comparison between his poetry and the hawthorn, he expresses his view on what poetry can be:

> Poetry is human existence come to life,
> The glorious energy that once employed
> Turns all else in creation null and void,

The flower and the fruit, the meaning and goal,
Which won all else is needs removed by the knife
Even as a man who rises high
Kicks away the ladder he has come up by.

The poems he has already written are to be to him what the innumerable points of ruby decking the stark hawthorn tree are in the winter – "flame-points of living fire," glimpses of the ideal which is itself expressed in the passage just quoted. He realizes, in other words, that at the most his poems thus far are merely indications of the "terrible crystal," as he has termed his ideal in the past.[8]
    The Scottish theme enters briefly:

[I] turn Scotland to poetry like those women who
In their passion secrete and turn to
Musk through and through! (36, *CP* 757)

And once again the idea of transmutation from substance to word recurs.
    His gaze widens, and instead of one hawthorn he sees a great number of trees in magnificent autumn colours, trees which are easily taken as symbols of realms of reality which are a preoccupation of his poetry as a whole:

They are not endless these variations of form
Though it is perhaps impossible to see them all.
It is certainly impossible to conceive one that doesn't exist.
But I keep trying in our forest to do both of these,
And though it is a long time now since I saw a new one
I am by no means weary yet of my concentration
On phyllotaxis here in preference to all else,
All else – but my sense of sny! (37, *CP* 758)

We are back in the world of words. Phyllotaxis refers to a careful study of the leaves, symbolizing the words which preoccupy him, and sny is "the bent or direction of the curvature of branches" which in turn symbolizes the relations among the words, as the leaves are brought into a spatial relation by this bent or curvature.[9] These lines are followed by the last stanza of section II of "In the Caledonian Forest," that intimidating exhibit of recondite vocabulary.
    There has been a markedly unsatisfactory symbolic shift here, as the poet first of all compared his poetry to a hawthorn, thereby investing the latter with certain symbolic properties, but then became

a wanderer through a forest. The two parts of the poem are only tenuously associated. Nevertheless, his essential concerns remain clear. His poetry contains traces of a pattern: he goes on to seek a state in which the ideal poetry he wants is realized, the hawthorn becoming entirely ruby, as it were. His concern with the foliage of trees reveals a desire to penetrate the mystery of their trunks, securely rooted in the earth. The leaves and branches change and move, but the trunk (the "something he never mentions" in this case?) remains immobile, an underlying reality. The world of phenomena is the foliage of truth. And these phenomena, as was shown a little earlier, are the stuff of language. His concern with words is phyllotactic.

We are, at any rate, brought sharply back to the world of language by the "Caledonian Forest" stanza, a clever shift in substance which prepares us for ensuing lists of grammarians, facts about language, descriptions of various languages, including a long passage on Greek and one on Chinese, a list of dance forms (a type of language as a set of symbols, just like the movement of the recording angel in "The Glass of Pure Water"), of the homes of Kazaks, Kurds, etc. (reflecting the differing realities or environments with which language must deal), and a further list of languages, until he comes to the role of the poet, once again the ideal poet he wants to be (38ff, *CP* 759ff).

The poet, like a farmer, knows languages as the latter "surveying his fields / Can distinguish between one kind of crop and another." The poet must emulate the "performance of two Basque Bersolaris / Involving, with more than Finnish *sisu*, the whole being, / All the senses at once" (40, *CP* 763). Then comes yet more information about languages, and a passage, like the one about the farmer, taken from his own poem "My Heart Always Goes Back to the North," concerned with the synthesis of "intranational differences" (41, *CP* 763).[10] Then a passage from *The Islands of Scotland* appears, a list of Norn words for aspects of the sea (41-2, *CP* 763-4). (The sea has almost always symbolized, for MacDiarmid, the chaotic modern environment in which he finds himself; naming aspects of it means exerting power over it.) This is followed by a passage on regional differences in Italian literature (42, *CP* 764). By this point it should have become obvious to any reader that the poet, by means of this continual itemization, is suggesting a possible state of omniscience through language.

After contrasting the efforts of regional Italian writers to the methodological limitations of science and the debased state of the masses in "our great industrial centres," MacDiarmid gives a famous (or infamous) passage on Karl Kraus and Hölderlin taken from Erich Heller's article in the *Times Literary Supplement* of 8 May 1953.[11] Kraus, and to some extent Hölderlin as well, become ideals for the poet. "Kraus whose thinking was a voyage / Of exploration in a landscape of words" was concerned with the power of language, and believed that in the debasing of language, its loss of power, its misuse, lay the doom of Germany:

> Oppressed by the confusing chorus of apparent triviality,
> All the seething sciolism of the conventional world
> His ear was tuned to the pitch of the Absolute.
> People gossiped about a War; he heard them
> Lament the loss of their souls; at every street corner
> Acts of high treason were committed.

Kraus, as a satirist, endeavoured to show by "creating another context for the trivial" the awful portents hidden in the chatter of people around him. To show the underlying truth, his concern of necessity was with words. In contrast, Hölderlin achieved

> the miracle of speechlessness
> Bursting into speech ...
> ... Hölderlin sought,
> And often miraculously found,
> The word with which silence speaks
> Its own silence without breaking it.

Silence too reveals truth, for it indicates the gulf between our present state and ideal understanding, the latter silent because it is yet to be revealed. That this curious interpretation of Heller's use of the word "silence" is the one MacDiarmid adopts, rather than the alternative, that truth is silence because it is beyond expressing in language, is revealed by the following passage:

> So beyond all that is heteroepic, holophrastic,
> Macaronic, philomathic, psychopetal,
> Jerqueing every idioticon,
> Comes this supreme paraleipsis,
> Full of potential song as a humming bird
> Is full of potential motion,
> When, as we race along with kingfisher brilliance,
> Seeking always for that which "being known,
> Everything else becomes known,"
> That which we can only know
> By allowing it to know itself in us,

Since "determinatio est negatio,"
Suddenly "chaos falls silent in the dazzled abyss."

This is MacDiarmid's paraphrase of Heller's commentary on Hölderlin quoted previously. MacDiarmid calls Hölderlin's achievement a "paraleipsis," this being a rhetorical device by which something is emphasized by pretending to pass over it without notice, using phrases such as "it goes without saying that." To sing of silence is indeed paraleiptical, but silence itself has only a dialectical function – it is no end in itself, no realm beyond the limits of language where truth resides, but merely the antithesis of song in the Hegelian sense. The "supreme paraleipsis" is a dialectical process "full of potential song." Beyond all the intricate concerns with language which MacDiarmid names, and most of which are quite clearly his own, a poet's song is about silence, for at the very height of his poetic expression, as he says a little earlier, silence supervenes; as he notes later on in the poem, it is "ever just beyond." It reveals the unfinished nature of his work. He sings directly about silence, and about the lack of certainty of which this is a manifestation, when he has actually conceived of certainty – when, searching for it, the abyss from which he struggles to free himself is dazzled momentarily by a visionary gleam of the truth for which he longs. But song, not silence, is what he is after. This, then, is MacDiarmid's conception of silence at this point, but, we suspect, it is not quite what either Heller or Hölderlin had in mind.

For MacDiarmid's former transitory misgivings about language cannot be found in this poem, except of course in his implied dissatisfaction with language as it is now. He wants a world language, the Omnific Word, not a mystical silence. Thus, after a few examples of silence ending with Hindemith's questioning the importance and relevance of sound to music, and a bit from Heidegger about the "silence / Of the 'existent' potentiality of being"[12] (MacDiarmid, having latched onto a concept, is reluctant to let it go without talking about it and making a category out of it), he returns to Karl Kraus. He praises Kraus, in fact, for believing that everything worth saying can be said in language. He does not go back to Hölderlin. It is curious and noteworthy how MacDiarmid seizes upon the concept of silence, but ends up by talking of several different silences: the silence of chaos in the dazzled abyss has little to do with Hölderlin's "paraleipsis," and Hindemith's query has even less to do with Heidegger's concept. In this he evidences his own confusion, but one can see a common concern here, nevertheless, the gap between actual and potential, real and ideal, which has concerned the poet almost from the beginning.

Music without sound is ideal, or unrealized, music, for example; silence is linked to potentiality by Heidegger.

But by returning to Kraus, MacDiarmid is once more in the realm of words. In a key passage following, he writes of

> The unity of thing and word
> Of feeling and its articulation,
> Which is the essence of poetry.

These are Heller's words, but in context echoes the similar idea in "On a Raised Beach." Being, he affirms, can be grasped in language. He still believes in the possibility of a God-like omniscience/omnipresence. Doubts do surface, however:

> The terrifying race between the material
> And its realization seems still in progress.
> It may even be in the materials' very nature
> That it will forever resist
> The attempt to raise it to a sphere
> Which permits its artistic contemplation.
> For it is more than material
> It is in itself perversely realized art,
> The *ne plus ultra*
> Of an infernal spiritualization of the real.

Specifically, this "infernal spiritualization" refers to events in Kraus's Germany. But here too is the threatening nature of MacDiarmid's materials as they resist his efforts to come to grips with them. Perhaps, he is implying, understanding will forever escape him because of some infernal reality which is opposed to his efforts. (In his open letter "To a Young Poet" in *Saltire Review* four years later, he describes a nightmare in which all the trivial objects which surround him acquire immortality but remain trivial.) One can sense his unease in this passage even though it is only implicitly concerned with himself. Borrowed from Heller, it readily acquires a new context in *James Joyce*.

But such doubts are, as usual, momentary:

> ... in this poem at least I will leave
> Thoughts of these difficulties
> As no more than the dark green glossy leaves of black bryony
> Which strike an exotic note in our hedgerows. (44ff, *CP* 767ff)

And then we are back in the lists: examples of his poetic diversity are given in terms of, or rather, reflected by, the diversity of musics in the regions of Spain, or the composition of racial types at Yale and their respective studies; then a list of languages and dialects, a passage on Breton etymology and its ramifications in Romance languages; then a list of Welsh poetic terms, some more references to singing ... (51ff, *CP* 776ff). These are a continual series of affirmations about language, about its range and power, the material MacDiarmid must absorb. For, as he says,

> We must know all the words, even as in chess ...
> Despite the great difficulty of reducing the mass
> Of available material to system, Spielman and Znosko-Borovsky
> Have laid the foundations of a science of combination
> By classifying its types and devising
> Some sort of terminology, still weak in giving guidance
> On the marks of a position in which the moment has arrived
> To look for a swift decision by combinative play. (54, *CP* 780-1)

A system is possible, an ideal language is possible in which words are systematically combined. A chess player, like a poet, faced with a time-limit (for the latter, his life-time),

> ... hopes his patient pursuit
> Of a strategic plan will be crowned
> By some sudden foray to seize a decisive advantage
> And has not had time to examine the changes
> Of such a foray at every move. What he needs is to acquire
> A kind of subconscious faculty for recognizing the positions
> In which a combination ought to be discoverable. (55, *CP* 781)

And in language, there "lie hidden ... elements that effectively combined / Can utterly change the nature of man." Comparing the action of growth hormone to this in an example of what David Craig quite rightly points out as a purely intellectual associationism,[13] he concludes,

> So perchance can we outgrow time
> And suddenly fulfill all history
> Established and to come. (55, *CP* 781)

So the goal of understanding is realizable: it depends upon the two mental activities which concern MacDiarmid from the very beginning – intuition (revelation) and learning. The idea of synthesizing these activities is expressed a little further on:

I seek ...
The point where science and art can meet,
For there are two kinds of knowledge,
Knowing about things and knowing things,
Scientific data and aesthetic realization,
And I seek their perfect fusion in my work. (55, *CP* 782)

Following these clear passages, however, we find ourselves once more in a quicksand, this time one of ideas. Count Korzybski figures largely here. Because he was concerned with semantics, the relationship of language to thought, and so on, he is inevitably of interest to MacDiarmid. Hence ringing phrases such as the following:

So we must get rid of all semantic blockages.
Above all, the old "unknowable" becomes abolished
And limited to the simple and natural fact
That the objective levels *are not* words. (56, *CP* 784)

This carries with it a tone of authority, but the assertion it contains is completely at variance with MacDiarmid's expressed desire to fuse thing and word. This passage is Korzybski speaking, not the poet. Korzybski's earnest but rather silly book, *Science and Sanity*, presents the argument that the root cause of wars, poverty, disease, and other ills is "Aristotelian thought." It is not his specific theories which are important here, however, but rather his attractiveness to MacDiarmid.[14] For Korzybski presents a world view, a system, which reflects the poet's own attempts to do so. He is concerned with words; so is the poet. He has easy solutions to complex problems; and MacDiarmid seeks such assurances since his task appears so formidable. He too seeks such answers, and must inevitably be attracted by the idea that they are easily understandable ones which will relieve him of the burdensome chore of "documentation." In terms of *James Joyce*, the quotation from Korzybski merely reveals certain attitudes of MacDiarmid, not specific beliefs. In the above passage, besides a borrowed tone of authority, the poet's concern with forging ahead to understanding is indicated. "Semantic blockages" suggest, for example, that the way to understanding is impeded. (Even the contextual contradiction of the last line might conceivably be resolved by reading *"are not"* as *"are not* yet.") In keeping with his feeling that a true genius is a voice in the wilderness, he finds a kindred spirit in Korzybski – but remains essentially oblivious to the man's ideas, or at least unaffected by them. He is no one's follower.

The powers of language are reaffirmed after this encounter, and the poet talks of "the speech to which all our efforts converge":

> No voice not fully enfranchised,
> No voice dispensable or undistinguishable
> Like a man who needs uses words from many dialects
> To say what he has to say as exactly and directly as possible.
>
> (59, *CP* 786-7)

He is writing of a linguistic Utopia, in fact, in which the personal language of each individual is open to all. MacDiarmid continues, still generalizing his struggle (seeing it in terms of "all men") to write of the time when "the Paneubiotic synthesis is grasped in its totality," implying once again the concept of reaching his own synthesis. But at the moment, there is speech

> With, ever just beyond, the stillness of light into which
> Vanish the multitudinous waves of speech,
> Ever just beyond,
> For is perfection desired
> Or an average of imperfection
> Such, for instance, as makes
> A tutti of twenty strings
> Playing together
> Distinguishable from one violin
> Magnified twenty times? (59-60, *CP* 787)

This clearly refers back to the poet's exegetical paraphrase of Heller on Hölderlin, where, in a momentary gleam of vision, "chaos falls silent in the dazzled abyss." The vision (light) seems to enclose the poet's speech rather than the other way round. MacDiarmid is obviously aware that his task is unresolved, and once more the actual/ideal polarity is presented. The question suggests a momentary acceptance of his present situation, almost a rationalization for not having achieved perfection. In the context of the poem as a whole, however, it is perfection which is desired, and the possibility of achieving it is continually affirmed.

The world of language is again examined in the odd quasi-scholastic manner to which we have grown accustomed. I.A. Richards is attacked, as Pape was at the beginning of the poem, for suggesting English as the future universal language. After a few observations about Esperanto and the "vast international vocabulary which already exists," the poet lists more lists, of linguistic problems of etymology, history, dialects, and so on. More facts on linguistics follow. Then he suggests that perhaps the complex rather than the simple should be the climax of achievement; at this point in the poem it seems an obvious self-justification. Then comes more data having to do with the history, use, and diversity of words, languages, and writing. Cassirer's statement that "speech actually shapes and extends our experience" is used to affirm once more the essential power of language (61ff, *CP* 787ff).

The poet seems to be back in the same mire which he laughed at earlier, and once again he appears to stand back from his work in order to poke fun at himself. (A rarity; it should be treasured!) In a quotation from *Hudibras* he clearly refers to himself:

> But, when he pleased to shew't, his speech
> In loftiness of sound was rich;
> A Babylonish dialect
> Which learned pedants much affect;
> It was a party-coloured dress
> Of patch'd and pyballed languages:
> 'Twas Irish cut on Greek and Latin
> Like fustian heretofore on satin.
> It had an odd promiscuous tone,
> As if h' had talk'd three parts in one;
> Which made some think, when he did gabble,
> Th' had heard three labourers of Babel;
> Or Cerberus himself pronounce,
> A leash of languages at once. (65, *CP* 795)

But this is followed by yet more information about languages, songs, and music, ending thus:

> Yes, I will have all sorts
> Of excruciating *bruitist* music,
> *Simultaneist* poems,
> Grab-bags and clichés, newspaper clippings,
> Popular songs, advertising copy,
> And expressions of innocence,
> And abstract sounds – taking care
> That one of them never turns out to be
> Merely the Rumanian word for *schnapps*;
> And all dada, merz, fatagaga. (66-7, *CP* 795-6)

If this is where language is, one concerned with language must be concerned with these things, so that the poem, a collage construction of a type similar to that described here, is being justified at this point.

That this is not indiscriminate, supposedly, is indicated by the rejection of trivia such as "the Rumanian word for *schnapps*"; the poet insists he is working with something in mind rather than being a mere magpie after "total speech." He can laugh at himself – but almost immediately afterwards adopts a defiant tone of self-justification. MacDiarmid is not one to make apologies. So once more we find ourselves adrift upon a sea of lists and data, such as camel-names and types of Scottish stone, and the idea of mixing languages. As a bit of wishful thinking, after bemoaning his lack of Greek, he writes:

> Virgil salutes him, and Theocritus;
> Catullus, mightiest-brained Lucretius, each
> Greets him, their brother, on the Stygian beach;
> Proudly a gaunt right hand doth Dante reach – (67, *CP* 797)

Here the actual and ideal poets are juxtaposed. As if to reinforce the concept of the ideal poet he wants to be, MacDiarmid immediately follows with a description of the kind of poetry he wants. Then come a few observations about religion, a list of woods used to make a house (symbolizing words), and a list of Athenian theatre festivals (68, *CP* 798).

Abruptly he gives a reaffirmation:

> All the world's languages as I see them then ...
> Are like the Albani polyptych of Perugino,
> – How cool in its warmth,
> With its space continuous through the various panels,
> Felt through beautiful arches,
> Stretching to enchanted distances,
> Evoking freshness and fragrance,
> Bringing back to us those rare moments
> When, new to life,
> In the early hours of a summer morning,
> For an instant we tasted of Paradise. (69, *CP* 799)

The build-up to the final word should be noted – there is a skilful technique evident here, used to emphasize that the vision of world language is a vision of understanding itself. The continuous space stretching through "the various panels" reminds one of the "seamless garment," for example.

But, not surprisingly, this passage is only a respite. The list of linguistic bits continues, and, in contrast to the above, appear such mundane lines as the following:

... unlike Basque, its detailed study is now made possible
Thanks to Lieut-Col. Lorimer and Professor Morgenstierne,
By Instituttet for Sammenlignende Kulturforskning,
And we can delight in a difficult phonetic structure,
And a grammar which with its four gender classes
Its intricate pronominal prefixes and infixes,
And its complicated verbal system, vies in complexity
With that of any other language in the world. (70, *CP* 800)

Perhaps MacDiarmid is trying to give language epic status, but he fails to communicate the delight he is talking about.

The easy answer is still sought, as he reveals in a passage about Patrick Geddes who "juggled words like algebraic terms" to gain a "synthesis of all view points," a "description of living / That included or could include / Every act and fact, / Dream and deed, / Of all mankind on this planet, / Revealing more on one sheet of paper / Than whole volumes of science or philosophy" (71, *CP* 801-2). Here once more the poet indirectly affirms that an answer is graspable, that language can encompass all the essences and qualities of being-in-the-world. And once more he implies that language is somehow distinct from the world of phenomena, a possible repository for them.

In order to write, he suggests, one needs the language and the facts as well. More data follow, more lists, and finally this section of the poem draws to a close. He writes of his "rich egocentric bulimian vision," which reflects his desire to swallow the universe (like Jimsy the idiot). Then comes a fine description of the ideal he seeks:

– Ah, good it has been even for a moment to lift
The heavy silk curtains and look
Through the porphyry-framed windows of the palace of Buda ...
And good to handle from the carved bookcases
With crimson silk draperies, the books, all bound in silk,
The workmanship of whose silver clasps and corners
Is splendid as the miniatures to be found inside
Which display the rich imagination of the Renaissance
Blended with that of antiquity,
Graceful garlands of flowers and fruit,
Cupids riding on fawns or playing with rainbow-coloured butterflies,
Triton and nymphs sporting, and, as a border,
Antique gems, and delicate climbing plants with golden flowers ...
(72-3, *CP* 804)

Through his study of language, he has, momentarily, glimpsed his goal: words, printed pages, embedded in the splendid matrix of the absolute. It is MacDiarmid's "rich imagination" which is referred to here, as he expresses his vision of certainty and of himself having achieved it. The Renaissance refers to his own personal renaissance, although on another level the Scottish Renaissance could be what is being alluded to. MacDiarmid never seriously questions the possibility of his eventually attaining this vision.

This section ends, then, on an affirmative note, with tones of confidence. The poet is dazzled by the enormity and complexity of his medium. The movement in this section, as has been shown, depends upon the dichotomy of actual and ideal, and is rather more intellectual than poetic. The next section, "The World of Words," is a coda, an appendix or addendum to the first, and contains nothing which really adds to what has gone before. Points of interest along the way will be noted.

MacDiarmid begins by quoting Yeats, "Words alone are certain good," and affirms once again the potential power of language by speaking of the power of the exact word upon readers. Then comes a list of authorities on everything to do with words, and, in general, perception. Then there is a list of such things as "verbal reflexes," "colour associations," psychology in relation to word use, and then a statistical breakdown of types of language in poetry. The power of language is again affirmed, the complexity of interaction between words and the self is explored, and more lists follow for page after page (75ff, *CP* 805ff).

Once more he expresses the faith in a pattern to be discovered in the complex assortment of experiences which is his own life:

> But, taking my life as a whole,
> And hovering with the flight of the hawk
> Over its variegated landscape,
> I believe I detect certain quite definite "streams of tendency"
> In that unrolling map,
> Moving towards the unknown future.
> For one thing I fancy the manner I have allowed
> My natural impulses towards romance and mysticism
> To dominate me has led to the formation
> Of a curious gap or "lacuna"
> Between the innate and almost savage realism,
> Which is a major element in my nature,
> And the imaginative, poetical cult
> Whereby I have romanticised and idealized my life. (88, *CP* 821-2)

His life may be an "unrolling map," but he shows little signs of being able to read it. Understanding is still an undiscovered continent. The two "streams of tendency" he notes have been examined throughout this study; not only do they reflect intuition and knowledge, but also the ideal and the actual, and the gulf betwen the latter is, on one level, the "gap or 'lacuna'" he writes about.

A little further on he insists that the objective "astronomical universe" is only part of life (88, *CP* 822). His self, in-the-world, is obviously not going to be allowed to become an integer in some Cartesian scheme. Understanding, involving the astronomical universe, and even if objective in some senses (such as the "discovery" of a metaphysics, of the purpose of life), cannot reduce the self to just another phenomenon. MacDiarmid almost always insists upon the fundamental importance of the self, which is the undoubted reason why he attacks the scientific method in "Ode to All Rebels" and elsewhere,[15] even if he, himself, strives for a super-scientific detachment as in "On a Raised Beach."

> The vision of a perfect language is reiterated, one which expresses
>   the complex vision of everything in one,
> Suffering all impressions, all experience, all doctrines
> To pass through and taking what seems valuable from each
> No matter in however many directions
> These essences seem to lead. (88-9, *CP* 823)

All these essences will become facets of one gemstone, he says, echoing the lines of an earlier poem on Scotland as a polyhedron in the brain. Here the symbolic quality of stone briefly re-emerges, for he is directly equating understanding and the jewel (89, *CP* 823).[16]

After further examples of what he himself terms "a vast panoply of knowledge / That seems more and more fantastic" comes a series of passages centred on the image of the archer. Here all that MacDiarmid is getting at is encapsulated. The situation of a person trying to reach a target is given and factors such as winds, the bow, the clearness of the target, and so on, are mentioned. Amid a host of other allusions, the poet writes of archery in Japan as a spiritual exercise, the target being hit when the correct spiritual state has been reached. Then, with the acknowledged help of T.H. White, a subpoem on the death of Dylan Thomas takes shape. The crow of death took his arrow before it could reach its mark. The crow, more explicitly, comes to represent war. "And how I shall rejoice when the War is over," says the poet. (One can perhaps infer here that the section on Dylan Thomas, who died in 1953, has been inserted before an older passage written before the end of the Second World War.)

The war can be taken to refer to MacDiarmid's struggle, over and above any literal significance it may have, although any struggle in this poem, as has been stated, is fairly theoretical. The poet goes on to write of recovering the arrow of a giant bow strung by Arjuna, again referring to his ambitions for realizing his goal. This is clinched by a reference to Indians with stanza-forms shaped like a bow. The link beween mental and physical, between thought and the object of thought, is emphasized by a passage dealing with the actual mechanics of bow-making and arrow-making, including a list of woods and threads (90ff, CP 827ff).[17]

This series of passages forms the high point of the section. MacDiarmid's associationism is relatively controlled here, and results in a strong, coherent statement based upon the image of the archer, expressing the poet's situation as he sees it. But his world remains as chaotic as ever. It still eludes control and intuitive grasping:

> [I] have had to go at times, like the hare
> That "limp'd trembling through the frozen grass,"
> Amid the haunting swarm of half-things dissolving each into each,
> Changing and intermixing monstrously in a fluctuating putrescence.
>
> (95, CP 831)

What arrow could penetrate such a world? "The artist imitates the Creator and tries to achieve unity," he says, but such affirmation seems empty indeed when set beside this chaos. How is he to win though? And perhaps, after all,

> The vision is in no sense dynamic or prophetic.
> It is a vision of understanding, not creation;
> Of some vast wisdom deepening into twilight,
> The glimmering light of intuition
> Fading into mental complication ...

Perhaps,

> Even the subject-object antithesis
> Is only an approximation.
> Life is an element like other elements.
> ... Much less of a miracle
> Than is the fact of matter at all. (98-9, CP 835-6)

But the poet is expressing what proves to be only a passing doubt. He never rejects intuition entirely, nor the central role of self. Fears that his vision is dulling and darkening are quickly dispelled by ensuing affirmations of the potential of language, literature, and himself. He concludes this section with references to the immense mental possibilities of the human race, ending with the conception

> of what the process of literature could be,
> Something far more closely related
> To the whole life of mankind
> Than the science of stringing words together
> In desirable sequences. (102, *CP* 839-40)

It is not beauty or craftsmanship for its own sake that he seeks, but the unity of senses, heart, mind, action, and the whole world. And this, he affirms, is possible.

"The Snares of Varuna" introduces a political element into the poem, and from here on in MacDiarmid shifts focus from language itself to the general problems which he has in the past associated with his central poetic concerns, problems which, presumably, would cease to be problems when the ideal language, which is even capable of changing human nature, is found. The theme of this particular section is, at least to start with, the viciousness of capitalism. Varuna is like Eldridge Cleaver's "Omnipotent Administrator":

> The world is fast bound in the snares of Varuna ...
> ... The winkings of men's eyes
> Are all numbered by him; he wields the universe
> As gamesters handle dice. (103, *CP* 840)

Capitalism has no inbuilt concept of evolution towards a goal. It is merely the "art of teaching fish by slow degrees / To live without water." And yet, he avers, even if humanity in its present state were freed, we would be at a loss to know what to do:

> And the only hopeful element
> Evidences here and there in quarters
> Where even that was hardly to be hoped for
> Of suddenly awakened, and therefore bewildered, panic.
> Bren guns, Devoitine fighters,
> Pylons and petrol pumps,
> Tinned frogs, more laws,
> More licences, more verbots,
> More inspectors,
> More and redder red tape

In every phase of life.
But *everywhere*! (104-5, *CP* 843)

So the potential of humanity, indicated by a list of human types and a comment on the great sense-sensitivity of some people, is kept from realization by a squalid economic system. The potential of the individual (such as MacDiarmid?) is thwarted by a system which creates insanity. A list of mental aberrations seems to indicate what individuality means in the context of capitalism: madness, not self-realization.

In a sudden contrast, the poet expresses in a reflective passage the life that is open to us when freed of the trivial and oppressive life of economic, social, and spiritual deprivation:

> We must look at the harebell as if
> We had never seen it before.
> Remembrance gives an accumulation of satisfaction
> Yet the desire for change is very strong in us
> And change is in itself a recreation.
> To those who take any pleasure
> In flowers, plants, birds, and the rest
> An ecological change is recreative. (106, *CP* 844)

MacDiarmid reveals himself as a very strange communist indeed; his attack on capitalism has an unmistakeably anarchist ring to it, and here he sees himself leading the masses out of the capitalistic wilderness into a Utopian garden. "Come. Climb with me," he exhorts his supposed followers on the mountainside, and then describes different varieties of sheep. Clearly implicit here is his self-image as shepherd! The freedom he is offering the masses is, as in "The Glass of Pure Water," the freedom to face the essential problem of existence itself. "Everything is different, everything changes," he says – so that freedom is at once an affirmation and a challenge (106-7, *CP* 845). Capitalism prevents people from being aware of the chaos of experience that he, the poet, has resolutely faced. To come to grips with the world, it is necessary to become aware of it. The poet's own awareness is evidenced in part by the almost imagistic clarity of his natural descriptions; but it must be said that the garden recreation he offers the masses, supposedly to entice them from their stupor, is, if the poet's tortuous career is a sample of what "recreation" means, a decided pig in a poke.

This passage is followed by an excursion into Greek learning and philosophy, concerned with the possible resolution of divergent philosophies such as those of Plato and Aristotle. From awareness of the world we must progress to the concept of synthesis, he is saying. But as a passage on Mozart indicates, this desire for a synthesis (understanding) is fraught with dangers:

> It is infinitely protean.
> It means just what you mean.
> It is intangible, immaterial,
> Fitting your spirit like a glove.
> Then suddenly there will pass through you a tremor of terror.
> A moment comes when that tranquillity,
> That perfection, take on a ghastly ambiguity.
> That music still suggests nothing, nothing at all;
> It is still just infinitely ambiguous. (107-10, *CP* 845-9)

The revelation in Mozart escapes, his face becomes a mask whose "directness and clarity is [sic] completely baffling." Beware of illusion, the poet says. Just when understanding seems to have been attained, it is once more revealed that we are, as Sartre puts it, encompassed by nothingness. Directness and clarity, exemplified by the poet in his previously given natural description, reveal nothing. Everything becomes clear – but "infinitely ambiguous." Perfection is not perfection after all, but an illusion. Mozart's music and its pitfalls reflect MacDiarmid's fears for the poetry he wants which may, after all, not be what he wants at all. Everything is revealed – yet infinite uncertainty remains. Could MacDiarmid be indicating, alternatively, that he senses a contradiction between what he wants and the essential structure of consciousness "conceived as a lack of Being, a desire for Being" in Sartre's terminology? That, in other words, perfection, by the very nature of the self, is impossible? He concludes with an observation that is pure MacDiarmid:

> Puskin's Salieri who wanted
> To poison Mozart was right.
> He should have poisoned Pushkin too. (110, *CP* 849)

The fear of illusion, reflecting Kierkegaard's view that we are condemned to wait for revelation and can never have a guarantee that we have, in fact, had it, is reinforced as a theme in a passage on Adalbert Stifter which, despite the learned footnotes, is taken from another *Times Literary Supplement* review (110, *CP* 850).[18] The argument of this passage is that apparent harmony can hide fearful struggles; that, in other words, an illusory resolution of the problem of existence, in MacDiarmid's continuing context, is a fool's paradise. Continuing, the poet observes, on the subject of angling, that striking too soon loses the fish. The poet must not leap to conclusions, but must wait for certainty to dawn on him. He must be on his guard against premature claims to success, for this is the essence of failure. Waiting for revelation, being patient and allowing trivia and false clues to fall by the wayside of their own accord is the theme here:

> There is a genius
> In literature ... like the Zambesi crocodile
> That keeps its powerful jaws wide open
> What time a bird hops about in the gape
> Picking food from between the teeth;
> The bird is never injured. The crocodile
> Appreciates its service as a toothpick. (111, *CP* 850-1)

The crocodile is the poet, his jaws wide open to swallow the universe; but he must not close them prematurely, or else he will drive away the spirit of literature (the bird). The poet's capacities are kept at their best by his perpetual openness, which allows the genius to work in him. If MacDiarmid is not referring to intuition here, which, by penetrating beneath phenomenal chaos, separates that which is important from that which is valueless and "sticks in the teeth," dulling the power of the poet/crocodile, an alternative is that he is suggesting that understanding, the "genius" perhaps, reveals itself in a process – but this, of course, is much the same thing.

This section ends with MacDiarmid returning to the image of the angler, and affirming his own correct attitude in not jumping to premature conclusions. He says when he fishes it is for the exotic, the uncatchable, and gives a list of bigger and bigger fish, concluding,

> ... and even then
> I'd remember with Herman Melville
> That behind Leviathan
> There's still the kraken,
> And no end to our "ontological heroics."
> And McCaig [sic] has laughed and said
> "Let me see you catch anything yet
> Big enough not to throw in again."[19] (111-12, *CP* 851)

The white whale was an illusory understanding which, when run down, brought only tragedy. The poet is willing to bide his time until he has the biggest fish of all on his line.

This section of *James Joyce* is remarkably coherent, but the unfolding is more logical than is due to the poem's taking its own shape in an organic fashion. There seems to be almost an imposed development here, a step-wise contrivedness, a self-conscious working out of an argument. And yet this is not entirely so. The transition from "men" in general to the "I" of MacDiarmid himself is subtly accomplished and seems quite natural. Besides putting his supposed concern for the rest of humanity in perspective, this modulation from outer to inner is organically conceived and utterly unselfconscious. What is more, the use of language in this poem is relatively skilful; the spirit of capitalism is captured in flat, prosaic language which seems exactly right for it, and which contrasts with the intense language with which MacDiarmid evokes his own sense of situation, an intensity he explicitly offers to the masses in a rather self-conscious manner. The dull and the tedious are thus effectively compared to the alive and the intense by means of language itself, and once more there seems no trace of self-consciousness in the transition. Finally, imagery such as that of the angler, while obvious in itself, nevertheless provides the imagination with anchoring points which are frequent enough so that the elements of the poem are related to each other within an imaginative context far more cohesive than in (for example) the two previous sections of the poem.

The following section, "The Meeting of the East and the West," echoing the "Poems of the East-West Synthesis," is not nearly so satisfactory. The theme is synthesis: MacDiarmid says his aim is the unity of heaven and earth. But he presents instead a gingerly exploration of German scholarship on Indian texts. All of this remains only a potential source of illumination. One is not misled by this, for example:

> Some interpreters of Buddhism, such as F.O. Schräder,
> Regard the "Trishnâ" as a metaphysical centre-point
> Of Buddhistic doctrine, and thus give it a position
> Coinciding with Schopenhauer's will as the pith of every individual.
> But this interpretation does not, in my opinion,
> Correspond with the facts. (115, *CP* 855)

A little later we are offered two untransliterated lines of Sanskrit (117, *CP* 856). Here is an ideal MacDiarmid once again, as learned as Ezra Pound, who is, in fact, mentioned in this section (117, *CP* 857). The poet concludes with a brief mention of Chinese language and music (118, *CP* 857). Here the East functions as a symbol of unity contrasting with the chaos of the Western world. It is the source of influence which led to the achievements of Wagner, Nietzsche, and Goethe (113, 116, *CP* 852, 855-6). The East, as for Herman Hesse in quite a different way, is timeless and unified. At the outset of the poem, MacDiarmid writes of the *Shakuntala* poem and of the errors which have crept into the original; a sort of fall in literary terms, a unity become many, a "gigantic maze / Of faulty knowledge, indirections, and distortions of all kinds" (113, *CP* 852). Thus the East for the poet becomes a symbol of the timeless certainty he seeks. But as poetry this section suffers from the accruing of material which is not handled enough, and from the self-conscious posturing which seriously detracts from the authenticity of his expression. The use of the literary analogy to express the idea of a fall has at best only an intellectual appeal. It is worthwhile comparing this to the direct imaginative impact of "The Eemis Stane" which bears a similar concept.

The next section, "England Is Our Enemy," brings into the poem another series of concerns which are familiar. Here he attacks English literature and English literary criticism, the latter being lampooned in a long witty passage which does not seem to have originated with him. (The style is not his; in two places, once by implication, he refers to English literature as though he were of the nation which produced it, and refers to "our business men" when he clearly means English businessmen. "We" is applied to the English arts, and "our writers" clearly refers to English writers (123ff, *CP* 863ff). It is impossible to believe that MacDiarmid himself could be guilty of such slips of the pen, whereas such incidentals might easily be overlooked in a passage the general import of which makes it useful to him.)

The final section of the poem is "Plaited like the Generations of Men," which begins with a long, slightly adapted passage taken from Ferruccio Busoni's essay "The Realm of Music: An Epilogue to the New Aesthetic."[20] In this context it celebrates the underlying unity of things in terms of music (always equated with poetry for MacDiarmid). Then he introduces the image of the "hair that's plaited / Like the generations of men": "All the knowledge is woven in neatly / So that the plaited ends come to the hand" (132, *CP* 872).[21] This is what MacDiarmid has wanted from the start, and which continues to elude him. The promise that he "will again bind the braid together," a variation of an assertion made throughout his work, seems at this point at once defiant and pathetic (134n, *CP* 874). It is not at all surprising that, as the end of this vast poem (the longest single poem he has ever produced) approaches, the old doubts re-emerge. He writes of

– The reflection of ideas and values
Not yet wholly assimilated by the sensibility,
So that I seem to be resolving my conflicts
By a kind of verbal self-hypnosis
– Communicating an excitement that resides
Too much in a certain use of language
And too little in the ordering of materials?
Am I only fobbing myself off
With a few more of those opiate-like phrases
Whose repetition so readily operates
As a substitute for discovery –
Instead of realising the concept
Of an ultimate metaphysical scheme
Under which we have to suppose
A triadic movement of the Universe ...

He continues,

Have I failed in my braid-binding
At this great crisis
... At this moment when braidbinding as never before,
The creation of the seamless garment,
Is the poet's task? (134-5, CP 875-6)

These doubts are followed by a long series of affirmations which
bring the whole poem to a close. There is unity, he insists, in all the
"fleeting accidents of a man's life / And its external shows... / ...irrelate
and incongruous" (137, CP 878). All he has to do is to discover a way
of winning through to it. The systems of others are incomplete; he
lists philosophies with their shortcomings. Another possibility is
proposed as to why understanding remains hidden:

... nature may be but imperfectly formed
In the bosom of chaos, and reason in us
Imperfectly adapted to the understanding of nature. (138, CP 880)

Yet, even so, it may be possible to discover "the secret of peace though
bereft / Of Spinoza's consolation – the bare rationality of the
universe." Perhaps religion holds the key:

... perhaps the only solution
Lies in the faith, or the mystical perception
That the welter of frustration in the parts

Is instrumental to some loftier perfection
In the universe as a whole? (139, CP 881)

But he is grasping at a straw here and he knows it. He cannot bring himself to withdraw from the world in favour of the possibility of pure revelation, for he could wait forever to discover the "loftier perfection." This for MacDiarmid could be the coward's way out:

Ah! no, no! Intolerable end
To one who set out to be independent of faith
And of mystical perception. (139, CP 881)

Another possibility is that expressed in "Diamond Body," a section of which appears here, namely that one can break up the phenomena of nature and reassemble them according to one's will (140, CP 882).[22] But this merely begs the question. What is this will? How, no matter how powerful the will, does he know what to do?

The philosophical concept of necessity remains. There must be some purpose behind it all:

Yet, as Gaudapapa says, even as a bed,
Which is an assembly of frame, mattress, bedding and pillows,
Is for another's use, not for its own,
And its several component parts render no mutual service,
Thence it is concluded that there is a man who sleeps upon the bed
And for whose sake it was made; so this world
Of words, thoughts, memories, scientific facts, literary arts
Is for another's use. (141, CP 884)

The stuff of the world, transmuted into these words, thoughts, and so on, forms a coherent unity in terms of the poet, whom it is for. Together they comprise what the poet strives for, "the super-objective, / The final reality to which human life can attain" (142, CP 884). The "super-objective" is Being, embodying the subjective and the objective in a synthesis. A little further on, he promises that the bed will be filled (143, CP 886). This could come from a temporalized revelation: in embryological development, secreting tubules in the developing kidney meet collecting tubules in answer to a "mysterious 'call.'" So too, suggests MacDiarmid, it is with human and artistic evolution (143-4, CP 887-8). That is, we are evolving towards understanding through history. As pointed out in chapter 3, this evolutionary theory is a projection or symbol of MacDiarmid's own sense of potential. Evolution is a concept he imposes upon his strivings in order to justify them. He is in fact suggesting the likelihood of the process being completed in him.

MacDiarmid concludes this section and the poem as a whole with a series of fragmentary observations, such as "The supreme reality is visible to the mind *alone*," emphasizing that he is correct in what he is doing, that he can achieve this as a poet of the type he has set out to be (144, *CP* 888). So close to the end, such protestations seem hollow indeed, and the poet, taking his leave of James Joyce (using the Peruvian word for goodbye, and, almost inevitably, digressing on the disparities in South American Spanish, thus implying he has not yet given up his labours), finishes on a peculiarly ambiguous note:

> "Non me rebus conjugere [sic] conor!"
> Sab thik chha. (144, *CP* 889)

("I won't let things get the better of me." "Everything's OK" [Gurkhali].)[23] These phrases, like the last faint radio messages of an explorer who has become hopelessly lost, convey, more powerfully perhaps than any other lines in MacDiarmid's work, a profound sense of spiritual tragedy, a courageous defiance in the face of impossible odds.

The last section, for the most part, and indeed most of the poem itslf, is an intellectual definition and re-definition of a situation which has become so conscious and oppressive that the imagination is scarcely free to act. The often tedious and hollow affirmations, that a goal exists for the poet to reach in order to found himself, tinged sometimes with despair and sometimes with arrogance, reduce through repetition the intensity such affirmation should possess. Certainly the poem is in no way didactic, being directed at his own situation, not at those of his readers. At the most he only wants us to be impressed with him; he is not trying to teach us anything, or at least the poem does not suggest anything of the kind. His quotations, his lists, and so on are exhibits, counters, bits of material, an array of gadgets, and appear as such. But this is hardly a mitigation.

The poem is divided into six sections, as has been seen, which bring together all the concerns which have preoccupied MacDiarmid throughout his career, although the Scottish question is noticeably underemphasized almost to extinction. The first section establishes the theme, the potential of language, and the concept of a world language, the material the poet needs in order to write the kind of poetry he wants. The second provides a series of afterthoughts to the first. The next three parts of the poem introduce political and cultural concerns, and the last section is an attempted conclusion, although it may well be asked precisely what is being concluded. For the poet, having seen a vision of the plaited hair, finds that he is solely responsible for braiding it himself; and he never really begins the task. The question "Have I failed in my braid-binding?" is thus doubly significant. It is a rhetorical gesture conveying a sense of doubt; if, after such efforts, no braid can be found, is it possible to perform his task? But at the same time the question itself is deceiving, for MacDiarmid has made no effort in this poem to do any braiding beyond relating his various concerns to each other and to the central problem of existence. There is no struggle here, only a continuing attempt to delineate what the object of struggle should be after the means of struggle, world language, has somehow been obtained. The question therefore serves the purpose of characterizing what has preceded it. By dramatically, in fact melodramatically, suggesting failure, the poet is actually conferring epic status upon a poem which does not possess it. For the poem has a hero of epic proportions, but one who fights no real battles. The effect of this question, however, is to suggest that he has been mortally wounded on the field of honour.

The six sections are not linked by a movement from one to the other, but by a common preoccupation. The bulk of the poetry consists of innumerable lists and references, which are the "sure ground for his feet," a bedrock of data offering a kind of foundation upon which the rest of the work is enacted. This material defines the world he is trying to encompass, comprising the "stony limits" within whose bounds his material is secure and total. The lists and references contain in themselves the affirmation that all there is to be known about language can be known, and that the world language the poet seeks can be discovered within their perimeter. As in "The Kind of Poetry I Want," he is mapping out areas to be covered (giving the impression, certainly, that he has covered them already) and these areas become the absolutes which give his search an authority and justification. The data and vocabulary are "hard," and in the context of the poem each item and list is a sign or indicator of a section of knowledge or experience equally hard, entire, well-defined. Mac-Diarmid's technique here is extended metonymy. Every reference to an authority, every piece of information, every list, signifies a little absolute, an area of completeness, part of the jigsaw puzzle and not open to question. They provide a substitute for a metaphysical system of belief or a universal myth. Of course these areas for the most part are known only potentially to MacDiarmid. They are small leaps of faith. He is coasting on them, taking them as read, and it is only the ideal MacDiarmid who is completely familiar with them.

Upon this bedrock, then, which the poet assumes to be firm (an assumption similar to that about the facts, the latter assumed to be hard and true, bits of the thing-in-itself made the poet's own by being transmuted into language, building blocks of understanding), is erected the rest of the poem, consisting of a continual definition of his existence in terms of the actual / ideal dichotomy. Even the MacDiarmid of the poem is very often an ideal, a MacDiarmid farther along the road to truth than is actually the case. But the theme of the poem, never in doubt, is not always mere reiteration; as the passage on the hawthorn tree indicates, the poet is able on occasion to express all the intensity his longing for the ideal should warrant. The truly grim business of documentation does throw into relief the poet's essential concern, his alternating moods of exultation and uncertainty combining to indicate the enormity and frustrations of the self-defined task he never begins. The poet gives the impression that what he seeks is just around the corner, that he can nearly reach out and seize it, but the poem amounts to talking about the means of doing this. He is now writing of the kind of language he wants in order to write the kind of poetry he wants.

In his search for the ideal language, for the ideal poetry, not to mention the ideal Scot (see *Lucky Poet*, 252-3), MacDiarmid has produced a poem which sums up the concerns of a lifetime. As a combination of lists, quotations, vocabulary, anecdotes, descriptive passages, borrowings, facts, and opinions, the poem is an excellent example of serial collage, an arrangement of material around the ever-present "I," bits which he has seized and recorded as of importance to him.

A prominent feature of the poem is the extensive use of borrowed substance, the significance of which has been noted throughout this study. By means of this practice he is able to incorporate intensity, imagery, feelings, ideas, and so on, ready-made as it were. For just like the facts, or the words in Jamieson's *Dictionary*, this material is available for use. There is only the world and MacDiarmid. If he can use facts derived from the observations of others, he can in like fashion use the writings of others, which are equally part of the poet's external world. If he uses material to give a false impression of his learning, it is to present a picture of the kind of poet he wants and feels himself capable of becoming. But he seldom makes it difficult to find him out, frequently even providing acknowledgment of sources. This is all part of the grim business of documentation. Most of the borrowed matter in *James Joyce* is given a new emphasis and context which enriches it; and it is no such passage in itself, but the patch-work effect of the poem as a whole, a loose arrangement which extends to the relation among its six sections, that one sees.

In keeping with this attitude towards found objects, whether these are found in the pockets of others or not, MacDiarmid has put together a poem of such objects, material to be kept within reach for the time when their potential is to be realized in the creation of world language. This is a poem of great energy, a courageous facing of dry and intractable material, in which the poet refuses to be distracted from what he sees as his crucial aims, even if at some points he seems aware that his problem is an insoluble one. But as a poem it is a profound failure.

This is not because understanding has not been achieved, of course, for such non-achievement, like unrequited love for the court poets, is merely the reflection of a given condition of his situation; besides, this poem is not an attempt to win understanding, and therefore is not a failure to do so. It fails because MacDiarmid's self-consciousness has led to a fetishistic obsession with his medium. Language has here become an abstract category; words have become objects which the poet observes rather than uses. Having placed language at a distance, it becomes as opaque as the stones in "On a Raised Beach." It is now an inaccessible plenitude. In order to possess words once more, he tries to approach them through knowledge, but the enormity of the task makes this a gesture only. "Words" become the category "language," and "language" becomes an ideal. MacDiarmid's relation to this medium becomes discursive rather than intuitive. This is the poem of one who has ceased to be a poet, in the same way that a carpenter who begins to be obsessed with the quiddity of hammer and nails ceases to be a carpenter, remaining only a potential one.

In *James Joyce* MacDiarmid has allowed his self-consciousness to paralyze him. As H.G. Porteous puts it, "the poetry is less a *fait accompli* than a pious hope."[24] W.S. Merwin points out that "the work ... does not seem to be going anywhere at all," and calls it "a series of notes for a poem."[25] He is quite right; the fact that this outlined poem, or rather, outlined language for a poem, cannot be achieved is neither here nor there. Poems can be written about poetry, but *James Joyce* is too much the bald statement. The construction process is overly intellectualized. By making language and poetry ideals, by making the very use of language a subject of conscious scrutiny, he loses his voice. Where the poetry of facts established a separation between the poet and his environmental material, so that he spent more time affirming the power of facts and describing what he wanted his poetry to be than he did in using the material he had amassed, *James Joyce* indicates a fatal rift between MacDiarmid and the very substance of his craft.

In the world of words he wanders about in a daze, handling a few objects, exulting in the fact that all of them are accessible to him, piling them up in what quickly becomes a tedious and repetitive exercise, but able at the end of it all only to affirm a potential to the realization of which he is unable actively to commit himself. Far from braid-binding, this poem is merely an essay on hair. Having created the ideal of a language and poetry, MacDiarmid has robbed himself of confidence; there seems no justification for any activity in the absence of the understanding he craves so desperately. Thus the poem is about activity but is itself a less than creative compilation for the most part. It is the inevitable result of the continual action of a corrosive self-consciousness which has denied his imagination the authority to act. Having reified his role he can no longer engage in it. He is limited to carrying out an endless inventory, clinging to the phantasmal hope, like Mr Micawber, that something will turn up. On occasion he is still able to convey his feeling of separation from the ideal, but too often he merely tells us about it. Despite isolated passages where the poet recaptures something of the old spontaneity, and the relative merits of "The Snares of Varuna," the poem as a whole is a helpless, prolonged stutter.

CHAPTER SIX

Conclusion: The Problems of the Modern Poet

A, a, a, Domine Deus

I said, Ah! what shall I write?
I inquired up and down.
(He's tricked me before
with his manifold lurking-places.)
I looked for His symbol at the door.
I have looked for a long while
    at the textures and contours.
I have run a hand over the trivial intersections.
I have journeyed among the dead forms
    causation projects from pillar to pylon.
I have tired the eyes of the mind
    regarding the colours and lights.
I have felt for His wounds
    in nozzles and containers.
I have wondered for the automatic devices.
I have tested the inane patterns
    without prejudice.
I have been on my guard
    not to condemn the unfamiliar.
For it is easy to miss Him
    at the turn of a civilization.

I have watched the wheels go round in case I
might see the living creatures like the appearance
of lamps, in case I might see the living God projected
from the Machine. I have said to the perfected steel,
be my sister and for the glassy towers I thought I felt
some beginnings of His creature, but *A, a, a, Domine Deus*,
my hands found the glazed work unrefined and the terrible
crystal a stage-paste ... *Eia Domine Deus*.
(David Jones, from *The Sleeping Lord and Other Fragments*)

Martin Heidegger, writing of Hölderlin in an essay entitled "Hölderlin and the Essence of Poetry," explains his choice of this one poet to illustrate the nature of poetry: "Hölderlin has not been chosen because his work, one among many, realizes the universal essence of poetry, but solely because Hölderlin's poetry was borne on by the poetic vocation to write expressly of the essence of poetry. For us Hölderlin is in a pre-eminent sense the *poet of the poet.*"[1]

In dealing with the problems faced by a modern poet, Hugh MacDiarmid has been chosen for a similar reason. MacDiarmid is the poet of the modern poet. His continual and explicit preoccupation with the theme of potential should not make one overlook the fact that this is always seen in terms of poetry, that it is poetry above all with which he is concerned. He is constantly absorbed by the questions, What shall I write? How shall I write? For what shall I write? The writing itself is never in question. It is a "given" of his existence. It is his essential self-consciousness as a poet which makes it valuable to examine his work in order to explore the problems of the modern poet. Because he is so concerned with what he is doing he faces these problems explicitly in a way that greater figures such as Yeats and Pound do not. As a poet he self-consciously confronts his age and reveals it to us as more than one man's vision, as an environment in fact within which many of his contemporaries live and breathe. By doing so he gives insight into much of the poetry of the latter.

The introduction attempted to provide a general description of the modern environment and the problems it raises. The manner in which modern poets engage themselves in this environment will now be considered. In a world where the word "truth" carries with it connotations of outrageous presumption, poets are left on their own to find a content and values for their work which they can accept as "true." The poet has a horror of illusions. It is the curious paradox of the age that truth is denied but in a very real sense demanded as well. The poet feels called upon to find meaning in an era which is hostile to metaphysical schemes. Poets who attempt a world view have no generally accepted frame available to them, and they are consequently forced to take note of the times they live in without reference to a transcendental reality. But to justify what is in essence an arbitrary choice of values, they must do more than merely observe. They have become empiricists; their attitude towards phenomena becomes almost scientific as they weigh observations and attempt to draw poetic conclusions from them.

Samuel Beckett, as a novelist, poet, and playwright, finds it possible to hold a mirror up to chaos, and finds justification in his art by affirming the truth of absurdity. Is there not something characteristically modern in the fact that he builds structures to affirm that structures are meaningless, that he produces ordered work to affirm universal disorder? It is like reasoning that reason is impossible. In a sense he has to stand above the world in order to judge it. Art is still, albeit implicitly, given supra-mundane status. The artist retains his role as giver of truth. The only way an artist can rejoin the chaotic world is to forget about creativity and produce gibberish, as the Dadaists did. But Dadaism was a short-lived movement, because gibberish is fundamentally boring and the point is made with few examples. Artists, to remain artists in a world with no apparent sense, purpose, order, or meaning of any kind, must, in the absence of a spiritual network of values, become their own transcendental realms. They must stand apart from the chaos they observe in order to avoid being swallowed up in it. To create, they must bring meaning into a world without meaning. T.S. Eliot doesn't merely present the Waste Land as a lot of fragments, but introduces a persona, Tiresias, who wanders about in it, a figure from Greek myth transplanted into the twentieth century. Tiresias gives coherence to the Waste Land both as poem and as the modern environment which is the poem's theme. He reacts to it, stands distinct from it, and the Waste Land is thus placed in a perspective. It acquires a meaning. As in "Gerontion," the modern chaos is set against what things were once like. Tiresias, although jaded, although lacking a clear identity (an idea conveyed here by sexual ambivalence), is nevertheless the representtive of another age which, unlike our own, had a mythology. Eliot himself, to write the requiem which the poem is, had to stand at a remove from the chaos he observed around him.

Poets, on their own, must pretend to be outside the world they confront. They must themselves become bringers of truth or meaning. But of course they are in-the-world, not at a remove from it. What is more, they often feel that any meaning they discover or create in the world has to be referred back to the world in that it has to be justified. Why do poets so often feel called upon to justify what is in fact their own creation in terms of something else? Simply because to face chaos they feel it necessary to have some sure ground for their feet. Fearing illusion, they want proof. Even revelation must be put to the test. Poets, like anyone else, crave certainty; they seek a relationship to the world which is absolute. To admit that they themselves are authors of meaning is to deny that poetry is anything more than arbitrary. But the age frowns on arbitrariness as all ages have done; no major poet of this age or of any other has taken this as a premise. In one way or another, truth is held to transcend the poet's existence or identity.

The very medium may be a factor here, since language is not the poet's own invention and does possess a structure. This might well give rise to a certain confusion, where a sense of order in the world is in fact derived from certain aspects of language itself. But there is no obvious meaning, no easily intelligible order arising from any source, which the modern poet can use. Where Dante, for example, could refer his values to the absolute of the Christian cosmic scheme, modern poets more often find themselves engaged in a search for meaning in their own experiences of the world they live in. Dante's search ended; the modern poet's search never ends. Even adopting a metaphysical scheme turns out to be a long and often arduous process which almost never resolves the gnawing sense of doubt. Perhaps only W.H. Auden managed to achieve a sense of being at ease in his world, a vantage-point from which he could view the rest of the world in comfort.

W.B. Yeats created such a scheme, but felt it necessary to justify it in his book *A Vision*, which is an attempt to give a personal mythology an objective status. Eliot, confronting the Waste Land, withdrew into a process of realizing Christianity, but never even at the height of his confrontation with it did he hold it up as the ultimate truth. He, like Pound, was concerned with rescuing fragments from it, values which the modern age threatens (the theme of "Gerontion" is this very threat) but which are a viable, if shaky, alternative. The modern age, for Eliot and Pound, disproved nothing; for them it was a destructive age, not an age free of illusions. For David Jones, too, there are only fragments left, but their substance, not the fragmentation, is where the truth lies. In one way or another poets such as Eliot, Pound, and Jones sing of the past, discerning vague shapes and meanings among the ruins. The modern environment is a cause for great sadness, but it is not "true." For Franz Kafka there is no readily available meaning in the chaos which surrounds us, and yet the existence of such meaning is continually affirmed. A situation, seemingly a random occurrence, is paralleled again and again in *Amerika*; there is no Aristotelian law of probability or necessity here, no plot in the usual sense, no beginning, middle, or end, merely a series of parallel situations indicating an order beyond reach, a connecting principle rendering the proceedings even more absurd. The existence of the castle (truth) is never in doubt in *The Castle*, nor is the existence of law doubted in *The Trial*. Kafka's pessimism arises, not out of the conviction that no truth exists, but out of our inability to grasp or recognize it.

Only the phenomenologists and the existentialist philosophers such as Heidegger and Sartre have been willing to start with the fact of human consciousness alone as the basis of understanding. *Dasein* ("being-there") or the *Pour-soi*, not truth or God, are all that one has available. The world is contingent. There is no inherent purpose or meaning in it at all. It is not too risky to assert that such philosophy is characteristically modern, despite the fact that some Greek philosophy, notably Epicureanism, has something in common with it. Faced with an environment apparently without meaning, these philosophers are willing to adopt the premise that it is in fact meaningless. They seek to clarify by description the situation of being-in-the-world. Such a methodically expressed preoccupation (and Gabriel Marcel eschews even the systematic or methodical exposition of his philosophy, feeling that to do so denies the reality he is trying to describe) illustrates the absence of a modern mythology or system of explanation which can be tested. They are realists in the sense that they take the world as they find it. They are descriptive in the sense that they describe the phenomenon of consciousess without asking the question why.

Logical positivism, the obverse of existentialism, is also an expression of concern with the modern environment. To Carnap and his circle, "philosophy is an activity," and that activity consists in part of determining what statements can logically be made and what statements are mere nonsense. The feverish concern with language, and with the oasis of logic in a Waste Land of nonsense, as well as the subsequent attempt to provide science with a firm logical foundation, are characteristically modern; this philosophy, as surely as existentialism, is a response to the age.

Modern poets, if they do not question the fact of their own existence, are full of questions about the world they live in and their own roles as poets. They are not philosophers. They are preoccupied with truth (a notion of little value to modern mainstream philosophy), which is missing or hidden, and for this reason much modern poetry seems to take the search for a world view as a predominant theme. Two apparent counter examples can be noted here: the Imagist movement and the concrete poetry movement. The poetry of the Imagists is a series of still photographs, that of the concrete poets a series of objects in which language is reduced to design. The first is an attempt to reproduce the clarity of an observation without interpreting it, a process of transmutation in which the poetry becomes purely descriptive. But language is not sacrificed to the observation. The poetry is not descriptive in the scientific or philosophical sense. Imagism is an experiment with language, an exploration of what language can do. It is a redefinition of poetry. Concrete poetry, however, reflects despair of language. Whatever its respectable origins, in the poetry of George Herbert, for example, concrete poetry is a denial of the function of language. The anteriority of language, implied or asserted by most modern poets, is rejected. Words and letters become a series of appearances. This is one extreme of a wide range of linguistic experimentation which characterizes much of modern poetry from Doughty to the present.

One notices in the two cases just described that language is the central topic of concern. Both schools are in a sense responses to language. Concrete poetry, certainly, is a negative response; it is a valid and exciting art form, but it is a moot point whether it can be called poetry at all. Nevertheless, language has, even for concrete poets, a distinct reality, if one which they are struggling to dissolve. The Imagists and the concrete poets share with other modern poets a concern with language, and are dealing quite clearly, if implicitly, with questions of the poet's role in-the-world. A world view is implied in their very methods. In fact these movements are not counter examples at all, but complementry to the other modern poetry which has been discussed. Both movements are responses to the Waste Land via language.

A number of modern writers explicitly equate art with truth. Pirandello, in *Sei personaggi in cerca d'autore*, and Yeats with his "Byzantium" are examples. The realm of art becomes extra- or supramundane, as was noted earlier in reference to Samuel Beckett. It becomes an end in itself. The order in art does not exist merely as a lattice whereby communication becomes possible, the explanation of the order in Sartre's and Heidegger's methodical treatises, but rather as its own object. In the realm of creative writing, it is obviously language which is the stuff of art, and the world of language is often given a status above the world "out there." "Words alone are certain good," said Yeats. Words cease to be part of the "concrete world of existents" and achieve, in Harold Rosenberg's phrase, a sacred otherness. (MacDiarmid writes, "Language towers above the ruins.") They become icons, and sometimes fetishes. Even for Imagists and concrete poets, language retains a reality distinct from other things. By adopting it as of central concern, it is removed from the chaos of the Waste Land and given a certain pre-eminence. Imagists attempt to turn the world into language, if only by a piece-meal process. Concrete poets attempt to do the reverse, but are forced to recognize the distinctness of language from the rest of the world in order to do so. They reject the anteriority of language yet assent to it implicitly.

It is now possible to understand how it is that poets are able to exist outside the world they inhabit and confront. They take refuge behind the screen of language. The world of language is a world where order can exist. From such a vantage point the world "out there" can be judged. The poet can stand apart. Order can be instilled into chaos through language. The world, become language, can be dealt with; the pieces can be put together again. The underlying unity of all things, felt to be there, can be revealed through language. Williams's microcosmic *Paterson*, Joyce's *Finnegans Wake* (a poem by Sartre's definition, anyway), Pound's *Cantos*, Jones's *The Anathemata*, Eliot's *The Waste Land*, Olson's *Maximus Poems*, and MacDiarmid's *In Memoriam James Joyce* all reflect in one way or another this belief. Language is the material out of which the world, at one remove, can be rebuilt. The contents of the world, all in a jumble, can be gone over and sorted out by the poet who stands above the lot.

One can notice two recurrent aspects of modern poetry, the striving for a world view based upon some principle or scheme as yet unknown, and what amounts to an obsession with the potency of the language material. The scraps of foreign languages in *The Waste Land* amount to incantations; the ideograms in Pound's Chinese cantos are likewise relics to conjure with. e e cummings made the world of language his home, and through his unique exploration of that realm came to grips with the rest of the world at second hand. It has already been shown what MacDiarmid makes of language. And through this magic medium, poets strive to make the world their own. Auden and Eliot turned to Christianity after excursions into the Waste Land (for the former a Waste Land of a socio-political nature, and for the latter one of culture and values), but poetry remains as the means by which this scheme is realized or possessed. Pound and Jones searched among the ruins for relics, once more to be handled in terms of poetry, through language. By juxtaposing fragments they seem to invite us to join in the search for the hidden meaning. Poetry holds the promise of revelation. Chaos is not ultimate, only an eclipse. Joyce and Yeats seek to apply myth to the modern environment, and once more they stand apart from the world in order to bring meaning into it. Poets are often preoccupied with metaphysical questions, and by such preoccupation they must needs stand apart from the phenomenal world, even if it is pointed out that this is a fallacy, that they are in-the-world, that language is a category of things of a being qualitatively no different from the being of other things. The content for so many modern poets has to be the entire world because they are concerned with the underlying meaning and are unable to trust interior revelation. The world becomes a series of clues, in which a pattern might be revealed as the survey continues, or a series of examples to justify an as yet unknown argument. The meaning could leap into focus as a result of thorough investigation: although this proposition is of dubious philosophical merit, to say the least, it has a certain aesthetic usefulness in that it allows poets to explore their world in what they feel to be not an arbitrary manner but one with some essential justification. Poets, engaged in-the-world, strive for something beyond it and hold up their art as, at least potentially, the residence of the meaning. At the very least their art consists of "getting their houses in order," although Kafka explains rather convincingly that this is an endless task in itself![2] This latter concept will be returned to below.

With this introduction, necessarily and yet perhaps unsatisfactorily sketchy, Hugh MacDiarmid's contribution to modern poetry can now be summed up. What has been described is a tendency in modern poetry which can be called mainstream in that the poets which have been discussed are major figures who seem to share common problems, and who in many ways epitomize what was described in the introduction as the phenomenon of modernism. MacDiarmid, in his poetry, lays bare these problems.

A survey of MacDiarmid's poetry indicates very clearly that the Scottish question is for him a means to a more fundamental end. Scottishness is for him a standpoint, possible firm ground which is subject to an exhaustive series of affirmations and reaffirmations. He is never content merely to be a Scot for very long, but feels it necessary to define what this means. To say "I am a Scot" in a sense merely exchanges one uncertainty for another. Hence his attempts to pin down the Scottish essence can be seen in his work over and over again. Relying upon Gregory Smith's study of Scottish literature, he adopted the "Caledonian antisyzygy" as a partial definition of Scottishness: the evidence of this antisyzygy in his early work, his lyrics and *Drunk Man*, can be said to be due at least in part to his acceptance of this definition. Even the theme of the drunken Scotsman in *Drunk Man* finds its origin, as noted earlier, in the first chapter of Smith's book. Scottishness is soon shown to be an ideal rather than a fact; to MacDiarmid the majority of his fellow countrymen are not Scots at all, except in name. The faith in a Scottish noumenon, which has been noted in this study, never seems to sit comfortably for long with the poet. He is always at pains to produce evidence that it exists. For all the mystical elements in his work, MacDiarmid is the practical man of experience, seeking verification in the outside world for his intuitive flashes. He accepts very little as "given" at any time. Wanting to make a unity of the "routh o' contrairies" that is Scotland, he finds that the problem widens to become universal. He realizes that "If there is ocht in Scotland that's worth ha'en / There is nae distance to which it's unattached." In attempting to reveal the Scottish essence he reveals instead his existential plight, which is far more fundamental than problems of nationality. His separation from certainty is a separation from the whole of Being.

This separation, this experience of *Geworfenheit*, is his essential theme almost from the beginning of his career, as has been indicated. Scottishness, as a channel to Being, remains as elusive as Being itself. For all his writing of national psychology, national physiology, the relation between the landscape and the people of Scotland, and so on, Scottishness remains an ideal which has to be continually affirmed. Far from leading to his goal, it becomes a symbol of that goal.

Yet the Scottish essence does have a living force in his Scots poetry. It is a faith which, however temporary in its immediacy, allowed him to produce the most intense poetry of his career. In later work it is largely an abstraction at a remove from the poet, who even writes of the kind of Scot he wants. In the early work in Scots, however, he writes as though possessed by this essence, before the inevitable uncertainty makes him think about it too much. The Scots vocabulary and idiom, in their richness and variety a powerful stimulant to the imagination, acquire added power by suggestion in MacDiarmid's poetry:the material of his craft has a significance to the poet which is carried into the poetry, almost as though he were speaking in tongues. The Scottish essence resides in Jamieson's *Dictionary*. The poet assumes this, letting it be implicit, and he uses the language rather than questioning it. Through its use he becomes Scottish. When he is a Scottish poet rather than concerning himself with what a Scottish poet is, the results are often magnificent. If he had stopped there one could dismiss his "Theory of Scots Letters" and so on as window dressing, as irrelevant to his poetry as Pound's broadcasts from Rome were to his. His use of Scots is a leap of faith to which no justification can add anything.

But as has been shown, dissatisfaction sets in. His triumph over the Scottish medium seems to answer none of the vital questions he has posed himself. His "marriage" to the Scottish mystical bride, as one observes in *Drunk Man*, is never consummated. The celebration of the Scottish essence, which so many of his lyrics implicitly comprise, never dispels a central gnawing sense of uncertainty which reaches new dimensions in *Drunk Man*, coinciding ominously with the peak of his fluency in Scots. The whole world is "eemis"; the poet feels it necessary to define himself as a poet and as a Scot. His use of Scots, the most convincing of definitions, fails to establish him in the universe. Wishing to be Scotland's voice, to be the means by which Scotland reveals herself, he finds himself on his own, giving voice only to his own uncertainty. As the height of his powers in the use of his medium, something seems to him to be lacking. The Scottish essence seems to be as remote as the moon; his use of the magic words conjures up visions which a moment later seem illusions.

The intensity of his early Scots work derives from two sources. One is the affirmation of the power of the Scots language. But the other source cannot be ignored; it is MacDiarmid's continual self-consciousness of his being-in-the-world, of being abandoned to an uncertain existence without absolute signposts to guide him. The poet is alone in the Waste Land without a map, and his career as a whole is a concern with finding his way out of it. As a theme (his search for certainty, his concept of potential-to-be-realized) this provides for a poetry which is an intense evocation of his sense of *Geworfenheit*. This intensity remains even when he abandoned Scots. It becomes destructive when, almost inevitably, the sense of uncertainty becomes focused upon the poetry itself, and when no work seems good enough, when the kind of poetry he writes gives way to outlines of the kind of poetry he wants. The word "inevitably" is used here because almost from the beginning MacDiarmid was facing the questions, What shall I write? How shall I write? Aware of his uncertain position in the universe, he could not but be aware of his activity and question that as well. Poetry is his life; his feelings of precariousness in-the-world are those he feels as a poet. Poetry is not the expression of his struggle for certainty, but is that struggle. His existence as poet is "eemis." His Scots lyrics are an active definition of the poet's role, but he soon turns to the reification of his activity as a poet, questioning his material and his form until even poetry becomes an ideal to be realized rather than a means of attaining that ideal.

The tone of *Drunk Man*, although varying, becomes despairing again and again, and ends with what is at once an affirmation of potential and a confession of failure: "Yet hae I silence left." In attempting to grasp the meaning of the thistle and win the moon, words quite literally have failed him. *Drunk Man* is a struggle to win certainty through intuition. The poet goes over and over his situation, desperately attempting to receive a revelation which will give him the certainty he wants. He wants a vision – but what appears is an endless series of what reveal themselves to be illusions or hallucinations. He struggles to open himself to the Scottish muse so that revelation can come flooding in – but there is only chaos, no truth emerges. His visions tantalize him, and then vanish into sober reality. He can conceive of understanding (the great wheel) but it is out of his grasp. The intensity truly present in this magnificent Scots epic arises from a profound sense of being lost. The promise of the Scots vocabulary, which could bring him closer to the Scots reality he seeks to become part of, is not fulfilled; at the end he has the silence he began with. In his earliest work, evoking a sense of "lostness", the poet gathered his forces, defining his situation and at the same time taking up Scottish nationalism and old Scots vocabulary in order to come to grips with it. In *Drunk Man*, this "lostness" is not only evoked, but remains, explicitly, at the conclusion of his struggle.

But *Drunk Man* is only a step in a development which can be traced from MacDiarmid's earliest work. The early lyrics in English indicate MacDiarmid's realization of his situation. At that point, as the *Annals* make perfectly plain, MacDiarmid is not actually struggling, but is becoming aware of himself and what he wants to do. These poems, mostly exercises, reveal only that poetry as a vocation is becoming a distinct possibility for him, and that he is aware of the uncertainty which characterizes being-in-the-world. The ideal of certainty is presented, in a highly stilted manner, in "A Moment in Eternity," his most ambitious poem of this period if not his most successful. But he has not yet decided on a fruitful approach to his problem. "Hugh M'Diarmid," his alter ego, has not yet been born.

His adoption of Scottish nationalism, a persona, and Jamieson's *Dictionary* give him a content and an approach. The struggle to overcome uncertainty can now begin. Poetry is no longer a mere possibility but a way of life in the strictest sense. Being a Scot promises him a place in the universe, for Scottishness appears as an absolute. How to be a Scot? Through poetry, made of Scots words, the Scottish essence can be captured and revealed, and his existence can be "grounded." In the Scots lyrics MacDiarmid actively affirms his new-found material, and at the same time restates the problem – of finding the "a'efauld form o' the maze," of living in an "eemis" world and so on.

Drunk Man is the first attempt to put his medium and his approach to the test. The problem of uncertainty is, in the poem, continually confronted, and the ideal, a solution to that problem, is continually affirmed. Having established the foundation of his struggle, he here engages in it with fierce energy. He becomes aware of the distance to go, and affirms that he can, in fact, make that journey. The concept of potential assumes vast importance as a theme. But as has already been said, this struggle does not end in the hoped-for resolution. Only a clearer sense of uncertainty results. The Scottish symbols, such as whisky, the mystical bride, and of course the thistle, assume vague and indefinable positions in the poet's awareness. The Scots medium, far from proving to be incantations or spells to call up the muse or to reach the absolute, serves only to give shape to an unresolved struggle. He realizes that he does not know what the Scottish essence is, nor what his existence means. He continually questions himself, worries about supposed inadequacies, sees Scotland as a maze of contraries and the world as a sea of chaos. The note of assurance and jocularity with which the poem begins is quickly dispelled. The truth will not out. The sense of uncertainty attains grim clarity.

Intuition, interior revelation, fails to carry with it a sense of conviction. The poet, dealing with his situation, always keeps an eye upon the outside world which constantly challenges his intuitive flashes, rendering them illusory, because it remains chaotic. Intuition ebbs and flows while the world MacDiarmid sees himself in remains the same. He continually perceives himself pursuing a goal which remains elusive. He struggles and at the same time sees himself struggle in vain, as he attempts to win through to a vision which never comes. The poem is a decisive stage in MacDiarmid's career, for thereafter he refuses to trust in pure revelation and engages himself actively in his environment. His potential, of which vision was to have been the realization, is to be approached more actively in the future.

His next work (excluding the small pamphlet *Lucky Bag*), *To Circumjack Cencrastus*, bears this out. The hope for revelation assumes a different form, for although MacDiarmid invokes the curly snake, the symbol of the understanding he craves, and even quotes the whole of "A Moment in Eternity," which is a statement of revelation, or rather, about revelation, he clearly sets out to look for it not purely in himself but in the world he lives in. MacDiarmid no longer sits on a hillside waiting for truth to come, like Vladimir and Estragon, but sets out to explore the environment. Meanwhile, the initial enchantment of "synthetic Scots" has worn off. The Scots is noticeably less rich, and some parts of it are in pure English. (There is only one short English passage in *Drunk Man*: 78, *CP* 150–1.) The curly snake remains elusive, too. MacDiarmid knows it is there, but is unable to grasp it. In this poem the facts appear as a new means of approach – "Middle Torridonian Arkose and the pillow lavas at Loch Awe," not the purity of inspiration, are contrasted to the banal, false Scots tradition. The relation of stone to the solution of the problem of uncertainty is suggested here. A world to be investigated is revealed in *Cencrastus* as a whole. It might well be said that this poem serves the forthcoming poetry of facts in the same way that the Scots lyrics served *Drunk Man*. In the latter case, the grounds upon which the self-drama of *Drunk Man* took place were established. In the case of *Cencrastus*, the ground upon which the poetry of facts is enacted is in the same way established. Ideas and facts, this time, not Scots vocabulary and mystical Scottish nationalism, are to be comprised in a new method of approach to what remains the poet's essential preoccupation: the plight of being-in-the-world. However mystical the concept of

Cencrastus, the approach to it is to be a practical one. Where politics, for example, were in *Drunk Man* drawn into the arena of vision, in *Cencrastus* they become important in their own right. In this poem MacDiarmid even provides a partial list of what he feels it is necessary to read; clearly knowledge, rather than intuition, is established as a new avenue of approach, although the idea of ultimate revelation is by no means excluded. He must make the world his through knowledge before he can define his place in it. Perhaps revelation comes only to the learned; it has certainly escaped him so far.

The most important things to notice in *Cencrastus* are, first of all, that the poet is redefining his tasks and approach, considering what is to be done, and, second, he expresses grave doubts about the possibilities of language, questioning the ability of poetry to be used for the problem which besets him. He seeks a "miracle of expression," giving us the first hints of the concept of an ideal language treated in *James Joyce*, for, as he says, even French and German have not circumjacked Cencrastus yet. But this poem is a pause; MacDiarmid "considers," in Heidegger's sense of the word, ceasing his essential struggle in order to gather forces, to make himself aware of what must be done and how to do it. The poem is a plan of action. The movement of the poem derives from a growing awareness of what this task entails. What is in fact revealed, however, as he determines to plunge into the chaos which surrounds him, is that even his poetic method is fraught with uncertainty. Even at this stage it is possible to see the idea of poetry becoming an ideal indissolubly linked with the understanding he seeks. For unlike the Scots vocabulary, which was "ready-to-hand," in Heidegger's terminology, the world of knowledge becomes tricky to handle and, eventually, in later work, turns into an abstract category. Especially in his misgivings about language can be detected the beginnings of a process of idealization. When he talks of how he wants to approach the problem of existence, that is one thing, but when he shows signs of doubting his resources we come up against something quite different.

To explain what is meant by idealization, it must first of all be noted that MacDiarmid, when these doubts occur, never questions whether he should continue writing or not, for this is taken as a "given" of his existence. The ending of *Drunk Man* is an expression of a renewed confidence and determination; the questioning noted in *Cencrastus* is directed at the possible futility of his struggle, but does not contain the suggestion that he should give it up. If C.M. Grieve is unsure of his vocation, Hugh MacDiarmid is by definition a poet. What happens instead is that he reconciles the doubts by means of the concept of potential, which is a central theme throughout his work. He questions his place in the universe, first of all; the achievement of that certainty is an ideal. Taking his Scottishness as a premise, he then subjects it to questioning, and it becomes an ideal. Settling at last on the pursuit of knowledge, he idealizes the attaining of it. He questions his poetry throughout until it too becomes an ideal ("The Kind of Poetry I Want"). He questions his very language material, and an ideal language is posited, most explicitly in *James Joyce*. All these things are seen in terms of potential-to-be-realized. Language material and facts, for example, have a potential usefulness, which is just another way of indicating the poet's own felt potential to realize himself as a poet. The Scottish essence too can be realized in the ideal poetry he seeks, as can all essences. In short, since he exists through his poetry, his existential and aesthetic problems merge. His projected ideal state readily attains the substance of an ideal poetry and an ideal language. This cannot help but have a powerful effect upon the actual language he uses and the poetry he writes.

The process of idealization is founded on a paradox: the poet requires certainty as a means of achieving certainty. Using the analogy of a carpenter, it is as though the latter were faced with the task of building a house to live in. S/he is unsure of the materials available, and so speculates on ideal materials for this house. S/he is unsure of his or her tools, and so is driven to speculate on ideal tools for the purpose. S/he collects all sorts of materials and tools, hoping they will come in handy, but eventually his or her entire occupation consists of speculation and collecting. S/he is no longer a carpenter, but a theoretician. But here the analogy breaks down, because, for MacDiarmid, tools, material, and the house are all part of the same ideal, in that his questioning reveals the uncertainty of his being-in-the-world. The attaining of any of these ideals is much the same thing, in that they presuppose the certainty he seeks. One can only be certain of possessing an ideal language if ideal poetry comes of its use; one can only be certain of writing ideal poetry, of the type outlined in "The Kind of Poetry I Want," when one has achieved the ideal of certainty itself. One can only achieve certain knowledge by becoming God, another word for the ideal state MacDiarmid seeks to realize.[3] One exception can possibly be made here: the gathering of facts is an ideal (another affirmation of the poet's potential, here the potential to learn) as *Lucky Poet* reveals, where MacDiarmid becomes his own ideal polyhistor, but this can be regarded as a half-way house. In "The Ideas Behind My Work," the poet affirms that when enough of the facts (stones of a mosaic) have been put in place, one may assume through poetic juxtaposition, the pattern will be revealed and thus the continual search for clues, "the grim business of documentation," as he calls it elsewhere, can cease. But perhaps even this can be seen as part of the ideal certainty he seeks, after all. How can he know how to fit the stones together unless he already knows the pattern? What one observes in so much of the poetry of facts, "Once in a Cornish Garden," "Cornish Heroic Song for Valda Trevlyn," and the latter part of "Direadh III," for example, is the crudest sort of association-ism, without more sophisticated structures being in evidence, in a seemingly desperate effort to make it cohere. In *James Joyce* MacDiar-mid reveals another attitude to the material he accrues:

> There is much to be said today for reviving
> The poetical method of Jalal ud-Din Rumi
> Who has made use of every kind of anecdote
> And allowed his pen to run on unchecked
> With every idea, every fancy, every play on words
> Which suggested themselves to him. (26, *CP* 744)

The pattern might reveal itself thus, in a species of automatic writing akin perhaps to John Cage's composing of music using the *I Ching*.

After *Cencrastus*, the world of knowledge becomes the poet's province. And there the process of idealization becomes plainer. The poet actively struggles in some cases, but in others turns to what Heidegger calls "theory." It is worth looking at what Heidegger is referring to here, since it casts much light upon MacDiarmid's later development. Heidegger distinguishes two categories of things, defined by one's relation to them. These are things "ready-to-hand" and things "present-at-hand." The former constitute "equipment" – "those entities which we encounter in concern" – and exist for one "in-order-to." (The hammer, for the carpenter, is "ready-to-hand," for example.) The latter, however, are faced "theoretically." As Heidegger says, "The botanist's plants are not the flowers of the hedgerow; the 'source' which the geographer establishes for a river is not the 'springhead in the dale.'"[4]

"If we look at Things just 'theoretically,' we can get along without understanding readiness-to-hand. But when we deal with them by using them and manipulating them, this activity is not a blind one; it has its own kind of sight, by which our manipulation is guided and from which it acquires its specific Thingly character. Dealings with equipment subordinate themselves to the manifold assignments of the 'in-order-to.'" A person may stop to "consider," but this does not make him a theoretician. "Holding back from the use of equipment is so far from sheer 'theory' that the kind of circumspection which tarries and 'considers,' remains wholly in the grip of the ready-to-hand equipment with which one is concerned."[5] MacDiarmid, leafing through Jamieson's *Dictionary*, remains a poet, as he does during his meditation *To Circumjack Cencrastus*, a "consideration" of how best to go about being a poet. But in later work the process of idealization makes him withdraw from activity, transforming his material from "ready-to-hand" to the merely "present-at-hand." He turns from "circumspective concern" to "theoretical discovery." This is where the concept of potential becomes destructive in his work, for everything he confronts, including his own activity and material, is seen in terms of what it might be, or what it can evolve towards. These ideals remain abstract and of necessity rather vague, but they do serve to induce in the poet a lack of the confidence he requires to get on with the job. They haunt him and belittle his efforts until he is reduced to affirming a merely theoretical ideal which is ever beyond his reach, although the concept of the ideal is occasionally captured in the passages of natural description with their symbolic overtones.

If a carpenter begins to regard his or her hammer as a series of properties ("heaviness" and so on), s/he is shifting to the "theoretical" attitude. "In the 'physical' assertion that 'the hammer is heavy' we *overlook* not only the tool-character of the entity we encounter, but also something that belongs to any ready-to-hand equipment: its place. Its place becomes a matter of indifference. This does not mean that what is present-at-hand loses its 'location' altogether. But its place becomes a spacio-temporal position, a 'world-point,' which is in no way distinguished from any other." In fact, as Heidegger continues, "[t]he aggregate of the present-at-hand becomes the theme."[6] When MacDiarmid begins to deal with the facts and language as categories, this is precisely what happens.

It may be objected at this point that Heidegger is being put in a false context here, since all the above quotations are concerned with science and the scientific method. Heidegger, at bottom, is objecting to the depersonalizing effect of science, the reduction of the world to abstract concepts such as energy and mass. Surely, it might be asserted, there is no one less impersonal in his method, and less scientific, than Hugh MacDiarmid. This is true in a sense, but the process of idealization which has been outlined is in fact as depersonalizing as the scientific method. The ideal, whether the "a'efauld form o' the maze," "the law to pit the matter on a proper basis," Scottishness, the moon, Cencrastus, or the kind of poetry he wants, is continually "pushed away" from the personal. All that is immediate and personal is imperfect. MacDiarmid is always present in his work, but the ideal he seeks is made more and more remote, as has been seen, and the farther away it seems, the more impersonally and abstractly it is expressed.

Heidegger admits the difficulty of distinguishing exactly where "the ontological boundary between the theoretical and the atheoretical really lies," and to some extent this difficulty presents itself in the consideration of MacDiarmid's later work.[7] Facts and words are always seen as potential equipment, after all. But this is precisely the point: the concept of potential, linked of course to that of the hidden or unrealized ideal, renders what might be a "consideration" in Heidegger's sense of the word, an exercise in theory. As one traces MacDiarmid's development, one sees him move further away from his goal in the sense that he renders even his activity and material in potential terms until active struggle to win understanding is not merely placed in abeyance but falls by the board. One sees his self-questioning become more and more destructive until, in *James Joyce*, his very language material is revealed as shot through with uncertainty. At the end there is a world of equipment presented in theoretical terms, like the science of economics. Equipment retains its character as equipment, but loses its "place." MacDiarmid's attempts to use this material are almost invariably mere exercises, such as "In the Caledonian Forest." The paradox in *James Joyce* is (despite his mention of silence in reference to Hölderlin, which is given some importance by Burns Singer) that language for a poet, as the poem coalesces, is experience, is not merely about experience, but MacDiarmid is using language in order to write of this experience. In *James Joyce* he talks about words, implying no reality beyond, or greater than, or transcending language, so that by talking about words he is merely presenting words which, in the very means he deals with them, are incapable of use. The ideal is remote; language is not subordinated to anything else, it is only theoretically an "in-order-to." The paradox is resolved, in a way: talking about talking is only that, and no more. Words become the referents of other words. The process is endless. The "total speech" which MacDiarmid rejects at the beginning of the poem seems, in a sense, to be all that is open to him.

In the poetry written after *Cencrastus* one can observe instances of struggle and instances of theorizing. The contrast between the two modes is clearly indicated in the differences between "On a Raised Beach" and "The Kind of Poetry I Want." In the former, the poet is confronted by a world of stones, which can be taken both literally and symbolically, as material ready-to-hand. He is not content merely to write of an abstract category "stones" but painstakingly describes them and attempts to "get into this stone world now" by so doing. There is a clear movement in this poem as the poet strives to come to grips with the opaque, motionless, and speechless stones. The gulf between object and image, frequently glossed over by the poet, is here powerfully felt, and this consciousness brings him to the intense resolution of the poem. The only way he can become one with the stones, he realizes, is to die. The ideal is here related to death: the poet will be like a fossil crinoid ("song" being his whole life of poetry), dead, mute, turned to stone, the sum total, and the end, of life. The sense of struggle is everywhere apparent in the poem. The tone is one of measured desperation as MacDiarmid finally comes to the conclusion that "we have lost all approach" to the stones. He tries, and fails, to be at one with them, and the result is an unquestionably fine poem.

By contrast, "The Kind of Poetry I Want" displays no such movement. Despite the many clear images he provides, the poem remains essentially lifeless as a whole. By describing the kind of poetry he wants, he is describing only his parameters; his list of bridge terms, for example, while giving a general idea of bridge, tells us nothing of the ideal poetry he is projecting. What we have here is pure theory. All is potential. Even the areas of knowledge he self-consciously maps out are only potentially known by himself. The world of facts, which this poem is about, remains an abstraction, as does the ideal transmutation of human action and the outside world into language and poetry. Poetry, for MacDiarmid, is ideally the highest form of action (it is seen as action explicitly in the last line of *Cencrastus*) into which all other forms of action, all other things, are subsumed, but he remains incapable of showing this achievement. All he can do is to affirm that it is, ideally, so.

Throughout the later poetry, as has been demonstrated, occurs a sprinkling of descriptive passages which reveal the poet at his considerable best. Such description (see "Direadh iii," for example, the "poetry like the hawthorn" passage in *James Joyce*, or the passage describing sunset by the Urr in "Lament for the Great Music") is never impersonal. In them everything feels right, in its place, calm and harmonized in the poet's gaze. They are the glimpses of the impossible ideal. Far from the false enthusiasm of "A Moment in Eternity," he conceives in these exact and powerful descriptions a sense of peace which, in the context from which they must not be removed, add a tragic depth to his later work. This immediate world of the senses is profoundly grasped by the poet, but his welter of second-hand material refuses to take such shape and harmony. These passages are at once literal and symbolic. They are the ordering of the poet's immediate experience, one picture synthesizing myriad sense-data, and at the same time they symbolize the ideal order he seeks. They are poetry, and at the same time they symbolize the kind of poetry he wants.

James Joyce, which is really the culmination of MacDiarmid's development, is not this ideal made real and immediate, for in it the poet abandons himself almost entirely to the theoretical attitude. He has hemmed in this original struggle from all sides, as it were, until no struggle is left. Affirmation after affirmation is given, revealing only the emptiness of the work at hand. Here is no struggle nor "consideration," only theory and despair that the "braid-binding" seems a failure after all. Every major ideological concern of the poet, from communism to Scottish nationalism, is introduced only to vanish (indicating their true significance in his work) in an all-embracing theoretical concern for an ideal language which is always an abstraction. Where a little earlier poetry became an abstract category, here language itself becomes the same. Even the solid rock of scholarly evidence, as has been shown, is more apparent than real. His encounter with language, here an explicit encounter, is devoid of intensity because there is no question of its being used. The poet, seeing everything in terms of a haunting, elusive perfection, finds himself at the end unable to engage himself in his craft because he cannot take his materials seriously as they actually exist – they are not good enough for what he wants.

MacDiarmid's career revolves about the two poles of revelation and observation, with language assuming the special status which has been outlined. "Towering above the ruins," it is the means by which the poet can at once engage himself in the world and set himself apart from it in order to set himself up as judge of it. The poet's engagement with language becomes a special case distinct from other (more worldly?) modes of concern, in his own eyes. Being-in-the-world remains his theme (objectively, the concern with language is a mode of being-in-the-world) but language, although revealed as a series of things or "equipment" in an existential sense like any other class of "equipment," like the tools of the carpenter, for example, is given an exalted, transcendental status, everything else being subsumed into it. From the pure revelation for which *Drunk Man* is a struggle, MacDiarmid, caught up in the observational spirit of the times, is unable to accept revelation without proof – that is, without reference to the outside world. He turns to knowledge, striving to know the world in terms of language and, ultimately, poetry; at the same time, he awaits the possible sudden intuitive flash by which this knowledge will become meaning. Not only does he seek the fusion of thing and word, of knowledge of things and knowledge about things, but he is ever in hopes of achieving the fusion of intuition and discovery. In the world he seeks a pattern, to be revealed through knowledge. He seeks the revelation of the meaning of that pattern through the poetry he wants. Knowledge is not understanding but a means of eventually achieving it, he evidently feels. To understand the world he must know it first. To understand his place in it he must know what "it" is, in all its complexity. But if knowledge *per se* had been his real source of concern, he would have abandoned poetry; as it is the world of facts is a theoretical one, and his triumph over it is as remote as the ideal of understanding. As a poet he has no time to be an expert linguist, bridge player, or gun-handler. He is caught in a trap. The choice of knowledge and the choice of poetry are two extremes which are simply incompatible. However, his approach has led to his insisting that neither one can have value without the other. The final result of this stubbornly held conviction, *James Joyce*, is a relegation of both to the theoretical realm.

MacDiarmid is engaged in-the-world, but at the same time frequently objectifies the world and makes it something to be treated at a distance – language is that distance – possessing its own pattern which ultimately involves him, though its outline can be discerned objectively, or at least is potentially discernible. The "detachment" he strives for – explicitly, for example, in "On a Raised Beach" – and which is an aspect of his entire work, in his objectification of the hidden pattern and meaning, is a false attitude in that he cannot remove himself from the world in order to establish himself in it. Although MacDiarmid's central concern, as has been shown, is with being-in-the-world, this is not a term or a concept which he himself uses, in the sense of accepting it as a preontological condition. It describes a perennial situation which the poet himself considers capable of resolution. It is not the definition of existence for MacDiarmid, but a condition to be overcome. When he comes to grips with his being-in-the-world, vague shapes of meaning and pattern arise before him always remaining out of reach, drawing him on, inexorably, out of his consciousness of his immediate situation and concern with it, into the realm of theory and vain hope. The attitude of "detachment," presupposed by his objectification of the ideal, eventually leads as has been indicated to a detachment from his very vocation. Language, in spite of his claims for it, takes its place among the "concrete world of existents"; MacDiarmid, haunted by his theoretical ideal, grows ever more reluctant to engage himself with it.

MacDiarmid casts light upon the problems of a modern poet, whose central problem consists of grappling with an age devoid of readily accessible myth or meaning. In what way does MacDiarmid's poetry reveal the particular problems which derive from this dearth of meaning?

The environmental material – that is, the raw stuff of experience as available to the poet for organizing into poetry, not excluding language itself – presents a problem of approach. This is of course a problem for the poet of any age, but it is an especially difficult one in the modern period.

Previously, poets and their world were linked by accepted metaphysical bonds. The order of their poems reflected and was justified by the order which was felt to be "out there." Their sense of relations was reinforced by this framework within which they moved and struggled, and which ultimately sanctioned their efforts. Their approach to their environmental material was conditioned by this sense of order, for the latter was a way of seeing which helped them to organize the former.

By a shift in perception, the world in the modern period has become a discordant mass of unrelated particulars. It has become inert and apparently without meaning. Poets, no longer at home, move restlessly about in it. It is not "theirs" nor anyone else's. Things are no longer "in place." The poets' perspectives vanish; there is no given sense of proportion. They find in it no harmony, unity, no justification of any kind, for the age offers no values, priorities, nor criteria beyond question: no way of seeing. Now poets can refer their activity only to themselves.

Modern poets, excluding the Dadaists, still need a sense of relations, but now have no outside reassurance. Their approach to the environmental material depends upon them alone. Since so little is taken for granted, a sense of relations is difficult to maintain. It is not surprising that the focus of their poetry is often, both implicitly and explicitly, upon the question of approach itself. The lack of a way of seeing the world obviously means that this question will be emphasized. How to deal with the environmental material, how to codify it, shape and organize it, make something coherent out of it, in the absence of this way of seeing, is revealed as a pressing problem in much modern poetry.

Some of the many approaches which arise out of this difficulty include the following:

• Dadaism, the most elemental approach, if it can be called one, of all. In a senseless world the poetry of the Dadaists, consisting of a meaningless welter of sounds and syllables, was to them the only permissable generalization they could make about their environment.
• Itemization, a recounting of particulars where they receive more attention in themselves than does any general scheme, which remains problematical. It is characteristic of such poems as *The Waste Land* and the *Cantos,* and is especially pronounced in

MacDiarmid's poetry. It is an approach which, by its emphasis upon them, invests particulars with an aura of significance, although the results can sometimes be tedious.

- Absorption/Reabsorption, a concentration upon a general scheme, into which particulars are absorbed; the emphasis is the converse of itemization. This is a way of establishing or re-establishing priorities in the environmental material. Yeats developed his own frame, as did Robert Graves, who attempted its objective validation in *The White Goddess*, whereas Eliot and Auden turned their attentions to making the Christian frame their own.
- Construction, where a scheme is attempted by a piece-by-piece building process, such as in Williams's *Paterson*. There is no clear-cut distinction between construction and itemization, only a difference of degree, and even this is arguable. For example, the *Cantos* were at first envisaged by Pound as having a distinct overall structure. Can the critic ever be certain that there is or is not an "a'efauld form o' the maze" in poetry such as the *Cantos*? Or that the poet did or did not attempt one?
- Archaism, where the environmental material is combed for relics which point to a golden past where things did cohere. This attempted resurrection therefore involves a heavy emphasis upon historical material. The *Cantos*, once more, Olson's *Maximus Poems*, and Jones's poetry all demonstrate this approach very strongly. The past, in a sense, becomes a hoped-for means of viewing the present.
- Isolation of the medium, where the approach becomes an approach to language itself. Language is part of the environmental material, but of course is not only this, for if it were it would be only incidental to the poet. In this approach the focus becomes the properties and structures of language itself, a fascination with the medium such as may be seen in concrete poetry and Imagism as sketched earlier, and in the poetry of e e cummings (where any word can become a noun: for example, "let's take the train / to because dear / whispered again / in never's ear").[8] So the emphasis upon language is not merely the selection of a category of environmental material, as in archaism, but a reflection of modern poets' self-consciousness. Becoming aware of themselves as users of language, their attention is naturally drawn to what they are using. As has been seen, it frequently takes on almost sacred qualities.

These approaches, with the obvious exception of Dadaism, are not mutually exclusive, nor are they ever anything more than partial aspects of the integrated, unique approach of any particular poet. No poet's work can be summed up in these terms. They are only indicators of a response to the modern world. Whether the mention of such aspects is mere speculation or something more depends upon the actual poetry which may reveal them to a greater or lesser extent. Such discussion is not meant to provide definitive conclusions about individual poems or even about any particular poet's writing as a whole. The difficulty in distinguishing "construction" from "itemization" has already been mentioned, for example; the critic cannot determine for certain whether the former or the latter is present in a poet's work. Perhaps a construction has been missed which the poet made – or perhaps one has been applied were none existed. To pose the problem of a poet's approach to his or her environmental material as a question would, if pursued too hard, become a completely fruitless discussion of the poet's intentions. The examination of this problem must remain fairly general. One is not interested in a particular poet's motives so much as a demonstrable response to the modern situation. Certain aspects of the approach can be isolated and examined as indicative of such a response, as has just been shown, but the chief concern is to show that there is a problem, and that the poet responds to it, rather than to try to define this response in precise detail.

MacDiarmid makes the problem of approach an explicit one in his poetry, as this book has borne out. In the early experimentation with Scots one can see a clearly "archaist" approach in which actual words, not historical data, are resurrected as a means by which the Scottish essence might be revealed, an essence which successive centuries of Anglicization have obscured and prevented from developing. When at length he discards this approach he, more than any other modern poet, adopts an uncompromising stance whereby he faces his environmental material directly as it is. Although determined to do something constructive with it, he often imposes little pattern upon it, hardly giving it even what is normally regarded as poetic shaping. A process of itemization, including the wide use of cataloguing, becomes a marked aspect of his work. (There is little evidence of a constructive approach in the sense outlined above, although the caution given in the last paragraph certainly holds.) Finally, although this has been an explicit aspect of his concern almost from the beginning, his medium itself assumes central importance in his poetry. Unlike e e cummings, however, MacDiarmid's later concern with language is, as has been seen, a passive one; in *James Joyce*, for example, he talks about language rather than experimenting with it as he did in his Scots work and in the synthetic English poems such as "In the Caledonian Forest." Words themselves are frequently itemized, as in the list of Norn vocabulary in "On a Raised Beach," for example; and itemization is certainly an aspect of poems such as "In the Caledonian Forest" and "Scots Unbound."

What makes MacDiarmid's work unique, and invaluable as an introduction to modern poetry in general, is the self-conscious and determined way in which he confronts poetic problems. The problem of approach is not excepted. His ceaseless self-questioning and doubt, which force him to follow his own remorseless logic in development, extend easily to the question of his approach to his environmental material, and by so doing reveal to us the nature of the problem itself, especially when his poetry is compared to that of his major contemporaries.

The problem of external structure also confronts the modern poet, and, as with the problem just discussed, this too has always been one but is exacerbated by the modern situation. In previous ages, forms existed and poets used them, for example the sonnet form, the heroic couplet, *terza rima*, and so on. These were a set of organizational rules or conventions by which environmental material was (and still is, of course) put into shape; they were in a sense methods of dealing with this material. So fundamentally can modern poets view their tasks, however, that frequently they find that they must develop their own forms: their way of saying must be entirely their own. In keeping with their sense of uncertainty, their lack of fixed points, they often discard traditional forms which seem somehow at odds with their purposes. This latter may be speculation; but imagine the *Cantos* put into rhyming couplets or a sonnet cycle. There are material and approaches which do not lend themselves to regular or formally elegant expression. In fact, a concern with expression *per se* rather than with beauty or elegance is itself a modern conception.

The "open-ended" poem, as Donald Davie calls it, is an example of a new, more personal, looser structure, characteristic of the *Cantos*, *The Anathemata*, and others. Such poems have no conventional resolutions: there is always room for additions. This is one approach to the problem of how to shape the material of the poem when traditional forms seem unsatisfactory. Free verse and sprung rhythm represent departures from the posed regularity of traditional poetry as well. The associationist technique, which Yvor Winters considers began with Shaftesbury, has become in modern times almost the only thing holding certain poems together; the associations do not even have to be particularly rich.

There are three general morphological characteristics of MacDiarmid's poetry which are interesting in this regard. The first of these is the "open-endedness" of many of his long poems. *Drunk Man* is not really open-ended although its structure is very loose; it does have an ending. *Cencrastus* has an ending too, but an unsatisfactory one which is preceded by no poetic suggestion at all. "Clann Albann" never achieved the quasi-integrated stage even of *Cencrastus*; it remained unrealized, a series of short poems not even turned into a cycle. Later poems such as "Cornish Heroic Song" are open-ended, no attempt at resolution being made. *James Joyce*, we are told, is only a part of a greater unfinished work called "Mature Art," and it too has no real ending. It has been indicated in this study that no resolution to the bulk of this later longer poetic work is possible, given the nature of the writing. MacDiarmid chooses his material and his tasks explicitly, and shows by so doing the necessity of the open-ended form for his work. It arises naturally as a consequence of the concerns he has.

The associationist technique, as has been seen, is an obvious feature of his poetry as well. In the absence of internal development in many of his later poems – that is, progressive unfolding – this seems necessary for coherence. Sometimes it is a rich and imaginative association which is made, and sometimes an intellectual one instead. It is rare that one finds serial associationism, however – that is, any term referring only to the one before and the one after it in the poem.

These two features arise almost organically in MacDiarmid's work, out of the demands of his approach to his environmental material. He approaches the particulars of his experience as particulars, rather than as parts of a scheme which is known in outline, and this process is implicitly without end. ("On a Raised Beach" is an important exception to this rule.) What is more, the particulars appear unrelated, and, in his insistence upon taking things as they are, MacDiarmid is loath to impose some pattern alien to their nature (and possibly obscuring some real pattern) upon them. Association in MacDiarmid's hands is a technique which sometimes provides only the bare minimum of linkage required to keep the poem in one piece. The argument in *James Joyce*, for example, is not developed in any even vaguely linear sense, but ranges where it wills. Open-endedness and associationism, characteristics of the work of other modern poets, are, in MacDiarmid's case, indicative of his explicit concerns as a poet: their importance in his work reveals the structural problems he is facing.

The third aspect of MacDiarmid's poetic structure which is of interest is his excessive use of quotation, which has sometimes led to outright plagiarism. The question has been examined above. At this point it might be added that it is possible that such wide use of opinions and writings of others indicates that MacDiarmid's confrontation with his material is not wholly on the elemental level. If some of his environmental material has an order to it, the poet is willing to let it remain. It might be part of the order he seeks. The poet makes no distinction between material from one source or another in his later work. It is all to be dealt with. If some of it comes in organized blocks, all the better. A quartz crystal is better than grains of sand. Even as early as *Drunk Man* this attitude suggests itself, in his "translations" from other poets which are embodied in the text. His landscape is not entirely level; some few substructures (in terms of the poetry he wants) appear dotted here and there on the terrain. Adapting them to his purposes, they still retain an essential integrity which the poet sees no reason to destroy.

These three structural characteristics of MacDiarmid's poetry clearly reflect, once again, a set of responses to the modern situation. His explicit preoccupations make these characteristics understandable in themselves. Comparison with the work of several other modern poets sheds light upon their use of allusion and quotation, as well as the open-ended and associationist aspects of their poetry.

The two problems, or rather sets of problems, which have been discussed reflect the fundamental problem of the modern poet, which might be expressed as "the question of poetry as a mode of being-in-the-world." This question centres upon language. At the outset, it may be noted that Sartre is in error when he states that "For the poet language is a structure of the external world."[9] He is mistaken, that is, in reference to much of modern poetry, although he is undoubtedly correct in some instances. Language, as has already been observed, is not part of the outside world for many modern poets but is a sort of screen by which they can at once be in-the-world and seem to stand apart from it. It has already been indicated how several poets use language (the realm of language) as a means of distancing themselves from the modern chaos. Language to some poets, moreover, seems at least potentially capable of being a means of transcending the outside world – that is, the world outside it.[10] Because the creative experience is profoundly linked to the sense of meaning, to revelation (that is, inspiration), to the transcendental realm, language, its substance in a sense, necessarily partakes of these characteristics. MacDiarmid, almost from the beginning, shows a reverence for the word which is almost religious: in his use of Scots the Scottish essence is to shine through, reborn; in his use of English, he handles esoteric vocabulary like incantations, or, as in *James Joyce*, keeps at a respectful distance from this potentially explosive material which holds the key to understanding. MacDiarmid makes vast, improbable claims for language. To do less would be to run the risk of seeing poetry as a frivolous occupation unsuited to his quest for

Being. If words are only things, then how could the use of them be justified over the use, say, of a hammer? Luckily this never seems to occur to him.

MacDiarmid mistakes the part for the whole. He wants the whole world, but possesses only language.[11] The problem of existence, for him, is tackled through poetry. The problems posed by his environmental material reflect the problem of being-in-the-world: this material, to the poet, is his world. Language, his medium, the coalescence of environmental material, contains that world. The doubts and uncertainties of modern humanity are faithfully reproduced in MacDiarmid's relationship to the stuff of his craft. The problem of structure, too, is really an aspect of his deeper and more fundamental problem. Making the material cohere is making the world cohere. The open-endedness of much of the poetry reflects the unending search for certainty; poetry as an occuption is the poet's life, and has no resolution but the poet's death.

Once again comparisons with other poets are valuable. MacDiarmid makes explicit his feeling that poetry as an activity, at least, ideal poetry, includes everything in it. He arranges the world as language about himself in an almost solipsistic manner. To him, then, poetry is quite obviously the means of resolving his existential plight. His emphasis on language is certainly paralleled by other modern poets; through a study of MacDiarmid new light is shed upon such phenomena as Yeats's use of the choric line, Pound's ideograms in the Chinese cantos, Eliot's use of quotations in foreign languages, and so on. (No trace of this exaltation of language occurs in the poetry of Auden, Day Lewis, Spender, Robert Lowell, and others, however.)A study of MacDiarmid allows one to compare alternative attitudes to language in modern poetry, and to examine more closely the fascination with language which other poets share. But a comparative study of approaches to the problems of environmental material and structure can be undertaken in more general terms; the approach to the environmental material typified by the fascination with language (the "isolation of the medium") is only one important aspect of what has been discussed. Poetry is revealed as a mode of being-in-the-world through all the attempted resolutions of material and structural problems, as we have tried to show. The modern predicament is, in terms of poetry, expressed as these problems.

We can see how poetry is a means by which poets tackle their own existence in-the-world and involve themselves in meaning by experiencing and using their medium. The various ways in which poets go about this can be observed by examining their approaches to the material and structural problems which have been outlined. The poetry of Hugh MacDiarmid serves as a measure, delineating a clear approach to the world (or rather, clear approaches) via poetry to which the approaches of other poets can be compared.

MacDiarmid's poetry, a forceful, uncompromising, courageous confrontation with the age, is in general valuable to compare to the work of other modern poets for this reason. In his concern with the word, with fragmentation which experience discloses and which no given scheme rectifies, with being a poet in such a situation, with experiment, with the outside world, and with interior revelation, he takes firm and explicit positions. This study has been an attempt to describe in precise detail what these positions are and how they are arrived at, with reference to the modern environment. By becoming aware of these positions one can more easily question and examine the work of other modern poets which is characterized by positions which are less explicitly *positions*. Comparison between MacDiarmid and any one of the other poets mentioned results in an exciting dialectic which would comprise a book in itself in order to be fully explored.

Hugh MacDiarmid makes us aware of the problems of the modern poet by voicing them or by making them explicit in other ways. He is not the greatest modern poet, but in his determination not to be deluded, in his courageous and ultimately tragic adherence to the inexorable logic of his own development, in his ceaseless questioning of what a poet and the poet's craft are, in his continual awareness of the modern environment, and in his sheer poetic excellence, he is undeniably the spokesperson for his contemporaries.

Appendix: MacDiarmid
and His Critics

As the foregoing study has indicated, MacDiarmid's poetry manifests, both structurally and thematically, a modernist sensibility. He writes not only as a Scot, but as an artist at grips with the modern world as a whole. His concern with the "Caledonian antisyzygy," and his poetry of facts, for example, acquire a larger significance in this context than as instances of idiosyncratic nationalism on one hand or equally idiosyncratic communism on the other. Fundamental aspects of modern poetry in general are clearly evident in MacDiarmid's work, and in particular can be demonstrated in poems which have been dismissed by some as incoherent.

Critics for the most part have tended only to scratch the surface of MacDiarmid's poetry in a plethora of short articles. Few as yet have attempted taking on his entire canon, and those who have either tend to give too much credence to the poet's rag-bag of philosophical ideas (Roderick Watson, Catherine Kerrigan, Harvey Oxenhorn) or anchor him too securely in his Scottish context (Kenneth Buthlay). In fact, it is fair to say that MacDiarmid criticism is still in an early stage, and has consequently not done him justice; more, that with the exception of a very few critics, those who have written about his poetry have done him a great deal of injustice. A number of factors account for this.

First of all, MacDiarmid cannot himself escape all blame for this state of neglect. He has actively, volubly, and repetitively placed himself so firmly in the middle of Scottish affairs, by means of political, polemical, and poetical activities of various kinds, that it has proven an easy temptation for the critic to leave him there and adopt a critical frame of reference in keeping with this position. If he insists that his later poetry is Marxist, it is once again easy to take him at his word. The trouble is that the word, for Hugh MacDiarmid, comes rather too easily when the scent of an audience is in the air. He is a poseur in the grand manner. (If critics find it difficult to separate the man from the mask, it is equally true that the poet himself appears to share this difficulty.) His opinions and ideas, or rather the opinions and ideas expressed by him (an important distinction), are numerous and contradictory. He will give his sanction to opinions and ideas which make no sense at all but which sound impressive, as this gem from an interview with Duncan Glen indicates:

> Glen: Pound goes inwards, you go outwards. Now in
> going inwards Pound also goes outwards, but
> in technique he goes inwards, doesn't he?
> MacDiarmid: That's quite true.[1]

MacDiarmid, it needs to be emphasized, is a poet, not a thinker — philosophical, political, or otherwise. Critic after critic, however, has made the serious error of arguing ideas with him, thus showing an inability to separate the literature from the notions (for such they usually are) which abound in it. His explicit Scottishness, his "Marxism," and his quasi-philosophical musings have been greatly overemphasized by incautious commentators who, however, in all fairness, have only accorded these aspects of his work the same attention and emphasis that the poet himself gives to them. It is difficult to find a more energetically voluble and disputatious person than Hugh MacDiarmid inside and outside his poetry. His blanket statements, rash judgments, and wrong-headed generalizations all cry aloud for rebuttal, for the application of good, plain common sense. And so good, plain common sense is applied, MacDiarmid's reflections on "the curst conceit o' bein' richt" are ignored, and the literature is lost in the polemics. But the poet himself, no shirker in the field of polemics, cannot entirely blame the critics who have taken him seriously.

Moreover, the sheer difficulty of MacDiarmid's work has engendered, in reaction, a number of critical stances which have contributed little to genuine understanding. The earlier work, for example, is written in an amalgam of Scots (much of the vocabulary obsolete) which came to be called "Lallans" or "synthetic Scots"; this has presented a problem for those unfamiliar with the language. One can only be grateful that the polemics over the legitimacy of this medium seem to have ended,[2] but even as late as 1954 the American critic Stanley Hyman, unwillingly to make the small effort necessary for comprehension, dismisses the Scots work (as he does nearly all the work in English) as mostly "unreadable."[3]

The consensus of more searching critics than Hyman seems to be that the early Scots work is MacDiarmid's finest achievement. But very often this assertion appears to be used as a stick to belabour the later work in English. Numerous critics adopt what might be called a pro-lyric stance, in fact, holding that there is of little value in the canon besides the early lyrics of *Sangschaw* and *Penny Wheep*. Others are willing to include in their selection *A Drunk Man Looks at the Thistle*, his long Scots poem which followed these two volumes, some holding in fact that it is his best work. But the work in English, culminating in long poems such as *In Memoriam James Joyce*, exposes a number of critical prejudices, raising as it does the perennial worthless question, What is poetry? Much of his later work is unique, and presents difficulties which are worth exploring in depth, as this book has shown. But it has characteristics, such as obscurity, prosiness, and repetitiveness, which are so obvious and overwhelming, and render so much of it tedious to read, that it is little wonder that timid critics are frightened off, impatient critics find it worth only a cursory glance and a curt dismissal, and critics with very firm ideas about what poetry should be dismiss it out of hand. Of course the reaction is not unanimously hostile to this work: on the other extreme we have Tom Scott referring to "Lament for the Great Music" as "classical verse which has never been equalled, let alone surpassed, since Milton, in these islands,"[4] and Anthony Burgess saying of his later work in general that "His capacity for fusing scraps of diverse learning into imaginative statements is as great as Pound's; his ear is as good in the free forms."[5] Law and Berwick take the "mere mortals" approach: "[It] is true that certain obscurities do occur in his poetry because he is dealing with very complex matters or because we are ignorant of his references or unfamiliar with the totality of his thinking."[6] All such statements are rather wide of the mark, and simply add to the critical confusion.

But it would indeed be unfair to suggest that no worthwhile criticism has been done. Kenneth Buthlay's introduction to the man and his work is very useful, for example.[7] Illuminating remarks can be found in two long articles, "Scarlet Eminence" by Burns Singer, and "The Piper on the Parapet" by Peter Thirlby, and in Roderick Watson's notes for an Open University course.[8] Edwin Morgan and David Craig have presented a series of valuable comments as well; Craig, in fact, has hinted at the wider context: "MacDiarmid's radicalism is belittled if it is seen as mainly nationalist/Marxist. It is these and at the same time it is existential. He is always striving to get at the essence and the conditions of being fully human at a particular time and place."[9]

More recently, a number of full-length studies of MacDiarmid's work have appeared, including Ann Boutelle's *Thistle and Rose*, Alan Bold's *MacDiarmid: The Terrible Crystal*, Harvey Oxenhorn's *Elemental Things*, and Catherine Kerrigan's *Whaur Extremes Meet*.

Boutelle's examination is not particularly revealing. While she correctly insists that MacDiarmid's poetry needs to be considered as a whole, her own study consists of a chronological tour through the canon, with textual analysis based narrowly upon a concept of "paradoxical vision"[10] which does not succeed in establishing the logic and integrity of MacDiarmid's development in any depth. Bold's underlying argument, too, seems a trifle thin: MacDiarmid's poetry is seen as "a consistent search for the source of universal creativity," with an accompanying evolutionary motif.[11]

Harvey Oxenhorn's critical analysis is even less satisfactory. Leaving aside such carelessness as placing the early "Cattle Show" in the wrong decade, there seems to be no clear thesis in this examination at all. Like Catherine Kerrigan, Oxenhorn takes MacDiarmid's philosophical pretensions too seriously, claiming, for example, that *Drunk Man* has a coherent philosophy underlying it, a highly questionable assertion.[12] (As critic, Oxenhorn sums up *Drunk Man* as "a sequence of fragments which cohere loosely by means of image and symbol," a less than illuminating observation.)[13] Kerrigan herself has done much useful spadework, uncovering the sources of many of MacDiarmid's ideas, and she provides a number of important critical insights into the poetry. But she does not appear to understand MacDiarmid's peculiar existential relation to ideas, and thus gives them far too much weight in themselves, as well as giving too much credence to MacDiarmid's own claims to philosophical knowledge and reflection.

As is always true, but especially so in MacDiarmid's case, one must seek the answers, the insights, and the understanding in the poetry itself. It might be briefly pointed out that critics have succumbed to critical fallacies in their consideration of the text that makes this all the more imperative. One telling example of the intentional fallacy is found in both Duncan Glen's and Kenneth Buthlay's books, in which the following quotation from MacDiarmid's poem "The Kulturkampf" is used to criticize his later poetry:

> But there was one virtue the meanest allotment-holders have
> Which he conspicuously lacked - they *weed* their plots
> While he left to time and chance
> And the near-sighted pecking of critics
> The necessary paring and cutting.[14]

Both Glen and Buthlay imply that MacDiarmid's intention is to leave his poems unfinished. They seem to accept that the poet is hewing stone for others to sculpt. This has led them to misinterpret a passage which is in fact an attack on critics and not self-criticism at all. MacDiarmid is only too happy to lack any virtue which "the meanest allotment-holders" possess. And weeding a mere plot of ground is a tiny perspective which the poem as a whole negates. This careful weeding, too, which Glen and Buthlay find lacking in MacDiarmid, is linked in the passage to near-sightedness and to the utterly random workings of time and chance. It is only the critics who regard "paring and cutting" as "necessary"; MacDiarmid is clearly being ironical. And two critics are hoist by their own petard.

In the same way, William Soutar's comment on *A Drunk Man Looks at the Thistle*, that the theme of drunkenness is "a brilliant manoeuvre by which he shifts the onus of responsibility upon his readers," is fallacious.[15] As a sympathetic critic, Soutar was trying to mitigate the seeming inconsistencies in the poem by referring to the author's supposed intention. But by doing this he has ignored the possibility that these inconsistencies are a necessary and (paradoxically) integral aspect of the poem *per se*, something which can in fact be demonstrated.

As a final example, or series of examples, there is the common charge of "didacticism" in his later work. Critics too numerous to mention have assumed that MacDiarmid's intention is to communicate ideas or to preach. By implication they have regarded his poetry as a series of ideas and little else, and some have averred that it could have been written as prose. This demonstrates extraordinary presumption coupled with careless reading of the material. Chapters 4 and 5 of this book indicate the part the ideas (and facts) play in what is essentially inward-directed rather than audience-intended work.

Against his own "didactic" passages and their introduction as evidence by critics might be quoted this unpublished poem which is here introduced not as evidence of MacDiarmid's intentions, but as an indication of the danger of searching the author's works for evidence of them:

> *On the Fishing Grounds*
> I am a poet
> And beliefs are to me
> No more than sunlight
> Is on the deep sea.
>
> Fishers know it's at night
> Their harvest is got.

Daylight's only of use
For disposing of the "shot."[16]

The practice of quoting MacDiarmid against himself, referred to above, leads to misinterpretation of his poetry in a more general way as well. MacDiarmid is an excessively self-conscious poet, and he often appears to be commenting upon what he is doing throughout his later long poems such as *In Memoriam James Joyce*. This leads to a critical assumption that these passages are somehow distinct from the "main" poem, almost as though they were not part of the poetry at all. When he asks, for example, "Have I failed in my braid-binding?" this is a question which cannot be answered by a simple yes or no, but must be taken as part of the movement of the poem as a whole, a dramatized moment of self-doubt at a crucial moment in *James Joyce*, a line which derives its meaning from its context. If it is argued that this context is his work as a whole, as the evidence indicates, then this does not alter the fact that the line is a rhetorical question, one moment of a continual self-questioning, and not, to use Henry Fielding's expression, "a crust for the critics." The answer to the question is irrelevant to the poetry, as are MacDiarmid's other self-questionings and self-examinations. (David Craig uses this line against the poet, although he does note that it occurs at "a striking point in *James Joyce*.")[17] Such taking advantage of the poet's self-consciousness, for that is what it is, besides leading to the intentional fallacy, implies a structural stutter or intrusion in the poetry for which there is no evidence.

One other critical error might here be mentioned, which could be called the psychological fallacy. Because MacDiarmid displays obsession and something approaching megalomania on occasion (see his autobiography *Lucky Poet*, for instance), explanations of his work have sometimes been made on the basis of a psychological judgment at second hand. This is often a mere polemical thrust, but it has been advanced to explain a supposed "shift" in his poetry after 1935.[18] This is not criticism, but speculation of a fairly worthless kind. As the present book is intended to show, a pattern of poetic development can be deduced from literary evidence alone.

One of the aims of this study has been to demonstrate, in fact, that the poetic work of Hugh MacDiarmid is not easily divisible into stages (*pace* Roderick Watson and others) but constitutes a unified, developing whole whose apparently diverse poetic tendencies are deeply interpenetrating. Walter Keir is on the right track when he says, "Grant his premises, and his development throughout is logical, direct and inevitable": although "inevitable" is a trifle strong,

MacDiarmid's development does have a logic of its own, and, as Keir implies, the important task is to uncover his premises rather than to impose artificial divisions.[19] Despite Rosenthal's claim that his use of Scots is not really a formal technique, it can in many ways be seen as such, and when this is done the question of a Lallans stage and two or more English stages becomes almost irrelevant to his main interests and preoccupations.[20]

If MacDiarmid's poetry transcends both his nationality and his critics, and can be more deeply understood within the wider context of modernism, it is equally true that modernism, and modern poetry in particular, can be better grasped through a careful study of MacDiarmid's work. It is hoped, in fact, that by placing his poetry in this larger setting MacDiarmid can be used as a sort of paradigm of the modern poet: several features of his work, as have been seen, render it invaluable for this purpose. The foregoing examination of his canon, then, is not so much the study of one poet as an effort to put his poetry into a context by which both are enriched.

A poet whose writing has a prodigious range and depth, as MacDiarmid's has, can be expected to express in any number of ways his confrontation with the milieu in which he is working, in a manner which reveals to the reader a great deal about both. An examination of MacDiarmid's art indicates what should be fairly obvious by now: his milieu is far wider in scope than the Scottish tradition, and the problems arising from this milieu are far deeper than those raised by the particular exigencies of the Scottish Literary Renaissance which he founded. Hugh MacDiarmid is more than a modern Scottish poet. He is a modern poet, no more restricted to the Scottish tradition than is David Hume, and his poetic environment is the modern age itself.

Glossary

a'efauld   *single (lit. "onefold")*
aiblins   *perhaps*
airt   *direction*
ava   *at all*
ayond, 'yont   *beyond*
begink   *cheat, deceive*
ben   *in*
blainy   *applied to a field with frequent blanks in the crop*
blanderin'   *diffusing or dispersing in a scanty and scattered way*
bombination   *buzzing*
brak   *break*
breenage   *burst*
broukit   *neglected, with a dirty face*
crockets*   *lit. to be impudent*
datchie   *sly, secret*
dirl   *pierce, thrill*
dule   *grief*
eemis   *insecure, precariously balanced*
een   *eyes*
ettle   *aspire*
faurer   *farther*
ferlies   *wonders*
flee   *fly*
fozy   *diseased*
fug   *moss*

gang   *go*
gangrel   *wanderer*
gar   *make*
gin   *if*
glisk   *glimpse*
glumpin'   *looking gloomy*
grugous   *ugly*
hazelraw   *lichen*
heteroepic   *involving pronunciation differing from the standard*
hiraeth (Welsh)   *longing, nostalgia*
holophrastic   *expressing a whole phrase or combination of ideas with one word*
howe   *hollow*
idioticon   *dialect dictionary*
jerque   *carry out a customs search*
keethin'   *lit. ripples in water signifying presence of fish below surface*
lammergeir   *the Bearded Vulture, largest European bird of prey*
lave   *rest*
lear   *learning*
leddy   *lady*
lift   *sky*
loup   *leap*
lozen   *window*

*(correct sp. crockats), "thraw c. up"

macaronic *designates a kind of verse written in one language but in the form of another*

maun *must*

noo *now*

on-ding *downpour*

ootby *outside*

ootrie *outré*

or *before*

orra *worthless*

owre *over, too*

peerieweerie *very little*

philomathic *devoted to learning*

plumm *deep pool*

psychopetal *tending towards the mind*

ramel *branches*

ratchel *fragments of loose shivery stone lying above the firm rock*

rice *twig*

rouch *rough*

sair *sore(ly)*

scunner *disgust*

scurl *a dry scab*

sesames *magic passwords*

sibness *relationship*

sic *such*

sisu (Finnish) *intestinal fortitude, stamina*

skimmer *gleam*

sma-bookin' *shrinking (from "sma'-bouket"; of small bulk, shrunken)*

soon' *sound*

syne *since*

taigled *entangled*

tesserae *stones of a mosaic*

thole *bear, suffer*

thrang *busy*

thrawart *perverse*

thriddin' *lit. dividing into thirds*

thunner *thunder*

tint *lost*

toom *empty*

trauchelt *troubled*

trauchlin' *troubling*

tyauvin' *struggling*

undeemis *countless*

watergaw *fragment of a rainbow appearing on the horizon (MacDiarmid's gloss: an indistinct rainbow)*

whuds *moves numbly and noiselessly*

whummle, dish o' *lit. an overturning dish*

widdifow *wrathful (MacDiarmid's gloss, "perverse," does not seem to be justified)*

xenolith *a crystal of xenolite, a silicate of aluminum*

yad *piece of bad coal*

yirdit *buried*

Notes

CHAPTER ONE

1 Young, "The Nationalism of Hugh MacDiarmid," 106.
2 Fraser, "Hugh MacDiarmid: The Later Poetry," 41.
3 Some lesser personae appear in the guise of critics, commentators, and one poet-commentator, A.K. Laidlaw: some of the others are Arthur Leslie, Pteleon, Mountboy, Isobel Guthrie, and Gillechriosd Mac a'Ghreidhir.
4 Wood, "Mod and Great," 19-21.
5 Watson, "Hugh MacDiarmid and the 'Poetry of Fact,'" 28. See also Watson, *Hugh MacDiarmid*, 8: "[This verse is] not an attempt to write poetry 'with facts in it' ... [but] to make the reader aware of the poetry that resides *in* facts."
6 "Perfect" was later replaced in the *Collected Poems* – by a passage, as Edwin Morgan has noted, from Hart Crane's *The Bridge*. For correspondence on "Perfect" and other borrowings see the *Times Literary Supplement*, 21 January-20 May 1915. As some of the correspondence indicates, even the line arrangement of "Perfect" may have been borrowed, from Kerdrych Rhys.
7 Buthlay, *Hugh MacDiarmid*, 72ff.
8 Watson, "The 'Cencrastus Theme,'" 15. See also Buthlay, *Hugh MacDiarmid*, 101.
9 Daiches, "Diversity in Unity," 33.
10 Howe, introduction to *The Idea of the Modern*, 11.
11 Richards, *Science and Poetry*, 4.
12 Lowith, "Heidegger: Problem and Background of Existentialism," 346.
13 Neil Young, "Don't Let It Bring You Down," *After the Gold Rush*.
14 Fromm, *The Fear of Freedom*, 216-17.
15 Steiner, *Language and Silence*, 44.
16 Sontag, *Styles of Radical Will*, 3ff.

17 McLuhan, *The Gutenberg Galaxy*, 170, 278; *Understanding Media*, 80. Cf Steiner, "On Reading Marshall McLuhan," in *Language and Silence*, 280-5.
18 Steiner, "McLuhan," 282.
19 Pearce, *The Continuity of American Poetry*, 114-15.
20 Stephen Spender, *The Struggle of the Modern*, 34.
21 Ibid., 50.
22 Leavis, *New Bearings in English Poetry*, 93, 91.
23 Richards, *Science and Poetry*, 40.
24 Spender, *Struggle*, 17.
25 Sartre, "Baudelaire," in Howe, *The Idea of the Modern*, 241.
26 Howe, *The Idea of the Modern*, 21.
27 Ibid., 30.
28 Sartre, *Literature and Existentialism*, 40.
29 Ibid., 91.
30 "A Manifesto of Italian Futurism," in Howe, *The Idea of the Modern*, 169.
31 Zamyatin, "On Literature, Revolution, and Entropy," in Howe, *The Idea of the Modern*, 173-4.
32 Kafka, *The Great Wall of China*, 259.
33 Richards, *Science and Poetry*, 60.
34 MacDiarmid, "Lament for the Great Music," in *Stony Limits and Other Poems*, 130.
35 Richards, *Science and Poetry*, 75.
36 Leavis, *New Bearings in English Poetry*, 41.
37 Glen, *The Individual and the Twentieth-Century Scottish Literary Tradition*, 25.
38 The term is Heidegger's: see *Being and Time*, 53ff. "Being-in-the-world" does not define a merely spatial relation but the fundamental condition of existence.
39 Leavis, *New Bearings in English Poetry*, 103.
40 Winters, *The Function of Criticism*, 47.
41 Buthlay, *Hugh MacDiarmid*, 99.
42 Quoted by Whalley, *The Poetic Process*, 46.
43 Quoted by Harold Rosenberg in "Aesthetics of Crisis," in Howe, *The Idea of the Modern*, 122, 119.
44 Rosenberg, "Aesthetics of Crisis," 122.
45 Yeats, "The Statues," *The Poems of W. B. Yeats*, 336-7.
46 Wood, "Mod and Great," 21.

CHAPTER TWO

1 *Early Lyrics*, ed. Annand, 26. And see *The Complete Poems of Hugh MacDiarmid*, ed. Grieve and Aitken, 1113. For the convenience of the reader, all succeeding quotations from MacDiarmid's poetry will be referenced to this edition after the original citation, eg, *CP* 1113.

2 MacDiarmid, *Penny Wheep*, 1, *CP* 45.
3 *Early Lyrics*, ed. Annand, 28, *CP* 1115.
4 *Northern Numbers*, ed. MacDiarmid, 68, *CP* 1200.
5 Glen, *Hugh MacDiarmid*, 72.
6 Buthlay, *Hugh MacDiarmid*, 15.
7 Singer, "Scarlet Eminence," 60ff.
8 Sartre, *Being and Nothingness*, 480.
9 Daiches, "Diversity in Unity," 33.
10 *Northern Numbers*, 69-70, *CP* 1201.
11 *Northern Numbers* (second series), 49, *CP* 1204.
12 Ibid., 50, *CP* 1201-2.
13 Ibid., 52, *CP* 1206.
14 Ibid., 54, *CP* 1207.
15 *Northern Numbers* (third series), 56, *CP* 1251-2.
16 Ibid., 55, *CP* 462.
17 Ibid., 54, *CP* 1212.
18 Ibid., 58, *CP* 1215.
19 *Scottish Chapbook*, ed. MacDiarmid, 6-10,*CP* 3-8.
20 Chiari, *Impressions of People and Literature*, 98.
21 Watson, "The 'Cencrastus Theme,'" 92ff.
22 Daiches, "The Early Poems," 22.
23 *Chapbook* 1, (October 1922): 79, *CP* 1217. And see ibid. (September 1922): 35, where he complains, "What are the best of us but fitful lights in chaos?"
24 Ibid. (December 1922): 133, *CP* 1209.
25 Ibid. (November 1922): 105, *CP* 1220.
26 Ibid. (November 1922): 99-101, ibid. (March 1923): 218-19, *CP* 1218-19, 1226-7.
27 Ibid. (December 1922): 134, *CP* 1210.
28 MacDiarmid, "A Russo-Scottish Parallel," in *Selected Essays of Hugh MacDiarmid*, ed. Glen.
29 *Chapbook* 1, (May 1923): 270-2.
30 Ibid. (June 1923): 300, 302.
31 Ibid. (March 1923): 214.
32 Carswell, "Perfervid Scots," 573-4.
33 Smith, *Scottish Literature, Character and Influence*, 4.
34 Speirs, *The Scots Literary Tradition*, 161.
35 MacDiarmid, *To Circumjack Cencrastus, or the Curly Snake*, 198, *CP* 289.
36 MacDiarmid, "Lament for the Great Music," in *Stony Limits and Other Poems*, 128, *CP* 472.
37 MacDiarmid, *Annals*, Introduction.
38 Sartre, *Nausea*, 33-4.
39 *Northern Review* 1 (August 1924): 182.

40 Ibid., 183.
41 *Chapbook* 2 (November-December 1923): 63. See *Scottish Nation*, 5 June 1923, 14. *Complete Poems* does not reproduce "Braid Scots" in its entirety. See *CP* 1234-5.
42 *Chapbook* 2 (November-December 1923): 68, *CP* 1234.
43 Ibid., 69.
44 Ibid., 70.
45 See *Chapbook* 1 (March 1923): 213, for example, or "The New Movement in Vernacular Poetry," *Contemporary Scottish Studies* (first series), 193.
46 "Braid Scots and the Sense of Smell," *Scottish Nation* 1 (15 May 1923): 10.
47 *Northern Review* 1 (May 1924): 16-21.
48 Ibid., 66.
49 "Programme for a Scottish Fascism," *Scottish Nation*, 19 June 1923, 10.
50 "The Caledonian Antisyzygy and the Gaelic Idea," in *Selected Essays*, ed. Glen, 70ff.
51 Called "To Lenin," this was first published in *New English Poems*, ed. Lascelles Abercrombie.
52 *Northern Review* 1 (August 1924): 161, *CP* 1242.
53 Davidson, "The Gleeman," in *In A Music-Hall and Other Poems*, 22, 24.
54 Davidson, "The Vengeance of the Duchess," in *Fleet Street Eclogues*, 41.
55 Davidson, "Lammas," in *A Second Series of Fleet Street Eclogues*, 41.
56 Davidson, *The Triumph of Mammon*, 144.
57 Davidson, *Mammon and his Message*, 173.
58 Davidson, "L'Envoi," in *Holiday and Other Poems*, 128.
59 MacDiarmid, *Albyn, or Scotland and the Future*, 5.
60 MacDiarmid, *Sangschaw*, 2, *CP* 17.
61 Ibid., 38-9, *CP* 34.
62 MacDiarmid, *Penny Wheep*, 1, *CP* 45.
63 Ibid., 46, *CP* 64.
64 Ibid., 23-4, *CP* 54.
65 Ibid., 51, *CP* 66.
66 MacDiarmid, *Sangschaw*, 23, *CP* 27.
67 Ibid., 1, *CP* 17.
68 Quoted on the cover of Trotsky, *Literature and Revolution*.
69 MacDiarmid, *Sangschaw*, 2, *CP* 17.
70 Ibid., 18-19, *CP* 25.
71 MacDiarmid, *Penny Wheep*, 3, *CP* 45.
72 MacDiarmid, *Sangschaw*, 23, *CP* 27.
73 Buthlay, *Hugh MacDiarmid*, 27. See Smith, "Hugh MacDiarmid," 174, also Daiches, "Hugh MacDiarmid," 26, for example.
74 MacDiarmid, *Sangschaw*, 14-17, *CP* 23-5.
75 MacDiarmid, *Penny Wheep*, 8, *CP* 24.
76 Ibid., 18, *CP* 51, 52.

77 Ibid., 28, *CP* 56.
78 Ibid., 45, *CP* 60.
79 MacDiarmid, *Sangschaw*, 21-2, *CP* 26.
80 MacDiarmid, *Penny Wheep*, 7, *CP* 47.
81 MacDiarmid, *Sangschaw*, 31, *CP* 31.
82 Ibid., 27-8, *CP* 29.
83 Ibid., 38-9, *CP* 34.
84 Watson, "The 'Cencrastus Theme,'" 256.
85 Thirlby, "The Piper on the Parapet," 58.
86 MacDiarmid, *Penny Wheep*, 4, *CP* 46.
87 MacDiarmid, *Sangschaw*, 5-9, *CP* 18-21.
88 MacDiarmid, *Penny Wheep*, 48-9, *CP* 65.
89 Ibid., 5, *CP* 46.
90 MacDiarmid, *Sangschaw*, 36-7, *CP* 33.
91 Ibid., 13, *CP* 23.
92 Ibid., 41-2, *CP* 35.
93 MacDiarmid, *Penny Wheep*, 9, *CP* 48.
94 Ibid., 29.
95 Ibid., 57.
96 MacDiarmid, "The Dead Harlot," in *New Tales of Horror*, 145ff.
97 MacDiarmid, *Sangschaw*, 43-52, *CP* 36-40.
98 MacDiarmid, *Penny Wheep*, 64-71, *CP* 72-5.
99 Ibid., 11-15, *CP* 48-51.

CHAPTER THREE

1 William Soutar notes this "recurrent ingathering of the thought to the moonlit hill" in "The Poetry of MacDiarmid," 9.
2 This metaphor was probably picked up from the first chapter of Smith's *Scottish Literature*, 20.
3 A stylized thistle and an octopus have similar silhouettes; one imagines the body of the octopus with tentacles pointing upwards like the thistle's jags. For Watson's view see "The Symbolism of *A Drunk Man Looks at the Thistle*," in *Hugh MacDiarmid: A Critical Survey*, 109.
4 Lovejoy, *The Great Chain of Being*, 244ff.
5 Sartre, *Being and Nothingness*, 566.
6 Watson, "The Symbolism of *Drunk Man*," 109.
7 For an alternative interpretation of this silence see, for example, Weston, 35.
8 Reid, *Modern Scottish Literature*, 19.
9 MacDiarmid, *Drunk Man*, Appendix B.
10 Buthlay, "Call Me Anti," 89-90.
11 MacDiarmid, *Drunk Man*, Author's Note.

12 Buthlay, *Hugh MacDiarmid*, 50.
13 Buthlay, *Hugh MacDiarmid*, 74-5.
14 See, for example, his co-adaptation "from the Swedish" of Harry Martinson's *Aniara*, done almost three decades after the lapse of his Lallans experiment.
15 Craig, "Jettisoning the Chaos," 46.
16 See Craig, "Hugh MacDiarmid's Poetry," 15.
17 Watson, "The Symbolism of *Drunk Man*," 94. The poem can drive critics off, as well: see Davie, "A'e Gowden Lyric," in which it is dismissed as "tedious reading as a whole."
18 Weston, *Drunk Man*, 7-8.
19 Thirlby, "The Piper on the Parapet," 61.
20 See Morse, "Contemporary English Poets and Rilke," 272-4.
21 MacDiarmid, *Cencrastus*, 92ff (see 88), *CP* 230ff, 228.
22 Latin corrected in *Collected Poems*, 109.
23 MacDiarmid's explicit sense of Godliness, or Godliness-to-be, might reflect the influence of John Davidson. Take this passage from the latter's poem "A Ballad in Blank Verse of the Making of a Poet," in *Ballads and Songs*, 22, for example:

> Henceforth I shall be God; for consciousness
> Is God; I suffer; I am God; this self
> That all the universe combines to quell,
> Is greater than the universe; and I
> Am that I am. To think and not be God? –
> It cannot be. Lo! I shall spread this news,
> And gather to myself a band of Gods –
> An army, and go forth against the world,
> Conquering and to conquer.

24 Watson, "The 'Cencrastus Theme,'" 311. See Filioque, "The Great Sea-Serpent," 223.
25 Berryman, "The Long Way to MacDiarmid," 66.
26 Smith, *The Golden Lyric*, 8.
27 Wittig, *The Scottish Tradition in Literature*, 287.
28 John Herdman, in "Hugh MacDiarmid's 'To Circumjack Cencrastus,'" 72, sums up the poem by stating that "The philosophic and linguistic issues which faced MacDiarmid in *Cencrastus*, and the failure of all his grapplings with them to produce the solutions he was seeking, give the work a pivotal place in his development."

CHAPTER FOUR

1 MacDiarmid, *Speaking for Scotland*, 64-5. See *Voice of Scotland*, June 1948,

17-20, and *The Battle Continues*, 85-6, *CP* 1122-3, 979-80. See also *CP* 840 and *CP* 937-8 for a passage occurring in *The Battle Continues* and in *James Joyce*.

2 Craig, "MacDiarmid the Marxist Poet," 99.

3 Morgan, "Jujitsu for the Educated," 225. Alexander Scott, in "MacDiarmid: The Poet," *The Hugh MacDiarmid Anthology*, ed. Scott and Grieve, xxii, writes: "All of MacDiarmid's late poems, even the bulky *In Memoriam James Joyce*, are eventually intended to be seen as parts of a mammoth 'work in progress,' 'Mature Art,' and it may be that in the perspective of the complete epic – should it even take form as such – the more prosaic passages will find their own level and play their part in the total effect, whatever that may turn out to be."

4 MacDiarmid, "O Ease My Spirit," in *Second Hymn To Lenin and Other Poems*, 28, *CP* 539.

5 MacDiarmid, "The Point of Honour (On Watching the Esk Again)," in *Stony Limits and Other Poems*, 17-21, *CP* 387ff.

6 MacDiarmid, "Ode To All Rebels," in *Stony Limits and Scots Unbound and Other Poems*, 99, *CP* 494-5.

7 MacDiarmid, "Whuchulls," in *A Lap of Honour*, 23-7, *CP* 1089ff, first appeared in *The Modern Scot*, January 1933.

8 MacDiarmid, "On Reading Professor Ifor Williams's 'Canu Aneurin' in Difficult Days," in *A Kist of Whistles*, 8, *CP* 691.

9 MacDiarmid, *First Hymn to Lenin and Other Poems*, 38, *CP* 314.

10 MacDiarmid, *Poems to Paintings by William Johnstone 1933*, 9, *CP* 1069.

11 Ibid., 11, *CP* 1070-1.

12 Ibid., 14, *CP* 1071-3.

13 MacDiarmid, *Lucky Poet*, 330, *CP* "Third Hymn to Lenin," 898.

14 MacDiarmid, *Kist of Whistles*, 26, *CP* 712.

15 MacDiarmid, *Lucky Poet*, 326-7, *CP* 653.

16 Watson, "Hugh MacDiarmid and the 'Poetry of Fact,'" 28.

17 See "Diamond Body" in *A Lap of Honour*, for example, or "On Reading Professor Ifor Williams' 'Canu Aneurin' in Difficult Days" in *A Kist of Whistles*, "Direadh III" in *Lucky Poet*, 300-5, or the vivid "Bagpipe Music" included in "Impavidi Progrediamur," *Collected Poems*, 428, *CP* 1084, 689, 1186, 665.

18 MacDiarmid, *Scottish Eccentrics*, 284.

19 MacDiarmid, *The Islands of Scotland: Hebrides, Orkneys, and Shetlands*, ix.

20 *Voice of Scotland*, March 1946, 14-19, and June 1946, 17-21, *CP* 675, 680, 683.

21 MacDiarmid, *The Islands of Scotland*, 26.

22 Ibid., 89-91.

23 MacDiarmid, *Lucky Poet*, 34.

24 Ibid., 324, *CP* 652.

25 MacDiarmid, *Scots Unbound and Other Poems*, 19, *CP* 345.

26 The earliest appearance of this quatrain was in *The Modern Scot*, July 1931, 127. Here, but in no subsequent reprinting, acknowledgments are made to Compton Mackenzie. The latter improvised the substance of this verse on a political platform: see Miller, "Scotch on the Rocks," 16; and Wright, *MacDiarmid*, 50.

27 MacDiarmid, "Towards a New Scotland," in *Stony Limits*, 101, 102, *CP* 452.

28 MacDiarmid, *Lucky Poet*, xxi, 28, 343, 356, for example; but other references are numerous.

29 Ibid., 341.

30 Ibid., 348.

31 Craig, "MacDiarmid the Marxist Poet," 99.

32 *Voice of Scotland*, January 1956, 25-6, *CP* 1397.

33 MacDiarmid, *First Hymn*, 13, *CP* 298-9.

34 Ibid., 22, 23, *CP* 304, 305.

35 MacDiarmid, *Three Hymns to Lenin*, 19ff, *CP* 893ff.

36 Watson, *Hugh MacDiarmid*, 39.

37 MacDiarmid, *Lucky Poet*, 152.

38 Ibid., 158ff, *CP* 616ff.

39 MacDiarmid, *Stony Limits*, 43, *CP* 407, bowdlerized here as well.

40 Craig, "MacDiarmid the Marxist Poet," 90-1.

41 MacDiarmid, *Second Hymn*, 47, *CP* 548.

42 MacDiarmid, *First Hymn*, 33-7, *CP* 311-14.

43 MacDiarmid, *A Lap of Honour*, 52, *CP* 1102.

44 Sartre, *Being and Nothingness*, xlii, 566.

45 MacDiarmid, *Scots Unbound*, 5-9, *CP* 333-7.

46 MacDiarmid, *A Lap of Honour*, 33, *CP* 1096-7.

47 MacDiarmid, *Lucky Poet*, 300-5, *CP* 1186-93.

48 MacDiarmid, *Stony Limits*, 14, *CP* 386.

49 MacDiarmid, *Scots Unbound*, 3, *CP* 332.

50 *Voice of Scotland*, March 1946, 14-19; and June 1946, 17-21, *CP* 675-84. In reference to MacDiarmid as civilization see "At the Cenotaph," *Second Hymn*, 26, *CP* 538.

51 Bruce, "'Between Any Life and the Sun,'" 65.

52 MacDiarmid, *The Islands of Scotland*, 29-36, *CP* 575-83.

53 MacDiarmid, *A Lap of Honour*, 52-8, *CP* 1102-9.

54 MacDiarmid, *Lucky Poet*, 316-18, *CP* 644-6.

55 Craig, "Jettisoning the Chaos," 48.

56 MacDiarmid, *Collected Poems*, 477, *CP* 1061.

57 Ibid., 437, first appeared in *Poetry Scotland* 4 (1949), *CP* 1054.

58 MacDiarmid, *A Kist of Whistles*, 16, *CP* 701-2.

59 Ibid., 19-24, *CP* 704-12.

60 MacDiarmid, *Lucky Poet*. The most complete version of the poem is found here, in the chapter of this title. MacDiarmid wants to be a poet in the sense that his gun-handler is a gun-handler – that is, in an absolute sense: see Sartre, *Being and Nothingness*, 59ff, 83.

61 Hugh MacDiarmid, *Cornish Heroic Song for Valda Trevlyn*, title-page note.

62 MacDiarmid, *Stony Limits and Scots Unbound*, 91ff, *CP* 487ff.

63 His outline of the "big new poem" to be is given in *The Modern Scot*, July 1931, 107n.

64 See MacDiarmid, *A Kist of Whistles*, 31.

65 MacDiarmid, *Cencrastus*, 77, *CP* 222. See MacDiarmid, "The Caledonian Antisyzygy and the Gaelic Idea," in *Selected Essays*, 67: the phrase there is "quadrilateral of forces."

66 MacDiarmid, *Lucky Poet*, 220.

67 MacDiarmid, *Stony Limits*, 59-61, *CP* 419-22.

68 Ibid., 62-75, *CP* 422-33.

69 The philosopher D.M. MacKinnon (*The Problem of Metaphysics*, 164-9) uses the poem as a means of distinguishing between theistic and atheistic ontologies. Although hardly the "valuable and profound discussion of the poem" Ruth McQuillan claims it to be ("Hugh MacDiarmid's 'On a Raised Beach,'" 91), a significant point is made: referring to the atheist, MacKinnon writes, "He is almost obsessively preoccupied with what there is and with the implications of the objectivity of which MacDiarmid writes." McQuillan is correct, however, in querying MacKinnon's bold conclusion "that out of an atheist ontology a great poem may spring": MacDiarmid's outlook is best described as reluctant agnosticism. He has none of the certainty of either the atheist or the theist. Nevertheless, MacKinnon's description of the atheistic perception can be extended to include MacDiarmid's precarious *Weltanschauung*.

70 MacDiarmid, "Lament for the Great Music," in *Stony Limits*, 138-9, *CP* 480.

71 MacDiarmid, *Stony Limits*, 130. See *Cencrastus*, 184, *CP* 474, 281.

72 MacDiarmid, *A Kist of Whistles*, 13, *CP* 696.

73 The *Stony Limits* volume brings together many of these experiments, for example, "In the Caledonian Forest," 22-3, "Ephyphatha," 24 (cf *Mark* 7:34, title corrected in *Complete Poems*), "The Sense of Smell," 51, and "Balefire Loch," 109-10, as well as the already noted "On a Raised Beach," *CP* 391-2, 393, 413-4, 458-60, 422-33.

CHAPTER FIVE

1 See *Lines Review* (summer 1956): 17n.

2 MacDiarmid, *The Battle Continues*, 99ff, *CP* 992ff.

3 As Philip Pacey puts it, the poem is "an invocation of a linguistic

complexity ... capable of matching the manifold world word for part and particle, relationship, thought and dream." "In Memoriam James Joyce," 101.

4 MacDiamid, "Charles Doughty and the Need for Heroic Poetry," in *Selected Essays of Hugh MacDiarmid*, 75-85.

5 Morgan, "Poetry and Knowledge in MacDiarmid's Later Work," 133.

6 This is part of a quotation.

7 In *Collected Poems*, "*welt literatur*" corrected to *Weltliteratur*.

8 For the probable source of this phrase see Read, *Form in Modern Poetry*, 51, 59.

9 These definitions are provided in the enlarged glossary prepared by John Weston for *Collected Poems* (1967). Weston's extrapolation of the literal meaning of the word "sny" (a ship-building term: a plank has *sny* when its edge has an upward curve) is undoubtedly correct in this context.

10 See MacDiarmid, "My Heart Always Goes Back to the North," 175-9.

11 See letter from G. Herdan in *Times Literary Supplement*, 6 May 1965, 351. He notes MacDiarmid's use of the Kraus article, although he does not attribute the original to Erich Heller. (See Heller's essay on Kraus in *The Disinherited Mind*, 236-60.) MacDiarmid does indicate the *Times Literary Supplement* as his source in a footnote.

12 The passage on Heidegger, 48, *CP* 772-3, is taken from a passage of *Existence and Being*, 82; see MacDiarmid's other use of this source in chapter 1, 10.

13 Craig, "Hugh MacDiarmid's Poetry," 7-8.

14 See MacDiarmid, *Lucky Poet*, 343ff.

15 See MacDiarmid, "Thalamus," in *Stony Limits*, 50, *CP* 411ff, for example.

16 See the quotation from Paul Claudel, chapter 4, 121.

17 See the discussion of the significance of expertise in "The Kind of Poetry I Want," in chapter 4.

18 See chapter 1, 10.

19 Norman MacCaig's surname is corrected In *Collected Poems*.

20 See Busoni, *The Essence of Music and Other Papers*, 188-9.

21 See *Cencrastus*, 80, *CP* 224.

22 See MacDiarmid, *A Lap of Honour*, 19, *CP* 1087.

23 Latin corrected in *Collected Poems*, "Non me rebus *subjungere* conor!"

24 Porteous, "Paging the Loch Ness Monster," 37.

25 Merwin, "Without the Reality of Music," 50-1.

CHAPTER SIX

1 Heidegger, "Hölderlin and the Essence of Poetry," *Existence and Being*, 293ff.

2 Kafka, "Abraham," *Parables*, 37.

3 See Alexander Scott, "MacDiarmid: The Poet," xxii, in *The Hugh MacDiarmid Anthology:* "Small wonder that ... he describes the kind of poetry he seeks to create as 'such poems as might be written in eternal life' – for it would seem that only the God who has been expelled from MacDiarmid's universe could experience and express the simultaneous synthesis of all knowledge which is the poet's aim."
4 Heidegger, *Being and Time*, 97-100.
5 Ibid., 98, 409.
6 Ibid., 413.
7 Ibid., 409.
8 e e cummings, *Collected Poems*, poem 211.
9 Sartre, *Literature and Existentialism*, 13.
10 The attitudes of Yeats and MacDiarmid in this respect have been noted.
11 Alexander Scott, in his poem "Great Eneuch," in *Mouth Music*, 7, recognizing the fundamental character of the phenomenon of consciousness, is well aware of being in this situation:

> And loss is great eneuch that wants the haill
> (Aa life, aa space, aa time) and aye maun fail
> To win thon prize, yet canna cease to sing
> The striving for't o ilka separate sel –
> And siccan sangs frae my ain lack I'd wring,
> Gin I was great eneuch.

APPENDIX

1 "The MacDiarmids. A Conversation – Hugh MacDiarmid and Duncan Glen," 32.
2 For a synopsis of the controversy see Glen, *Hugh MacDiarmid (C.M. Grieve) and the Scottish Literary Renaissance*, 29-41.
3 Hyman, "The Language of Scottish Poetry," 23.
4 Scott, "Lament for the Great Music," 20.
5 Quoted by William Cookson in "Some Notes on Hugh MacDiarmid," 38.
6 Law and Berwick, *The Socialist Poems of Hugh MacDiarmid*, xxii.
7 Buthlay, *Hugh MacDiarmid (C.M. Grieve)*.
8 Watson, *Hugh MacDiarmid*.
9 See Morgan, "Poetry and Knowledge in MacDiarmid's Later Work," and Craig, "MacDiarmid the Marxist Poet." Quotation is from Craig, "The Radical Literary Tradition," in *The Red Paper on Scotland*, ed. Brown, 297.
10 Boutelle, *Thistle and Rose*, 9 and throughout.
11 Bold, *MacDiarmid: The Terrible Crystal*, 4, 12.
12 Oxenhorn, *Elemental Things*, 100.

13 Ibid., 58.
14 MacDiarmid, *A Kist of Whistles*, 17. See Glen, *Hugh MacDiarmid*, 161, and Buthlay, *Hugh MacDiarmid*, 109.
15 Soutar, "The Poetry of MacDiarmid: A Cursory Survey from 'Sanschaw' [sic] to 'Cencrastus,'" 9.
16 Manuscript reproduced in Duval and Smith, eds., *Hugh MacDiarmid*, facing 193.
17 Craig, "Jettisoning the Chaos," 48.
18 Buthlay, *Hugh MacDiarmid*, 84.
19 Keir, "Hugh MacDiarmid and the Scottish Literary Renaissance," 14.
20 Rosenthal, *The Modern Poets*, 140.

Bibliography

BOOKS AND PERIODICALS EDITED BY HUGH MACDIARMID

Northern Numbers, Being Representative Selections from Certain Living Scottish Poets. Edinburgh and London: T.N. Foulis 1920.

Northern Numbers, Being Representative Selections from Certain Living Scottish Poets. Second series. Edinburgh and London: T.N. Foulis 1921.

Northern Numbers, Being Representative Selections from Certain Living Scottish Poets. Third series. Montrose: C.M. Grieve 1922.

Scottish Chapbook. August 1922-November/December 1923.

Scottish Nation. 8 May 1923-25 December 1923.

Northern Review. May 1924-September 1924.

Voice of Scotland. June/August 1938-June/August 1939; December 1945-June 1949; January 1955-(? August 1958).

WORKS BY HUGH MACDIARMID

Annals of the Five Senses. Montrose: C.M. Grieve 1923.

Sangschaw. Edinburgh and London: Blackwood 1925.

Penny Wheep. Edinburgh and London: Blackwood 1926.

A Drunk Man Looks at the Thistle. Edinburgh: Blackwood 1926.

Contemporary Scottish Studies. First series. London: Leonard Parsons 1926.

Albyn, or Scotland and the Future. London and New York: Kegan Paul, Trench, Trubner 1927.

To Circumjack Cencrastus, or the Curly Snake. Edinburgh and London: Blackwood 1930.

First Hymn to Lenin and Other Poems. London: Unicorn Press 1931.

Scots Unbound and Other Poems. Stirling: Eneas MacKay 1932.

Five Bits of Miller. London: C.M. Grieve 1934.

Stony Limits and Other Poems. London: V. Gollancz 1934.

Second Hymn to Lenin and Other Poems. London: Stanley Nott 1935.

Scottish Eccentrics. London: Routledge 1936.

The Islands of Scotland: Hebrides, Orkneys, and Shetlands. London: Batsford 1939; New York: Scribners 1939.

Lucky Poet: A Self-Study in Literature and Political Ideas. London: Methuen 1943.

Cornish Heroic Song for Valda Trevlyn. Glasgow: Caledonian Press [1943].

Speaking for Scotland. Distinguished Poets Series, volume 3. Baltimore: Contemporary Poetry 1946.

A Kist of Whistles. Poetry Scotland Series, no. 10. Glasgow: Maclellan [1947].

"My Heart Always Goes Back to the North," *Poetry* (Chicago) 72, no. 4 (1948): 175-9.

In Memoriam James Joyce, from A Vision of World Language. Glasgow: Maclellan 1955.

Stony Limits and Scots Unbound and Other Poems. Edinburgh: Castle Wynd Printers 1956.

Three Hymns to Lenin. Edinburgh: Castle Wynd Printers 1957.

The Battle Continues. Edinburgh: Castle Wynd Printers 1957.

"To a Young Poet," *Saltire Review* 6, no. 18 (1959): 38-41.

Poems to Paintings by William Johnstone 1933. Edinburgh: K.D. Duval 1963.

Collected Poems. New York: Macmillan 1967.

A Lap of Honour. London: MacGibbon and Kee 1967.

Early Lyrics by Hugh MacDiarmid. Edited by J.K. Annand. Preston: Akros 1968.

A Clyack-Sheaf. London: MacGibbon and Kee 1969.

Selected Essays of Hugh MacDiarmid. Edited with introduction by Duncan Glen. Berkeley and Los Angeles: University of California Press 1970.

"The MacDiarmids. A Conversation - Hugh MacDiarmid and Duncan Glen." *Akros* 5, xiii (1970).

The Hugh MacDiarmid Anthology. Edited by Alexander Scott and Michael Grieve, with introduction by Alexander Scott. London: Routledge and Kegan Paul 1972.

The Socialist Poems of Hugh MacDiarmid. Edited with foreword by T.S. Law and T. Berwick. London: Routledge and Kegan Paul 1978.

Hugh MacDiarmid: Complete Poems 1920-1976 (2 vols.). Edited by Michael Grieve and W.R. Aitken. London: Martin Brian and O'Keeffe 1978.

The Letters of Hugh MacDiarmid. Edited by Alan Bold. London: Hamish Hamilton 1984.

GENERAL REFERENCES

Abercrombie, Lascelles, ed. *New English Poems*. London: V. Gollancz 1931.

Aitken, W.R., "Hugh MacDiarmid (Christopher Murray Grieve, b.1892): A First Checklist," *The Bibliotheck* 1, no. 4 (1958). A revised checklist is published in *Hugh MacDiarmid: A Festschrift*, ed. K.D. Duval and S.G. Smith, Edinburgh: K.D. Duval 1962; and yet another in *The Bibliotheck* 5, nos. 7-8 (1970).

– *Scottish Literature in English and Scots: A Guide to Information Sources*. Detroit: Gale Research Co. 1982.

Anonymous. "Growth and Consummation," *Times Literary Supplement*, 15 August 1952, 532.

Berryman, John. "The Long Way to MacDiarmid," *Poetry* (Chicago) 88, no. 1 (1956): 52-61.

Billings, R.G. "The Mood and Plan of Yeats' *Words for Music Perhaps*," MA thesis, Queen's University, Kingston, Ontario, 1972.

Bold, Alan. *MacDiarmid: The Terrible Crystal*. London and Boston: Routledge and Kegan Paul 1983.

Boutelle, Ann Edwards. *Thistle and Rose: A Study of Hugh MacDiarmid's Poetry*. Loanhead: MacDonald Publishers 1980.

Brown, Gordon, ed. *The Red Paper on Scotland*. Edinburgh: EUSPB 1975.

Bruce, George. "'Between any Life and the Sun,'" in *Festschrift*, ed. K.D. Duval and S.G. Smith.

Buchan, John, ed. *Northern Muse*. London: Nelson 1924.

Busoni, Ferruccio. *The Essence of Music and Other Papers*. Translated by Rosamond Ley. London: Rockliff 1957.

Buthlay, Kenneth. "Call Me Anti" (a review of *Drunk Man*), *Saltire Review* 1, no. 1 (1954): 89-90.

– *Hugh MacDiarmid (C.M. Grieve)*. Edinburgh and London: Oliver and Boyd Ltd. 1964.

Carswell, Donald. "Perfervid Scots," *New Statesman and Nation*, 11 April 1936, 573-4.

Chiari, Joseph. *Impressions of People and Literature*. Edinburgh: Moray Press 1948.

Cookson, William. "Some Notes on Hugh MacDiarmid," *Agenda* 5, iv-6, i (1967-8): 35-41.

Craig, David. "Hugh MacDiarmid's Poetry," *Voice of Scotland* 7, No. 1 (1956): 6-19.

– "Jettisoning the Chaos," *Lines Review* 19, winter (1963): 46-9.

– "MacDiarmid the Marxist Poet," in *Festschrift*, ed., K.D. Duval and S.G. Smith.

cummings, e e. *Collected Poems*. New York: Harcourt, Brace and World 1963.

Daiches, David. "Diversity in Unity," *Scottish Field*, August 1962, 33.

– "The Early Poems," in *Festschrift*, ed. K.D. Duval and S.G. Smith.

Davidson, John. *In a Music-Hall and Other Poems*. London: Ward and Downey 1891.

– *Fleet Street Eclogues*. London: E. Mathews and J. Lane 1893.

– *Ballads and Songs*. London: J. Lane; Boston: Copeland and Day 1894.

– *A Second Series of Fleet Street Eclogues.* London: J. Lane; New York: Dodd, Mead and Co 1896.
– *Holiday and Other Poems.* London: E.G. Richards 1906.
– *The Triumph of Mammon.* London: E.G. Richards 1907.
– *Mammon and his Message.* London: G. Richards 1908.
Davie, Donald. "A'e Gowden Lyric," *New Statesman,* 10 August 1962, 174-5.
Duval, K.D., and S.G. Smith, eds. *Hugh MacDiarmid: A Festschrift.* Edinburgh: K.D. Duval 1962.
Eliot, T.S. *The Waste Land.* London: Faber and Faber 1961.
Filioque. "The Great Sea-Serpent," *New Age,* 11 March 1926, 223-4.
Fraser, G.S. "Hugh MacDiarmid: The Later Poetry," *Akros* 5, no.14 (1970): 13-14.
Fromm, Erich. *The Fear of Freedom.* London: Routledge and Kegan Paul 1960.
Glen, Duncan. *Hugh MacDiarmid (C.M. Grieve) and the Scottish Literary Renaissance.* Edinburgh: W. and R. Chambers, Ltd 1964. (Includes extensive bibliography.)
– *The Individual and the Twentieth-Century Scottish Literary Tradition.* Preston: Akros 1971.
– ed. *Hugh MacDiarmid: A Critical Survey.* Edinburgh and London: Scottish Academic Press 1972.
Glenday, M.K. "Hugh MacDiarmid: A Bibliography of Criticism, 1924-78." *Bulletin of Bibliography* 36, no. 2 (1979): 91-8.
Graves, Robert. *The White Goddess.* London: Faber and Faber 1948.
Grimsley, Ronald. *Existentialist Thought.* Cardiff: University of Wales Press 1955.
Heidegger, Martin. *Existence and Being.* With introduction by Werner Brock. London: Vision 1949.
– *Being and Time.* Translated by John Macquarrie and Edward Robinson. Oxford: Blackwell 1967.
Heinemann, F.H. *Existentialism and the Modern Predicament.* London: A. and C. Black 1953.
Heller, Erich. *The Disinherited Mind.* London: Bowes and Bowes 1952.
Herdman, John. "Hugh MacDiarmid's 'To Circumjack Cencrastus,'" *Akros* 12, no. 34-5 (1977): 65-75.
Howe, Irving, ed. *The Idea of the Modern in Literature and the Arts.* With introduction by Irving Howe. New York: Horizon Press 1967.
Hyman, Stanley. "The Language of Scottish Poetry," *Kenyon Review* 16, no. 1 (1954): 20-37.
Jamieson, John. *Etymological Dictionary of the Scottish Language.* Revised and collated by John Longmuir and David Donaldson. Paisley: Alexander Gardner 1887.
Jones, David. *The Anathemata.* London: Faber and Faber 1962.
– *The Sleeping Lord and Other Fragments,* London: Faber and Faber 1974.

Joyce, James. *Finnegans Wake*. London: Faber and Faber 1964.

Kafka, Franz. *Parables*. Translated by E. and W. Muir. New York: Schocken Books 1947.

– *The Trial*. Translated by E. and W. Muir. London: Secker and Warburg 1956.

– *Amerika*. Translated by E. and W. Muir. New York: Schocken Books 1966.

– *The Castle*. Translated by E. and W. Muir. New York: A. Knopf 1968.

– *The Great Wall of China and Other Pieces*. London: M. Secker 1933.

Keir, Walter. "MacDiarmid's Poetry in the 1930s," *Festschrift*, ed. K.D. Duval and S.G. Smith.

Kerrigan, Catherine. *Whaur Extremes Meet: The Poetry of Hugh MacDiarmid 1920-1934*. Edinburgh: Mercat Press 1983.

Korzybski, Alfred. *Science and Sanity: An Introduction to Non-Aristotelian Systems and General Semantics*. Lancaster, Pa, New York: International non-Aristotelian Library Publishing Company 1941.

Leavis, F.R. *New Bearings in English Poetry*. London: Chatto and Windus 1950.

Lovejoy, A.O. *The Great Chain of Being*. Cambridge, Mass.: Harvard University Press 1936.

Lowith, Karl. "Heidegger: Problem and Background of Existentialism," *Social Research*, 15, no. 3 (1948): 345-69.

MacKinnon, D.M. *The Problem of Metaphysics*. London, New York: Cambridge University Press 1974.

Martinson, Harry. *Aniara*. Adapted from the Swedish by Hugh MacDiarmid and E.H. Schubert. London: Hutchinson 1963.

McLuhan, Marshall. *The Gutenberg Galaxy*. London: Routledge and Kegan Paul 1962.

– *Understanding Media: The Extensions of Man*. New York: McGraw-Hill 1964.

McQuillan, Ruth. "Hugh MacDiarmid's 'On A Raised Beach,'" *Akros* 12, no. 34-5 (1977): 89-97.

Merwin, W.S. "Without the Reality of Music," *Poetry* (Chicago) 88, no. 1 (1956): 48-52.

Miller, Karl. "Scotch on the Rocks," *New York Review of Books* 17, no. 9 (1971): 13-16.

Morgan, Edwin. "Jujitsu for the Educated," *Twentieth Century* 160, no. 955 (1956): 223-31.

– "Poetry and Knowledge in MacDiarmid's Later Work," in *Festschrift*, ed. K.D. Duval and S.G. Smith.

Morse, B.J. "Contemporary English Poets and Rilke," *German Life and Letters (New Series)* 1, no. 4 (1948): 272-85.

New Tales of Horror. London: Hutchinson and Co [1934].

Olson, Charles. *Maximus Poems 1-10*. Stuttgart: J. Williams 1953.

Oxenhorn, Harvey. *Elemental Things: The Poetry of Hugh MacDiarmid*. Edinburgh: Edinburgh University Press 1984.

Pacey, Philip. "A Gift of Tongues: A First Encounter (Twenty-One Years

after Publication) with Hugh MacDiarmid's 'In Memoriam James Joyce,'"
Akros 12, no. 34-5 (1977): 101-8.

Pearce, R.H. *The Continuity of American Poetry*. Princeton: Princeton University Press 1961.

Pirandello, Luigi. *Maschere Nude*. Milan: A. Montadori 1964.

Porteous, H.G. "Paging The Loch Ness Monster," *Nimbus* 3, no. 3 (1956): 34-40.

Pound, Ezra. *The Cantos of Ezra Pound*. London: Faber and Faber 1954.

− *Drafts and Fragments of Cantos CX-CXVII*. London: Faber and Faber 1970.

Read, Herbert. *Form in Modern Poetry*. London: Sheed and Ward 1932.

Reid, J.M. *Modern Scottish Literature*. Saltire Pamphlet no. 5. Edinburgh: Oliver and Boyd 1945.

Richards, I.A. *Science and Poetry*. New York: W.W. Norton and Co 1926.

Rosenthal, M.L. *The Modern Poets*. New York: Oxford University Press 1965.

Sartre, Jean-Paul. *Being and Nothingness: An Essay on Phenomenological Ontology*. Translated with an introduction by Hazel E. Barnes. London: Methuen 1966.

− *Literature and Existentialism*. Translated by B. Frechtman. New York: Citadel Press 1966.

− *Nausea*. Translated by R. Baldick. Harmondsworth: Penguin 1970.

Scott, Alexander. *Mouth Music*. Edinburgh: M. Macdonald 1954.

Scott, P.H., and A.C. Davis, eds. *The Age of MacDiarmid: Essays on Hugh MacDiarmid and His Influence on Contemporary Scotland*. Edinburgh: Mainstream Publishing 1980.

Scott, Tom. "Lament for the Great Music," *Agenda* 5, iv-6, i (1967-8): 19-26.

Singer, Burns. "Scarlet Eminence," *Encounter* 8, no. 3 (1957): 49-62.

Smith, A.J.M. *Poems New and Collected*. Toronto: Oxford University Press 1967.

Smith, G. Gregory. *Scottish Literature, Character and Influence*. London: Macmillan and Co 1919.

Smith, Iain Crichton. *The Golden Lyric*. Preston: Akros 1967.

− "Hugh MacDiarmid: *Sangschaw* and *A Drunk Man Looks at the Thistle*," *Studies in Scottish Literature* 7, no. 3 (1970): 169-70.

Sontag, Susan. *Styles of Radical Will*. New York: Farrar, Strauss and Giroux 1969.

Soutar, William. "The Poetry of MacDiarmid: A Cursory Survey from 'Sanschaw' [sic] to 'Cencrastus,'" *Free Man*, 7 April 1934, 8-9.

Spender, Stephen. *The Struggle of the Modern*. London: Hamish Hamilton 1963.

Speirs, John. *The Scots Literary Tradition*. London: Faber and Faber 1962.

Steiner, George. *Language and Silence*. London: Faber and Faber 1967.

Thirlby, Peter. "The Piper on the Parapet," *New Reasoner* (spring 1959): 58-73.

Times Literary Supplement. Correspondence on plagiarism, 21 January-20 May 1965. See *TLS*, 25 February 1965, for editorial on the subject.

Trotsky, Leon. *Literature and Revolution*. Ann Arbor: University of Michigan Press 1968.

Watson, Roderick Bruce."Hugh MacDiarmid and the 'Poetry of Fact,'" *Stand* 9, no. 4 (1968): 24-31.

– "A Critical Study of the 'Cencrastus Theme' in the Poetry of Hugh MacDiarmid." PH D thesis, Cambridge University, 1970.

– *Hugh MacDiarmid*. Milton Keynes: Open University Press 1976.

– "The Symbolism of *A Drunk Man Looks at the Thistle*," in Glen, D., ed., *Hugh MacDiarmid: A Critical Survey*.

Weston, John. *Hugh MacDiarmid's A Drunk Man Looks at the Thistle*. Preston: Akros 1970.

Whalley, George. *The Poetic Process*. London: Routledge and Kegan Paul 1953.

Whitman, Walt. *Leaves of Grass*. Edited by H.W. Blodgett and S. Bradley.New York: New York University Press 1965.

Williams, William Carlos. *Paterson*. Books I-V. London: MacGibbon and Kee 1965.

Winters, Yvor. *The Function of Criticism: Problems and Exercises*. Denver: A. Swallow 1957.

Wittig, Kurt. *The Scottish Tradition in Literature*. Edinburgh: Oliver and Boyd 1958.

Wood, Michael. "Mod and Great," *The New York Review of Books* 19, no. 4 (1972): 19-22.

Wright, Gordon. *Hugh MacDiarmid: An Illustrated Biography*. Edinburgh: Gordon Wright 1977.

Yeats, W.B. *A Vision*. London: Macmillan and Co 1937.

– *The Poems of W.B. Yeats*. Edited by R.J. Finneran. New York: Macmillan Publishing Co 1983.

Young, Douglas. "The Nationalism of Hugh MacDiarmid," in *Festschrift*, ed. K.D. Duval and S.G. Smith.

Young, Neil. *After the Gold Rush*. Warner-Reprise Records 1971.

Index of Poems by
Hugh MacDiarmid

General Index

DATE DUE

AUGUSTANA UNIVERSITY COLLEGE
LIBRARY